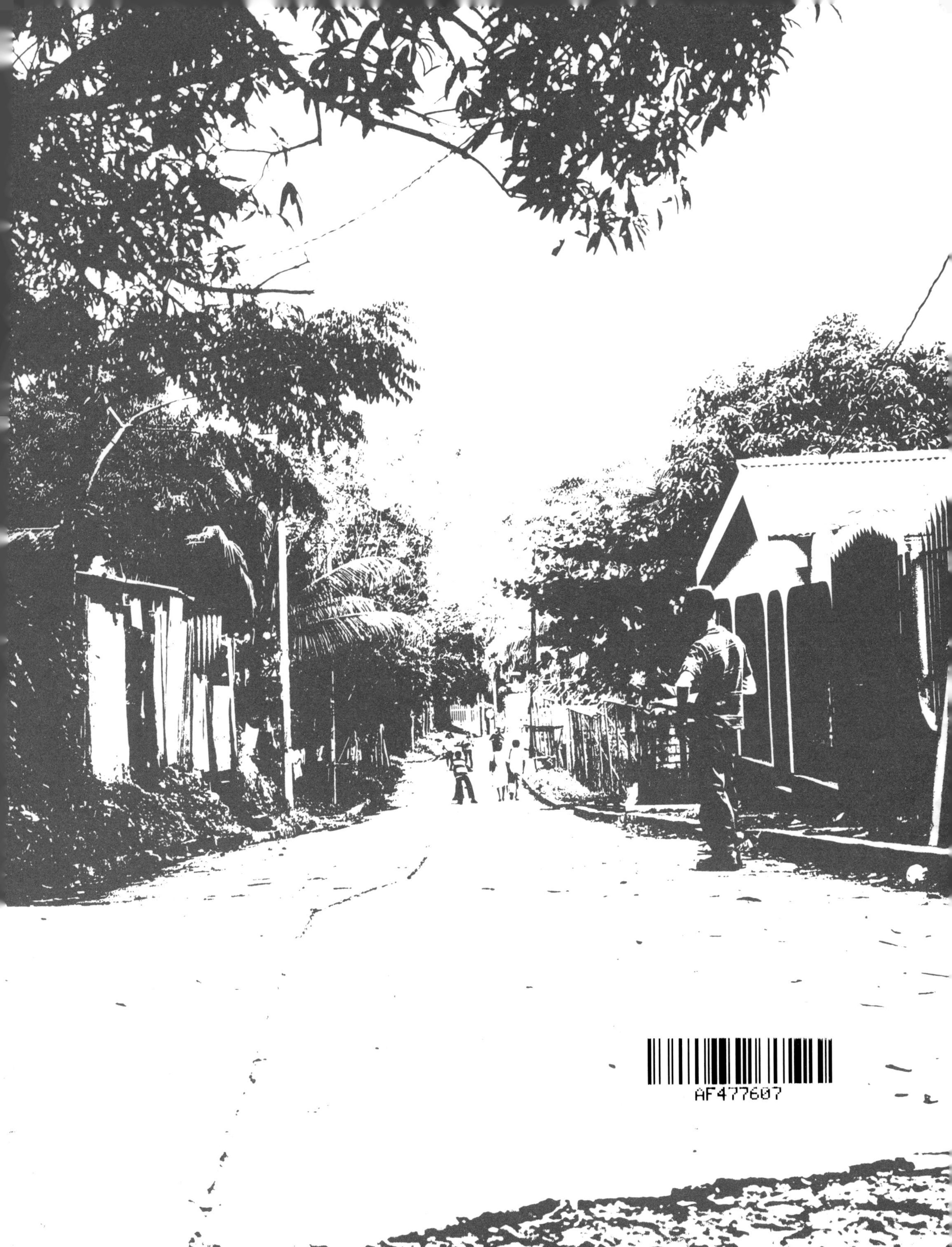
AF477607

Dan Rees

Road Back to Relevance

Contents

Contenuti

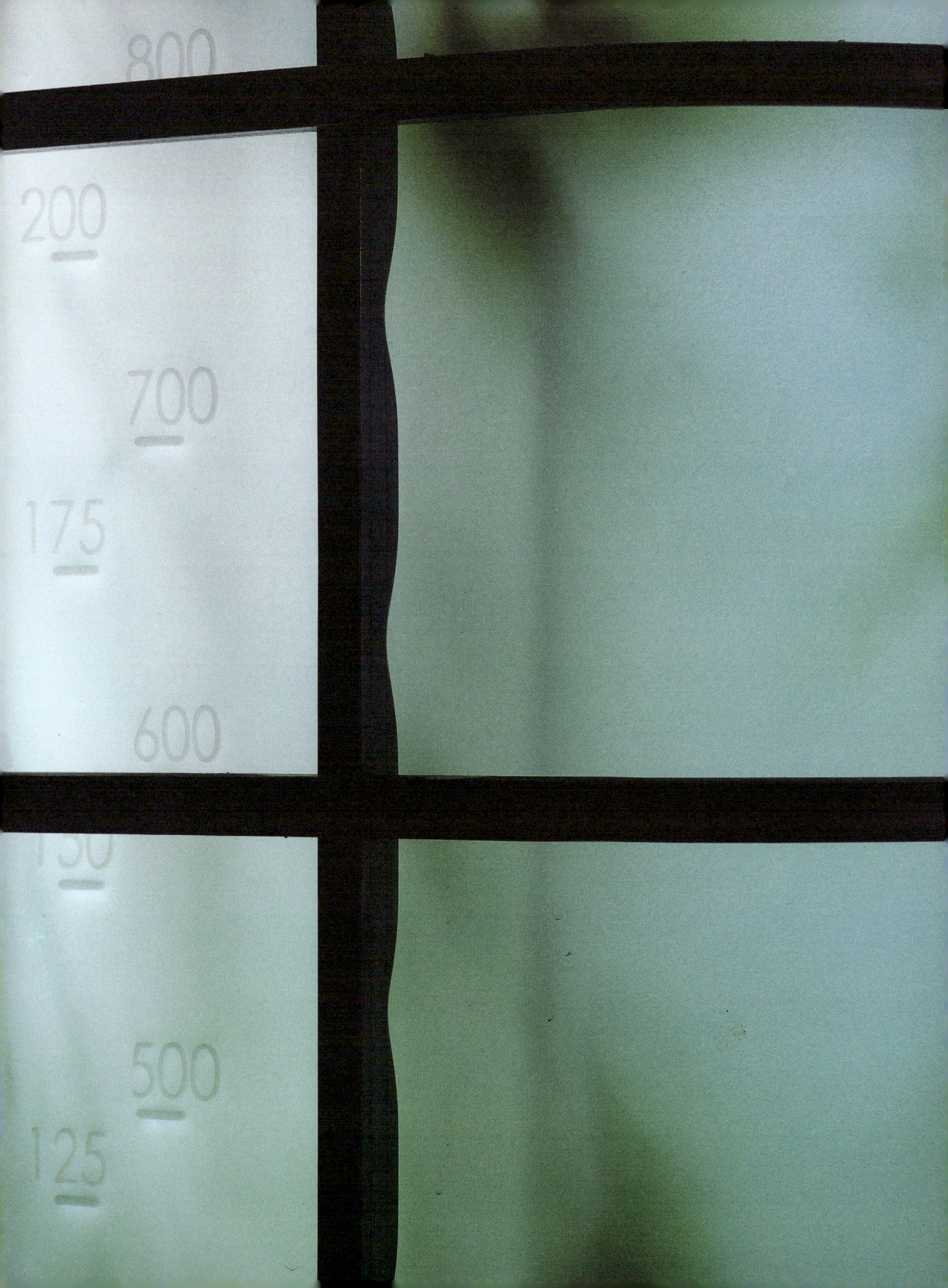
800
200
700
175
600
150
500
125

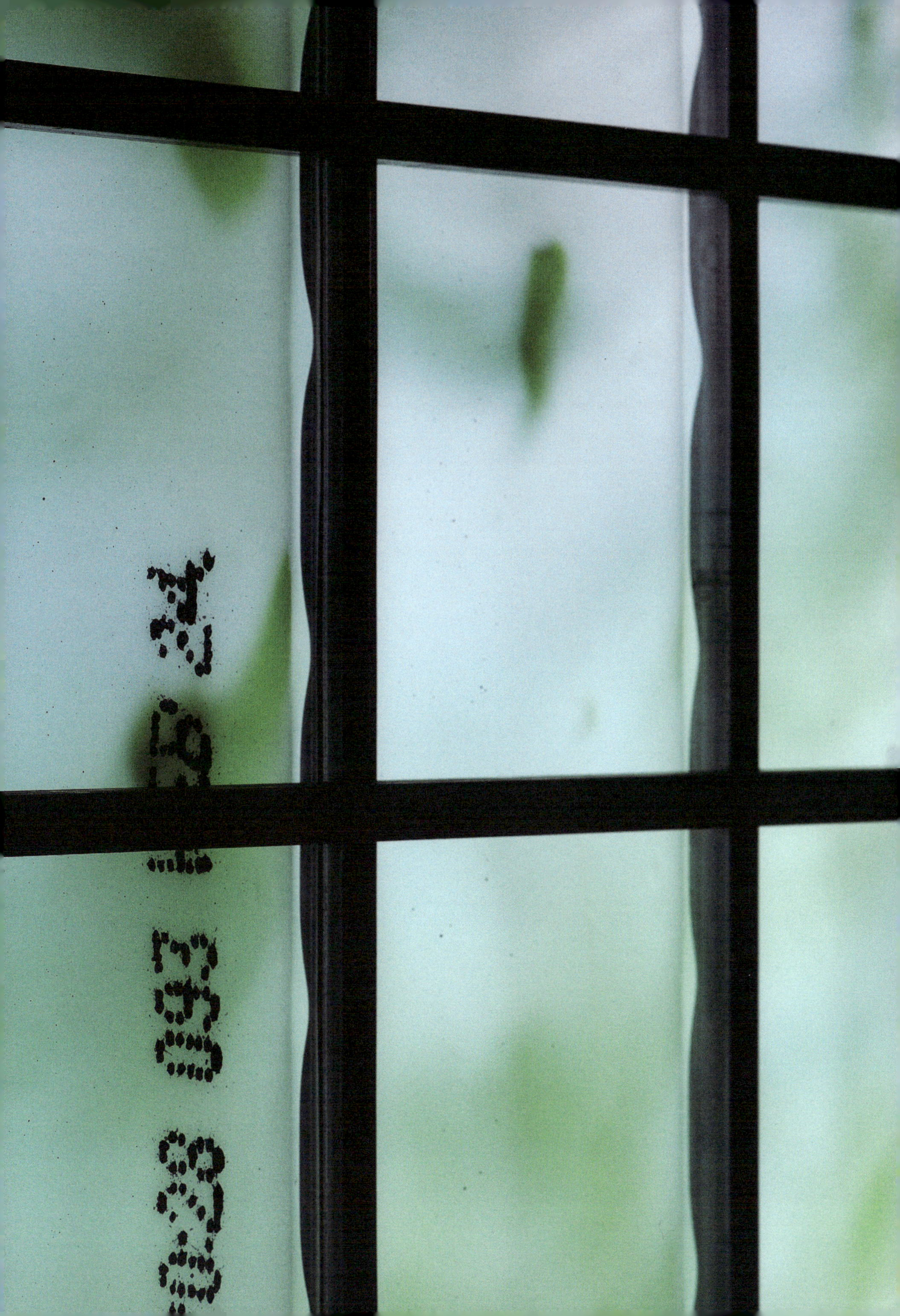

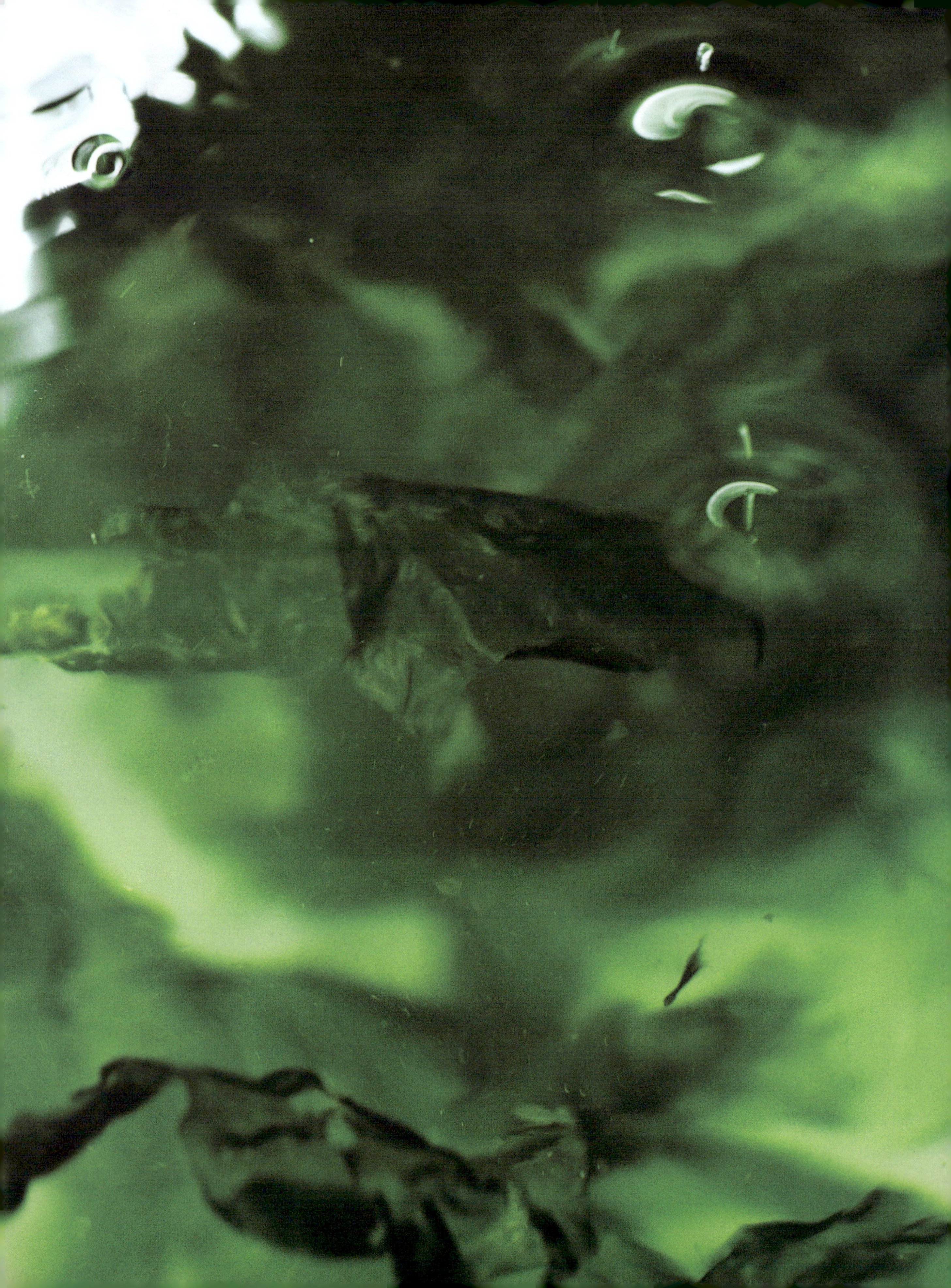

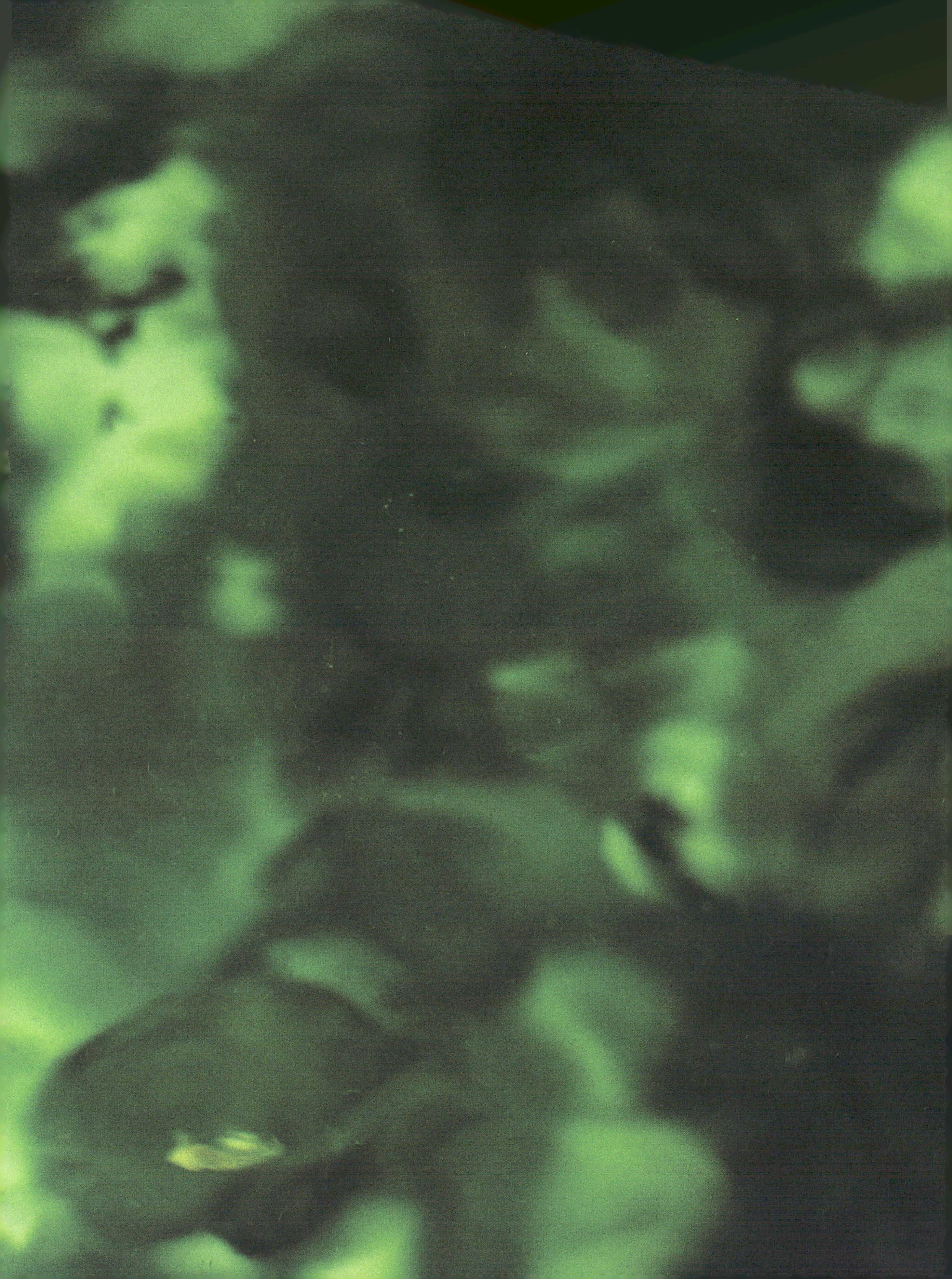

Two Views of Dan Rees's Work

by Dieter Roelstraete

1. Left

*Thus art becomes problematic precisely because
reality has become non-problematic.*
—Georg Lukács, *The Theory of the Novel*
(Cambridge, MA: The MIT Press, 1971), 17.

The work of Dan Rees touches upon a wide range of topics, subjects, and issues, but one dominant, recurring preoccupation doubtlessly concerns the *politics of taste*. 'Taste'—its cultural corollaries, its political over- and undertones, and most importantly its social sources—is one of Rees's preferred problems. And where it is addressed most directly and unapologetically—that is to say, in the so-called Artex paintings—is exactly where his work becomes most willingly, egregiously 'problematic.' The problem in question equates the question of taste with the tetchy issue of *class*: Artex, as a historical material, so to speak, is, in the context of Rees's own British working-class origins, a distinctive marker of class—hence, inevitably, its halo of aesthetic abjection. Artex, 'they' say, is *ugly*.

Interestingly enough, talk of taste in contemporary art is often considered tasteless—or, to use an especially telling predicate, plainly 'poor' taste. By its very definition, one could argue, contemporary art thrives *beyond* the boundaries of taste; it is typically art 'after' taste (much like it is art 'after' skill—both concepts are evidently related). Correspondingly, talk of *class* in today's presumably classless society is regarded with comparable suspicion, if not outright disdain. Such talk is likewise considered a hallmark of poor taste (try it, at your next New York gallery dinner!), that is to say, anything but 'classy.' Much like contemporary art is a species of art 'after taste'—art enjoyed *after* the demise of traditional Kantian standards of *Urteilskraft*, so to speak—its accompanying culture flourishes in the ideological vacuum 'after class.' (That said, our classless society has not necessarily made for more tasteless art—*or has it?*) However—and as a result—as Rees himself has remarked on occasion, 'The economy of the art world has produced its own process of class formation.' Indeed, this may well be contemporary art's secret social function: finding new ways of insinuating class distinctions back into a neoliberal world order supposedly weaned off the spectre of class consciousness.

Though it seems intuitively self-evident to 'date' the emergence of contemporary (as opposed to merely modern or even postmodern) art somewhere early on the timeline of the neoliberal consensus that has produced the mirage of a world in which traditional class distinctions no longer appear to matter much—and which constitutes much of the defining socioeconomic background against which some of Rees's more overtly political work must be seen—it is of course pointless to try to locate the historical origins of both the contemporary in 'contemporary art' and the perceived classlessness of contemporary society with anything approaching historiographic exactitude. Still, if a suggestion must be made concerning such an exact point of origin, Rees's own origins would most likely not be too far off the mark—early Thatcher-era Britain, more specifically its rapidly deindustrialising, deregulating fringes. The late 1970s, early 1980s, when a grocer's daughter from Grantham rode to Tory victory spurred on by Saatchi-engineered claims that 'Labour isn't working'; when across the pond Reagan unleashed his own brand of class warfare on what little remained of American class consciousness; when the abject failure of Soviet-style socialism in the original workers' state had long been plain for all to see—this was also the age, not coincidentally, that witnessed the rise of the *Pictures* generation; the emergence of Jeff Koons and his post-Warholian ilk; the blurring of disciplinary boundaries between high- and lowbrow culture as embodied by the popularisation of video art (among other media); and the passing of Joseph Beuys's baton to a generation of more pragmatically minded activist types. Decisive markers, all, in the development of what we now understand to constitute contemporaneity in art. A chapter in art history, also—*our* chapter, which we understandably have trouble understanding as anything other than a passing phase—that has seen Artex become a legitimate material for making art, for *being* art.

Right on the cusp of this historical moment, in 1979, the French sociologist Pierre Bourdieu published his magisterial *Distinction: A Social Critique of the Judgment of Taste* (it was translated into English in 1984), still required reading for anyone interested in the devious entwinement of class and taste. In it, Bourdieu basically makes the case that the rhetoric of taste is a sophisticated machine for producing and sustaining class difference—'distinction': 'Tastes (that is, manifested preferences) are the practical affirmation of an inevitable difference. It is no accident that, when they have to be justified, they are asserted purely negatively, by the refusal of other tastes. In matters of taste more than anywhere else, all determination is negation'—with 'bad' taste, from the perspective of class difference, always understood to be 'poor' taste, of course: fundamentally *lacking*. Indeed, Bourdieu continues, 'Aesthetic intolerance can be terribly violent. Aversion to different life-styles is perhaps one of the strongest barriers between the classes; *class endogamy is evidence of this*' (my emphasis).[1] As an aside, it is interesting to note the very distinctive use made by Bourdieu of the talismanic concept of *difference* precisely at a time when it was considered a philosophical panacea by so many of his contemporaries, Gilles Deleuze and Jacques Derrida foremost among them (towards the end of the book, Bourdieu takes issue with Derrida's reading of Kant's *Critique of Judgment*). The contrast between these positions is symptomatic of that larger shift so characteristic of the neoliberal dispensation: the migration of 'difference' from the real world of social relations to the innocuous realm of aesthetic pleasure and philosophical reflection. Or, in other words still: Artex—from the council flat to the gallery wall.

2. Right

Art always says 'And yet!' to life.
—Georg Lukács, *The Theory of the Novel*, cit., 72.

Underlying Rees's concern with the entanglement of class and taste, we may discern two interrelated queries—one that concerns the matter of access and accessibility (Can a vanguard art be truly 'popular'? Whence the cultural elite's instinctual scorn, by and large, for popular forms, even to this day? Why are we so often told that making art legible across a wider swath of the population inevitably leads to its being watered down?), and another that concerns the question of art's real impact in society (simply posed: Can art change or save the world?), with both converging in an ongoing interrogation of the (mostly failed) project of popular modernism, of a truly radical culture for the masses. Rees's most exemplary work in this regard, and the artist at his most emphatically political (and, perhaps not coincidentally, at his most broadly *autobiographical*), is probably the aptly titled video *Road Back to Relevance* (2015), which attempts to show us 'how the Wales Nicaragua solidarity campaign can inspire people today,' though it really asks the question as to how art can secure the longed-for intersection of 'social, cultural and political' relevance—that is, art's titular 'road back to relevance'—that Rees so clearly seeks. ('Solidarity' seems as anachronistic a notion as class in the previous discussion.) This road (back) to relevance, art's voyage back to the centre of a society's sense of self, may involve negotiating the oftentimes strained, simultaneously antagonistic and symbiotic relationship between *art* and *culture*—a distinction that is not without consequence for a better understanding of Rees's practice.

For what it's worth, I myself have long tended to err on the side of *art*—in the manner discussed by Alain Badiou in his introduction to *Saint Paul: The Foundation of Universalism*, where he notes:

> The contemporary world is doubly hostile to truth procedures. This hostility betrays itself through nominal occlusions: where the name of a truth procedure should obtain, another, which represses it, holds sway. The name 'culture' comes to obliterate that of 'art'. The word 'technology' obliterates the word 'science'. The word 'management' obliterates the word 'politics'. The word 'sexuality' obliterates love. The 'culture-technology-management-sexuality' system, which has the immense merit of being homogenous to the market, and all of whose terms designate a category of commercial presentation, constitutes the modern nominal occlusion of the 'art-science-politics-love' system, which identifies truth procedures typologically.[2]

Badiou, in short, confuses culture with the *culture industry* here—that old mainstay of Frankfurt School–style cultural criticism—in terms that inscribe his thought in the long history of the philosophical valuation of art above *all* other realms of human activity, a history that stretches back to the early days of German Romanticism and German idealism (which eventually gave birth to Marxism on the one hand, but also to other things on the other hand). What Dan Rees's art appears to aspire to, however—and this is precisely where it has most successfully challenged the occasional reactionary inclinations of this elitist, among others—is to question this insular tendency, that is, art's self-isolating ways, by way of the jargon and spirit of art itself: call it art setting out to save *culture* from the clutches of the *culture industry* if you like—an art of righteous populist inspiration (as well as indignation).

Antonio Gramsci, one of the primary theorists of a truly working-class culture and perhaps the single most influential philosophical signpost in Rees's world, observed many decades ago that 'it seems evident that, to be precise, one should speak of a struggle for a "new culture" and not for a "new art" (in the immediate sense).'[3] A new culture such as the one Gramsci had in mind may not necessarily (or no longer) be in the offing—it is certainly not Rees's most pressing concern, and not exactly in accordance

with his rather unassuming artistic temperament—but it certainly pays for 'new art'
to look back at the cultures of old for guidance going forward, and Dan Rees does so
by revisiting the forgotten legacies of a truly populist avant-garde culture: back to the
future, where art *can* change or save the world.

1. Pierre Bourdieu, *Distinction:
    A Social Critique of the Judgment
    of Taste* (Cambridge,
    MA:Harvard University Press,
    1984), 56.

2. Alain Badiou, *Saint Paul:
    The Foundation of Universalism*
    (Stanford, CA: Stanford
    University Press, 2003), 12.

3. Quoted in David Forgacs, ed.,
    *The Antonio Gramsci Reader,
    Selected Writings 1916–1935*
    (New York: New York University
    Press, 2000), 395.

Due letture del lavoro di Dan Rees

di Dieter Roelstraete

1. Sinistra

Sicché l'arte diventa problematica proprio perché la realtà perde ogni problematicità.
—Georg Lukács, *Teoria del romanzo*, SE, Milano 1999, p. 16.

L'opera di Dan Rees tocca un ampio ventaglio di argomenti, soggetti e problemi, ma una preoccupazione ricorrente è senza dubbio quella che riguarda la *politica del gusto*. Il "gusto" – i suoi corollari culturali, le sfumature e i sottintesi politici e, soprattutto, le fonti sociali – è uno dei problemi preferiti da Dan Rees, ed è quando lo affronta nel modo più diretto e privo di remore – ovvero nei suoi cosiddetti "dipinti Artex" – che la sua produzione diventa volontariamente e oltraggiosamente più "problematica". La questione mette sullo stesso piano il problema del gusto e quello delicato di *classe*: l'Artex, un materiale per così dire storico, è, nel contesto delle origini di Rees, che proviene dalla classe operaia inglese, un tratto distintivo dell'appartenenza di classe e quindi, inevitabilmente, porta con sé il suo alone di abiezione estetica. L'Artex, dicono "loro", è *brutto*.

È interessante notare che spesso, nell'arte contemporanea, parlare di gusto è considerato privo di gusto; o, per usare un'espressione particolarmente efficace, semplice "cattivo" gusto. Si potrebbe ribattere che, per sua stessa definizione, l'arte contemporanea prospera *oltre* i confini del gusto; in genere si tratta di arte "dopo" il gusto (proprio come si tratta di arte "dopo" la capacità: i due concetti sono chiaramente legati). Di conseguenza, parlare di classe nella società odierna, presumibilmente priva di classi, è visto con una diffidenza simile, se non aperto disprezzo: anche discussioni del genere sono considerate indice di cattivo gusto (provateci, alla prossima cena in una galleria di New York!), vale a dire tutto fuorché "di classe". Proprio come l'arte contemporanea è una specie di arte "dopo il gusto" – arte fruita *dopo* la rovina dei tradizionali standard kantiani dell'*Urteilskraft*, del Giudizio –, così la cultura che l'accompagna prospera nel vuoto ideologico del "dopo la classe". (Ciò detto, la nostra società priva di classi non è necessariamente fatta per altra arte priva di gusto – *oppure sì?*) In ogni caso – e di conseguenza –, come lo stesso Rees ha osservato in diverse occasioni, "l'economia del mondo dell'arte ha generato il proprio processo di creazione di classi". Di fatto, questa potrebbe essere la funzione sociale segreta dell'arte contemporanea: trovare nuovi modi di reinsinuare distinzioni di classe in un ordine mondiale neoliberista teoricamente disabituato allo spettro della coscienza di classe.

Benché d'istinto venga naturale far "risalire" la comparsa dell'arte contemporanea (contrapposta alla semplice arte moderna o persino postmoderna) agli albori del consenso neoliberista che ha creato il miraggio di un mondo in cui le tradizionali distinzioni di classe non sembrano più contare granché – e che costituisce gran parte del decisivo background socio-economico contro cui bisogna interpretare alcune delle opere più apertamente politiche di Rees –, è naturalmente inutile cercare di individuare le origini storiche del contemporaneo nell'"arte contemporanea" e quelle dell'apparente assenza di classi della società contemporanea utilizzando un qualsiasi metodo che si avvicini all'esattezza storiografica. Tuttavia, se si volesse suggerire un punto d'origine preciso, probabilmente le origini dello stesso Rees fornirebbero una risposta piuttosto accurata: l'Inghilterra agli inizi del tatcherismo, più precisamente le sue frange in rapida de-industrializzazione e deregolamentazione. La fine degli anni Settanta, i primi Ottanta, quando la figlia di un droghiere di Grantham guidò i Conservatori alla vittoria, spronati dalla campagna "Labour Isn't Working"[1] della Saatchi & Saatchi; quando, oltreoceano, Reagan dava libero sfogo alla sua versione di lotta di classe su quel poco che rimaneva della coscienza di classe americana; quando ormai il miserabile fallimento del socialismo sovietico negli stati proletari originari era sotto gli occhi di tutti da tempo (è stata anche l'epoca, e non si tratta di una coincidenza, che ha assistito alla nascita della *Pictures Generation*); l'ascesa di Jeff Koons e della sua stirpe post-Warhol; il confondersi dei confini disciplinari tra cultura intellettuale e popolare, incarnata dal diffondersi della video arte e di altri media; il passaggio del testimone da Joseph Beuys a una generazione di attivisti più orientati al pragmatismo: tutti segnali decisivi nello sviluppo di ciò che oggi riconosciamo come parte integrante della contemporaneità nell'arte. È anche un capitolo della storia dell'arte – il nostro capitolo, che comprensibilmente fatichiamo a interpretare come qualcosa di diverso da una fase di passaggio –, che ha visto l'Artex diventare un materiale legittimo per creare arte, per essere arte.

Nel 1979, sulla soglia di questo momento storico, il sociologo francese Pierre Bourdieu diede alle stampe il magistrale *La distinzione. Critica sociale del gusto* (tradotto in inglese nel 1984 e in italiano nel 1983), una lettura ancora oggi fondamentale per chiunque sia interessato all'infido intrecciarsi di classe e gusto. Nel saggio, Bourdieu sostiene essenzialmente che la retorica del gusto è una macchina sofisticata per produrre e sorreggere la differenza ("distinzione") di classe.

"I gusti (cioè le preferenze espresse) rappresentano l'affermazione pratica di una differenza necessaria. Non a caso, quando debbono giustificarsi, si affermano in forma tutta negativa, attraverso il rifiuto opposto a gusti diversi: in materia di gusti, più che in qualsiasi altra, ogni determinazione è negazione", laddove il "cattivo" gusto, dalla prospettiva della differenza di classe, è sempre percepito come fondamentalmente inesistente. Infatti, Bourdieu prosegue: "L'intolleranza estetica conosce violenze terribili. L'avversione per gli stili di vita diversi rappresenta senza dubbio una delle barriere più solide tra le classi: *l'omogamia lo dimostra*".[2] È inoltre interessante notare l'uso particolare che Bourdieu fa del concetto talismanico di *differenza*, proprio in un momento storico in cui era considerato una panacea filosofica da moltissimi contemporanei, primi fra tutti Gilles Deleuze e Jacques Derrida (verso la fine del libro, Bourdieu si dice in disaccordo con l'interpretazione fatta da quest'ultimo della *Critica del Giudizio* kantiana). Il contrasto tra queste posizioni è sintomatico del più ampio spostamento di significato che caratterizza il governo neoliberista: la migrazione della "differenza" dal mondo reale delle relazioni sociali al regno innocuo del piacere estetico e della riflessione filosofica. O, in altre parole, Artex: dalle case popolari alle pareti delle gallerie.

2. Destra

L'arte – in rapporto alla vita – è sempre un nonostante.
—Georg Lukács, *Teoria del romanzo*, cit., p. 64.

Alla base della preoccupazione di Rees per l'intrecciarsi di classe e gusto, dobbiamo distinguere due questioni interconnesse, una delle quali riguarda il problema dell'accesso e dell'accessibilità (un'arte d'avanguardia può essere davvero "popolare"? Da dove nasce l'istintivo disprezzo dell'élite culturale verso le forme popolari in generale, che sopravvive ancora oggi? Perché ci viene detto così spesso che fare arte leggibile da una fascia più ampia della popolazione conduce inevitabilmente al suo stemperamento?), e l'altra riguarda il problema del vero impatto dell'arte sulle società (in parole povere: l'arte è in grado di cambiare o salvare il mondo?): entrambe le questioni convergono in un'interrogazione in corso del progetto (in gran parte fallito) di modernismo popolare, di una cultura davvero radicale per le masse. Al riguardo, l'opera più esemplare di Rees, in cui l'artista dà il massimo sotto il profilo politico (e, forse non a caso, il massimo sotto quello ampiamente autobiografico), è probabilmente il video dal titolo calzante *Road Back to Relevance* (La strada per tornare alla rilevanza, 2015), che tenta di mostrarci come "la campagna gallese di solidarietà per il Nicaragua possa oggi ispirare la gente", benché in realtà si chieda come l'arte possa assicurare l'attesa intersezione della rilevanza "sociale, culturale e politica" – ovvero la nominale "strada di ritorno alla rilevanza" dell'arte – che Rees ricerca in modo tanto evidente. (Il concetto di "solidarietà" sembra anacronistico quanto quello di classe nella discussione precedente.) Questa strada (per tornare) verso la rilevanza, il viaggio di ritorno dell'arte verso il nucleo dell'autocoscienza di una società, può comportare la negoziazione del rapporto, spesso teso, antagonistico e insieme simbiotico, tra *arte* e *cultura*: una distinzione carica di conseguenze per una migliore comprensione della pratica di Rees.

Per quanto possa valere, io stesso ho avuto per molto tempo la tendenza a errare sul versante dell'arte, nel modo descritto da Alain Badiou nell'introduzione a *San Paolo. La fondazione dell'universalismo*, in cui sostiene che:

Il mondo contemporaneo risulta essere doppiamente ostile ai processi di verità. Il sintomo di questa ostilità è costituito da occultamenti nominali: là dove dovrebbe esserci il nome di una procedura di verità viene a stare un altro nome che lo rimuove. Il nome "cultura" viene a obliterare quello di "arte". La parola "tecnica" oblitera la parola "scienza". La parola "gestione" oblitera la parola "politica". La parola "sessualità" oblitera l'amore. Il sistema "cultura-tecnica-gestione-sessualità", che ha l'enorme merito di essere omogeneo al mercato e i cui termini designano tutti, del resto, un repertorio di merci, è il moderno occultamento nominale del sistema "arte-scienza-politica-amore" che identifica tipologicamente le procedure di verità.[3]

In sintesi, Badiou confonde la cultura con l'*industria culturale* – il vecchio pilastro della critica culturale sulla scia della Scuola di Francoforte –, con termini che inscrivono il suo pensiero nella lunga storia della valutazione filosofica dell'arte al di sopra di qualsiasi altro ambito dell'attività umana, una storia che risale agli albori del romanticismo e dell'idealismo tedeschi (che in definitiva hanno portato alla nascita del marxismo da un lato, ma dall'altro anche a cose ben diverse). In ogni caso, l'arte di Dan Rees sembra aspirare a mettere in discussione la tendenza alla ristrettezza – e proprio in questo aspetto ha sfidato con maggiore successo le sporadiche inclinazioni reazionarie di questo mondo elitario, tra le altre cose –, ovvero le modalità di autoisolamento dell'arte, operate attraverso il gergo e lo spirito dell'arte stessa: chiamatela arte per salvare la cultura dalle grinfie dell'*industria culturale*, un'arte di legittima ispirazione (e indignazione) populista.

Antonio Gramsci, tra i maggiori teorici di una cultura davvero operaia e forse la guida filosofica più influente nel mondo di Rees, diversi decenni fa ha osservato che sembra chiaro "che si debba parlare, per essere esatti, di lotta per una 'nuova cultura' e non per una 'nuova arte' (in senso immediato)".[4] Una nuova cultura come quella che Gramsci aveva in mente potrebbe non essere

necessariamente (o non più) nell'aria –
di certo non è la preoccupazione principale
di Rees, e non è in linea con il suo tempera-
mento artistico piuttosto dimesso –, ma
sicuramente alla "nuova arte" fa gioco ripensare alle culture degli antichi in cerca

di indicazioni su come proseguire, e Dan
Rees lo fa rivisitando i lasciti dimenticati di
una cultura d'avanguardia davvero populista:
un ritorno al futuro in cui l'arte è davvero
in grado di cambiare o salvare il mondo.

1. Lo slogan si basa su un gioco
di parole, e significa: "Il Partito
Laburista non funziona", ma
anche: "Il Partito Laburista non
lavora", un riferimento all'alto
tasso di disoccupazione inglese
nel 1979. *(NdT)*

2. Pierre Bourdieu, *La distinzione.
Critica sociale del gusto*, Società
editrice il Mulino, Bologna 1983,
p. 56, corsivo mio.

3. Alain Badiou, *San Paolo. La
fondazione dell'universalismo*,
Edizioni Cronopio, Napoli 1999,
p. 23.

4. Antonio Gramsci, "Cinema Nuovo",
1, dicembre 1952.

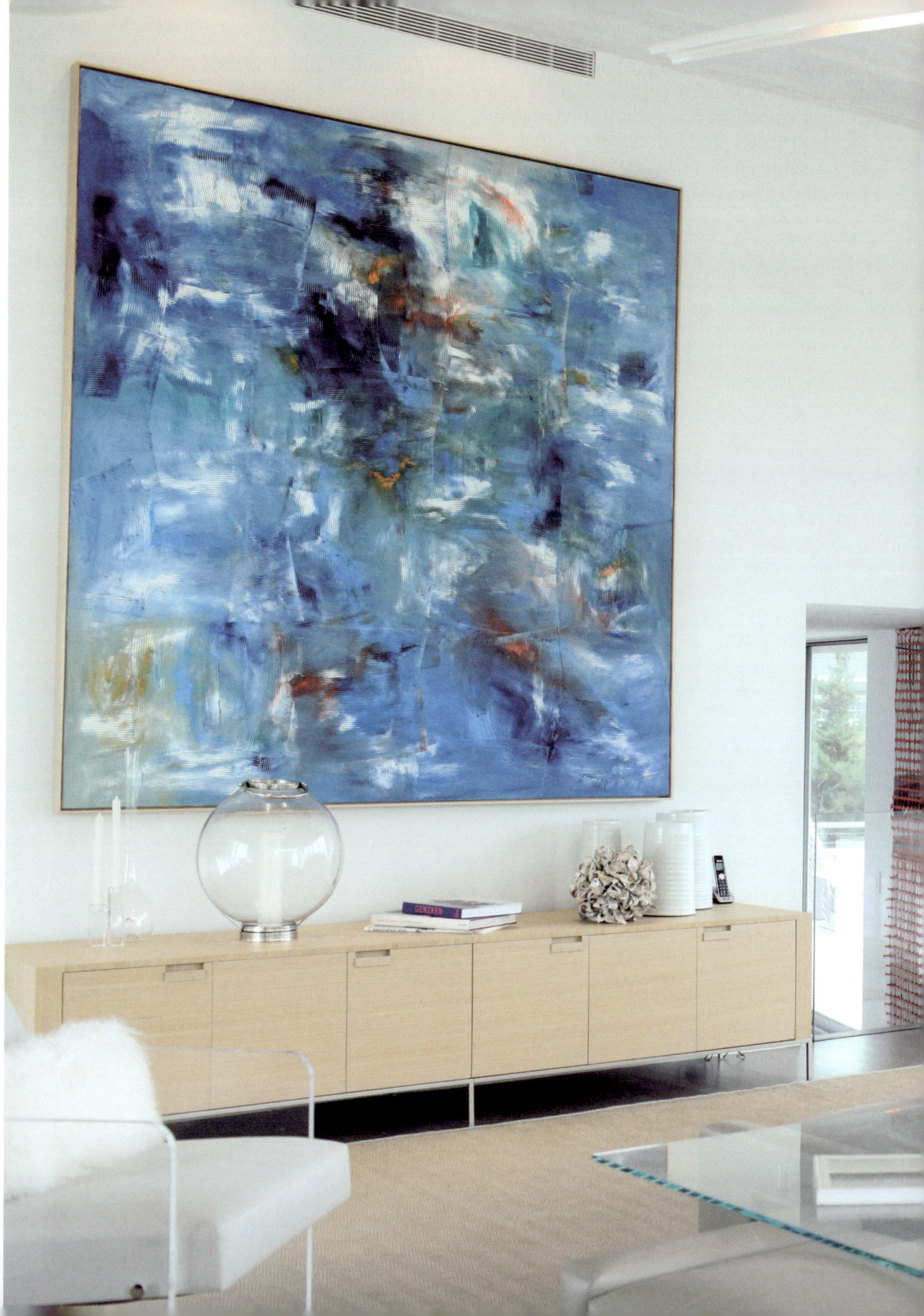

Intended Circulation, 2013–ongoing

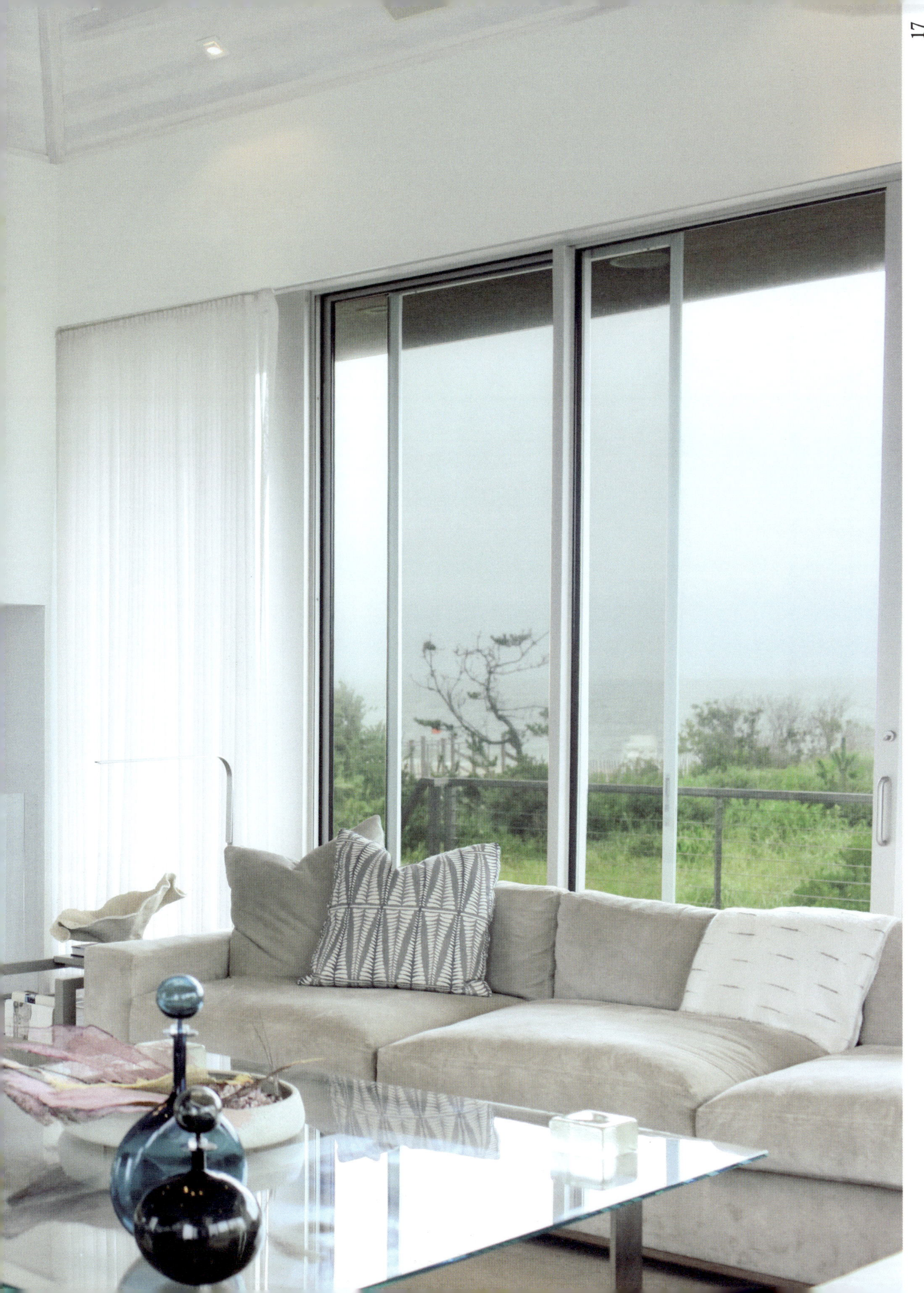

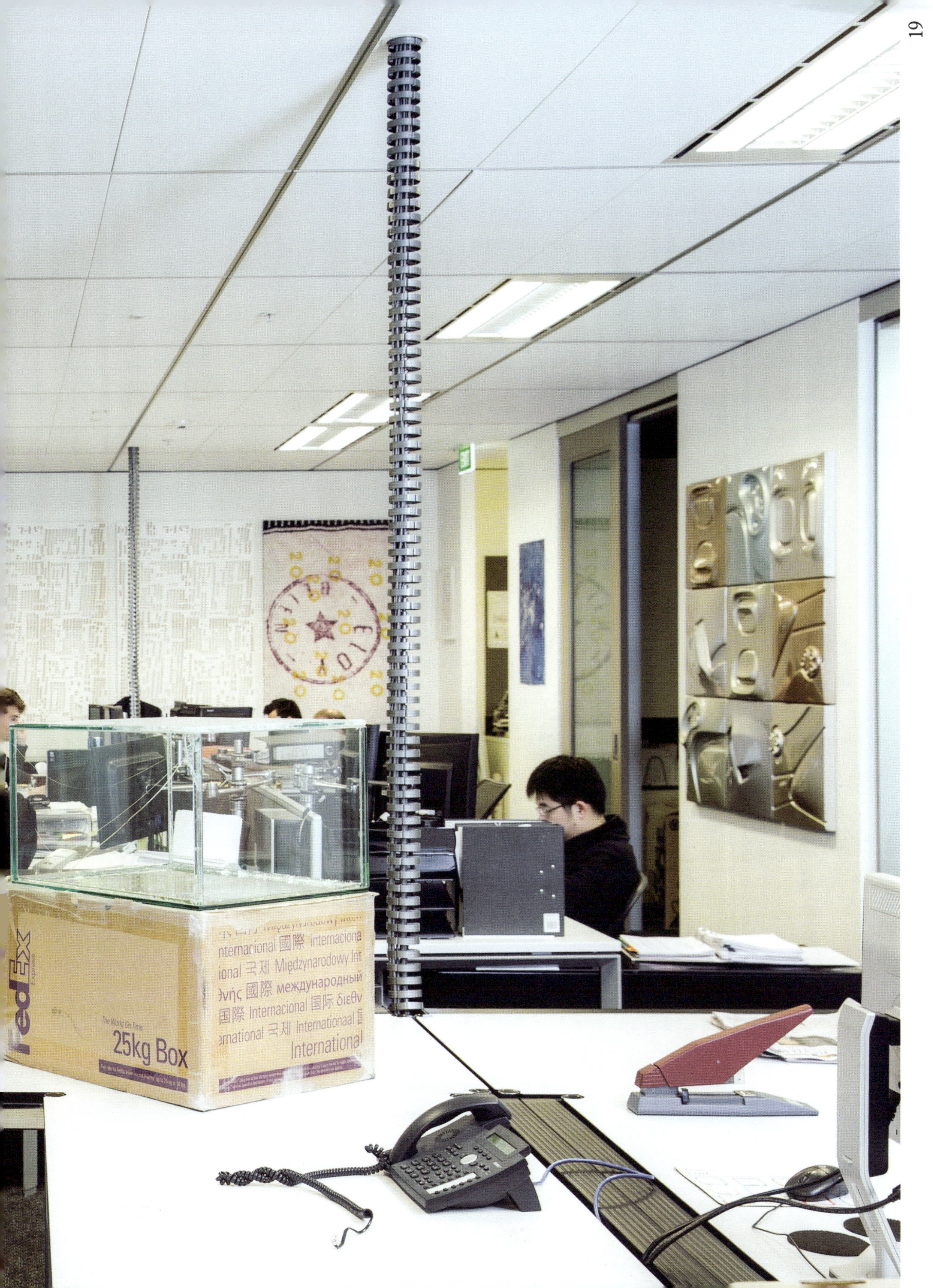
International 國際 Internaciona
ional 국제 Międzynarodowy Int
ǒνής 國際 международный
國際 Internacional 国际 διεθν
ernational 국제 Internationaal 国
International
FedEx
The World On Time
25kg Box

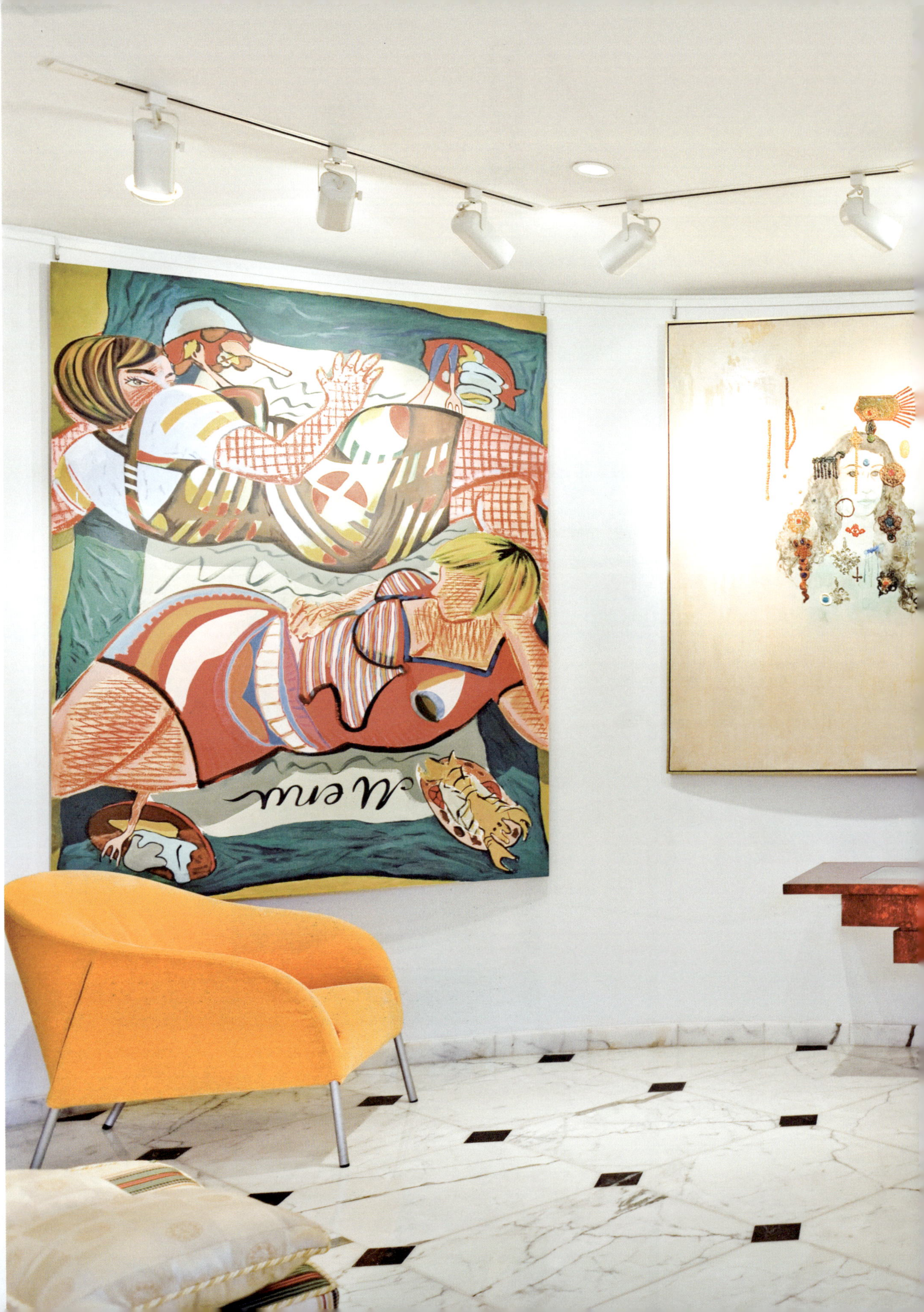

Intended Circulation, 2013–ongoing

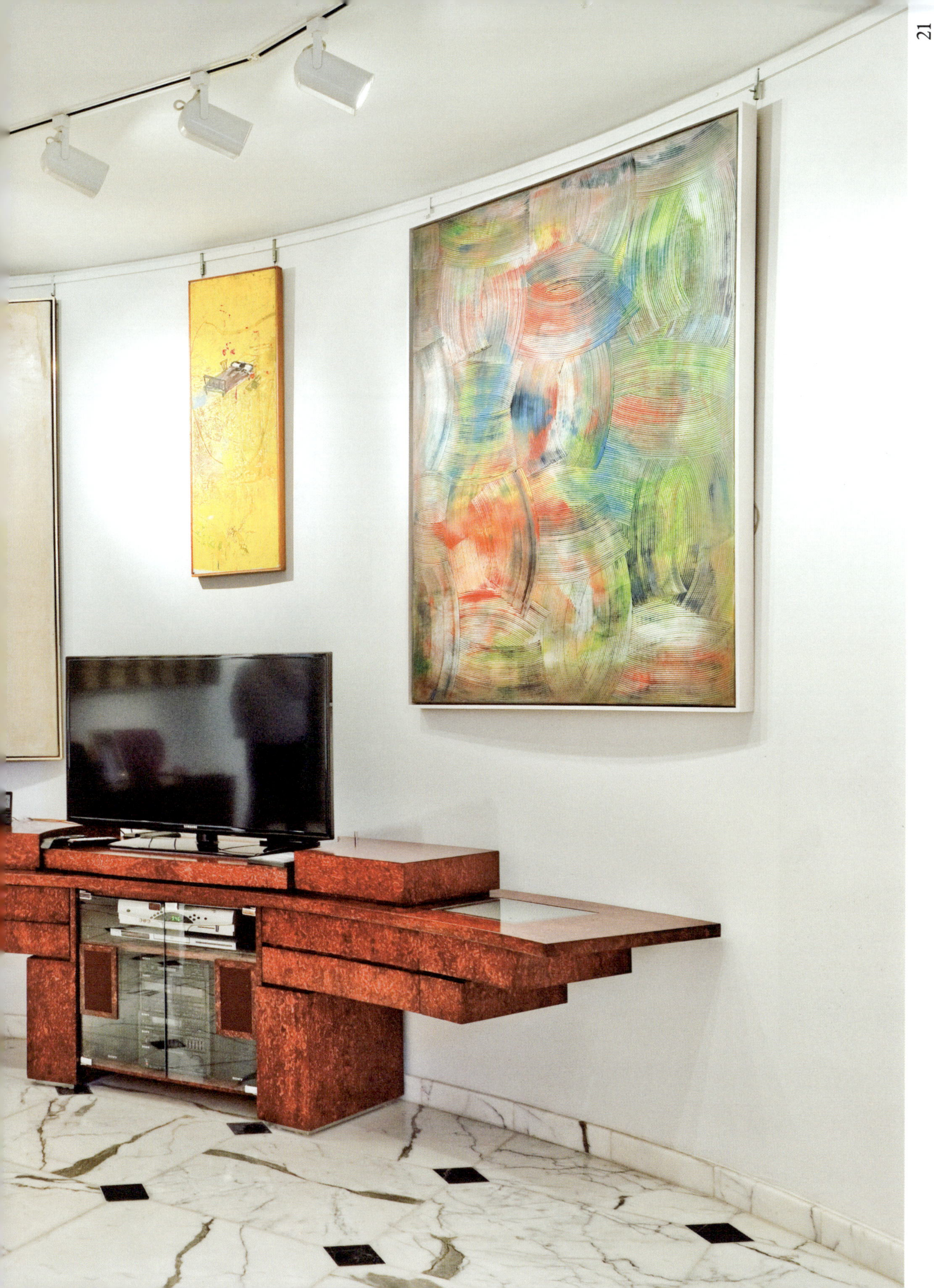

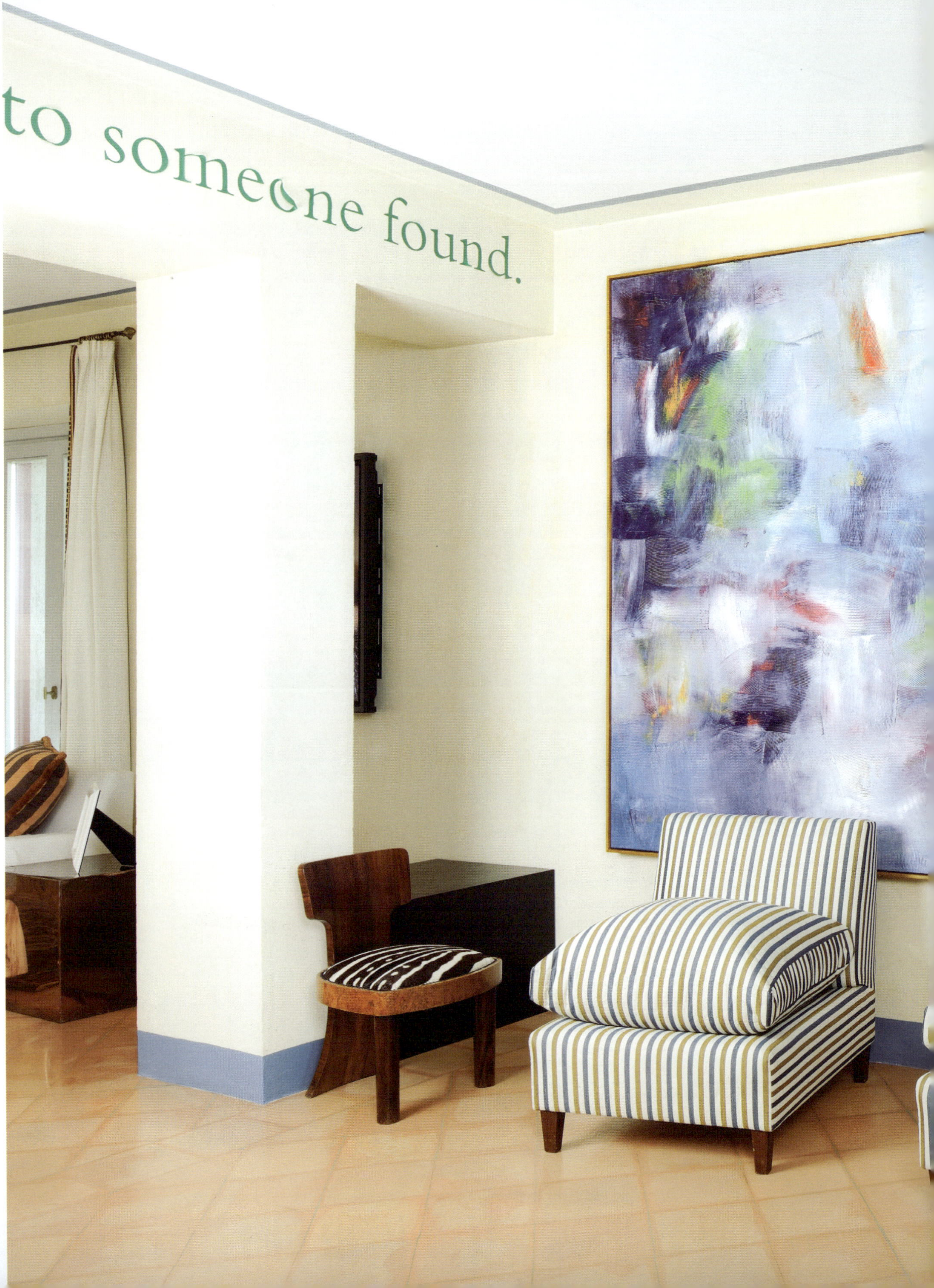

to someone found.

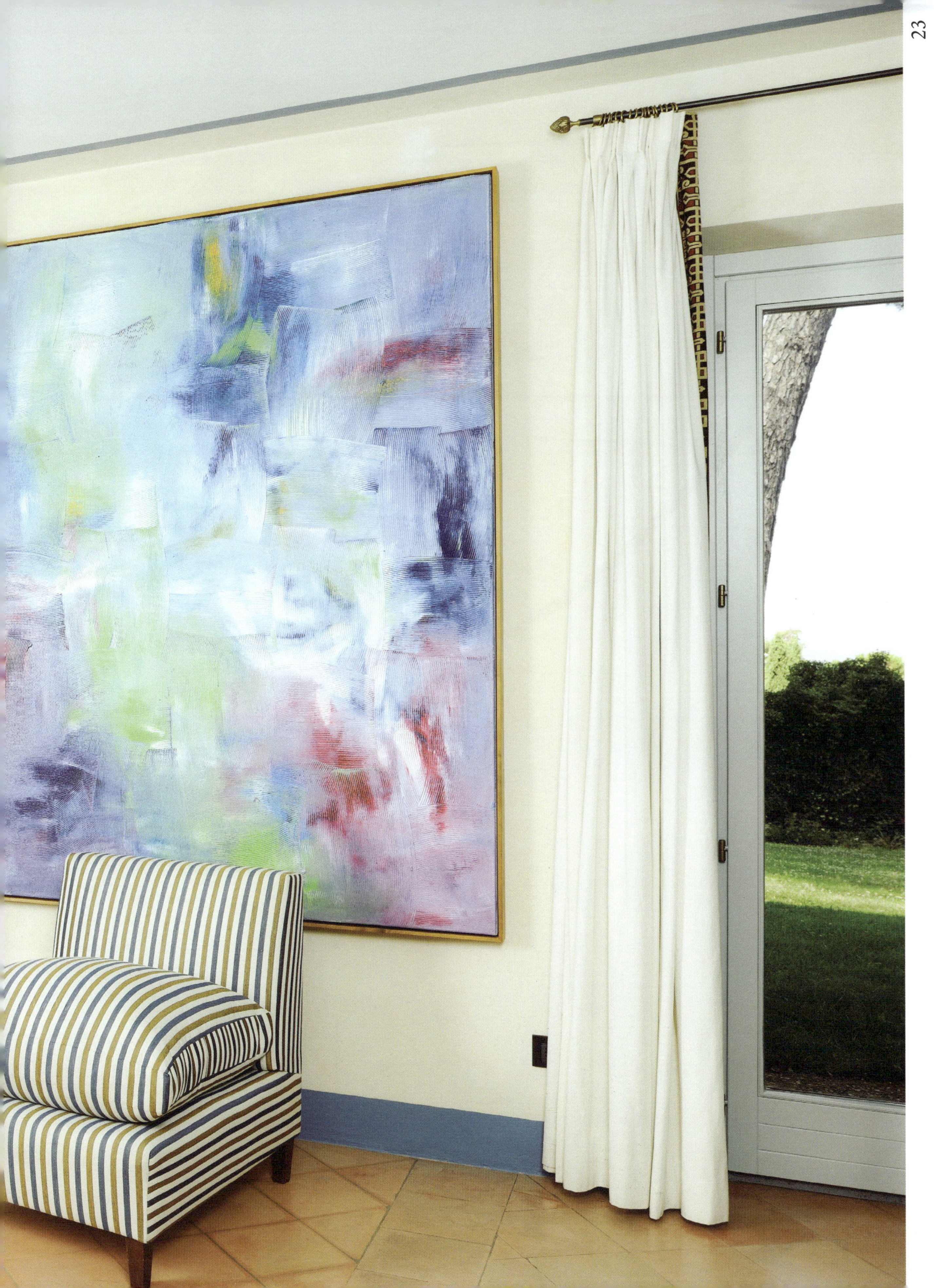

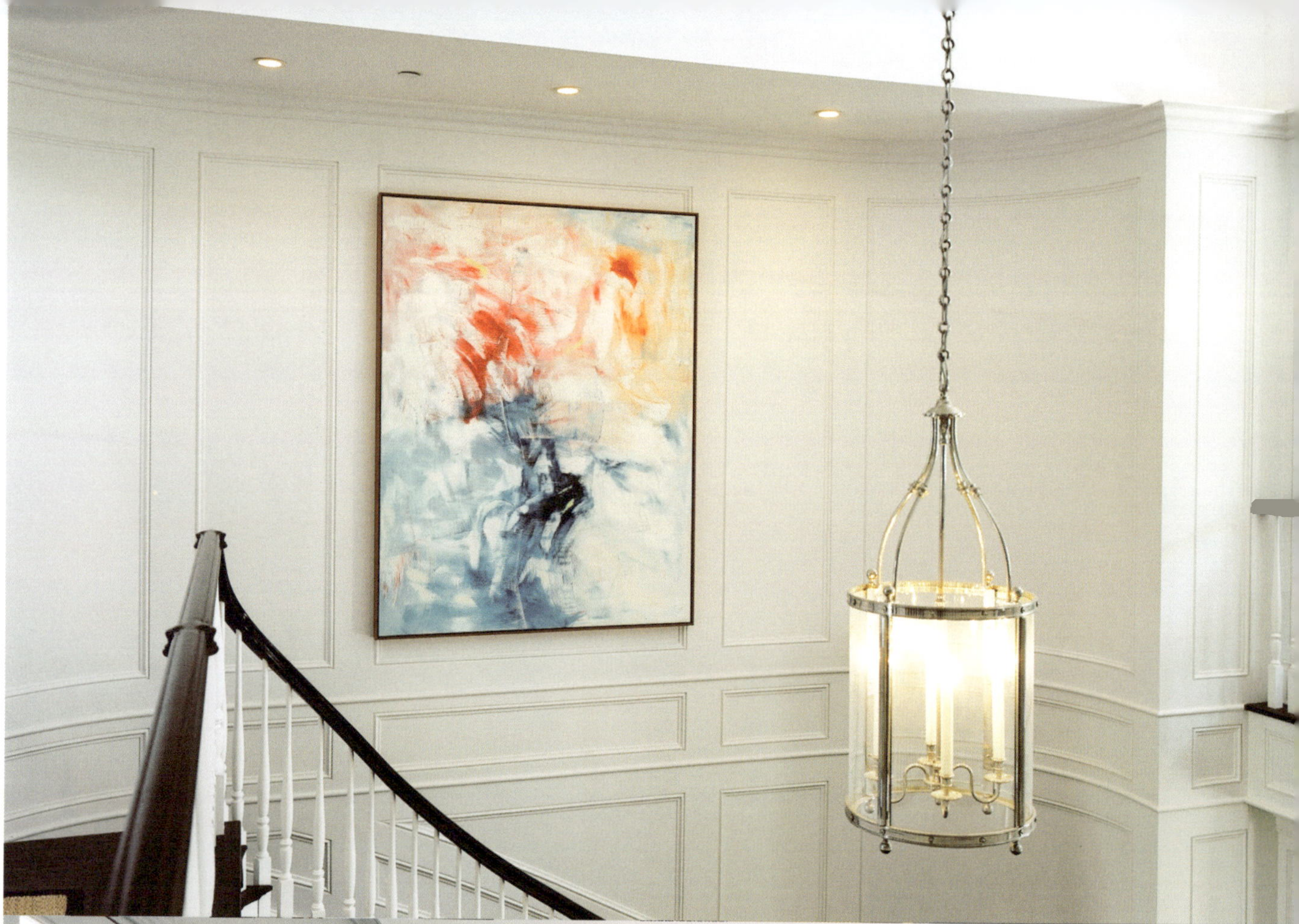

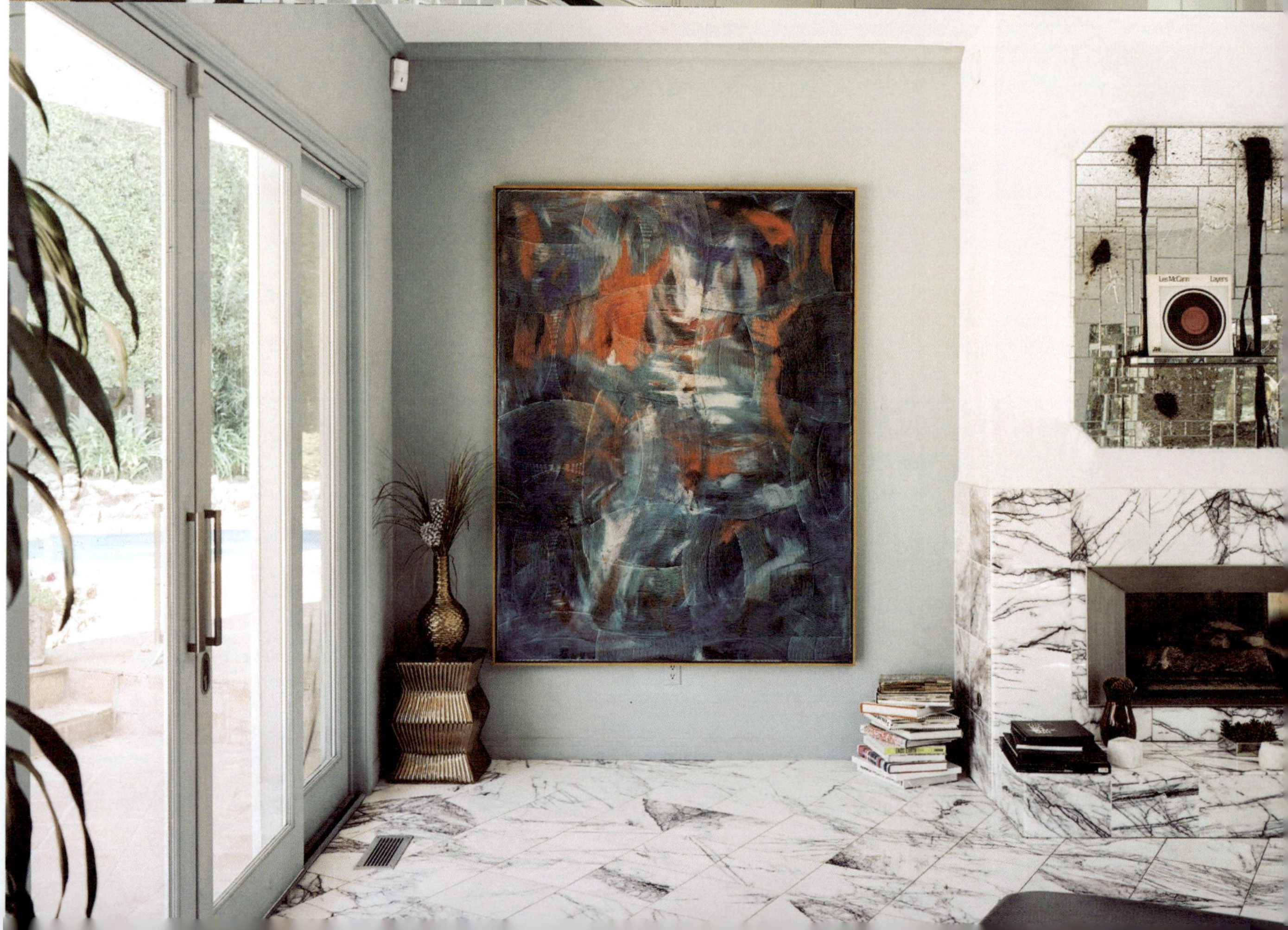

Intended Circulation, 2013–ongoing

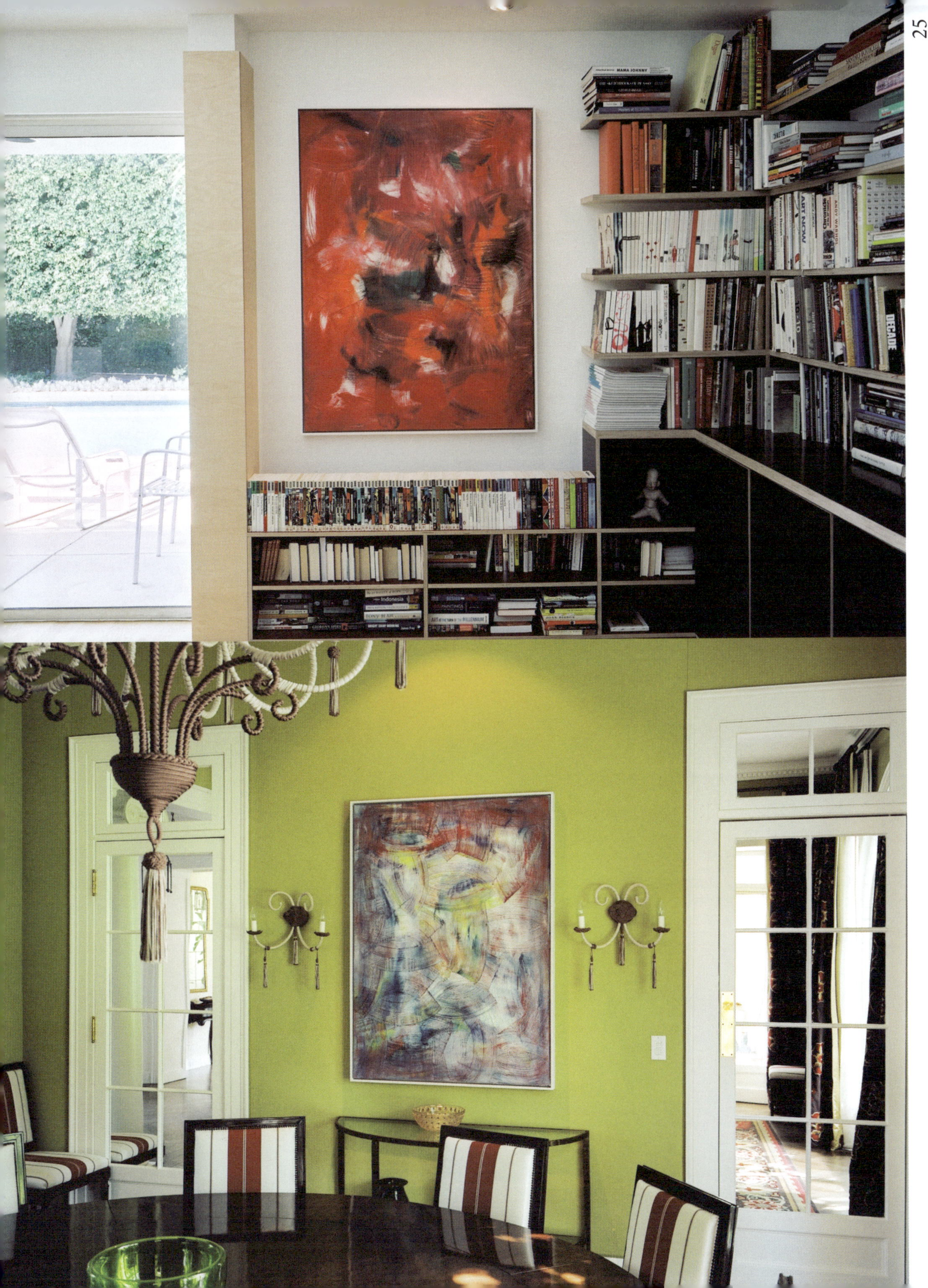

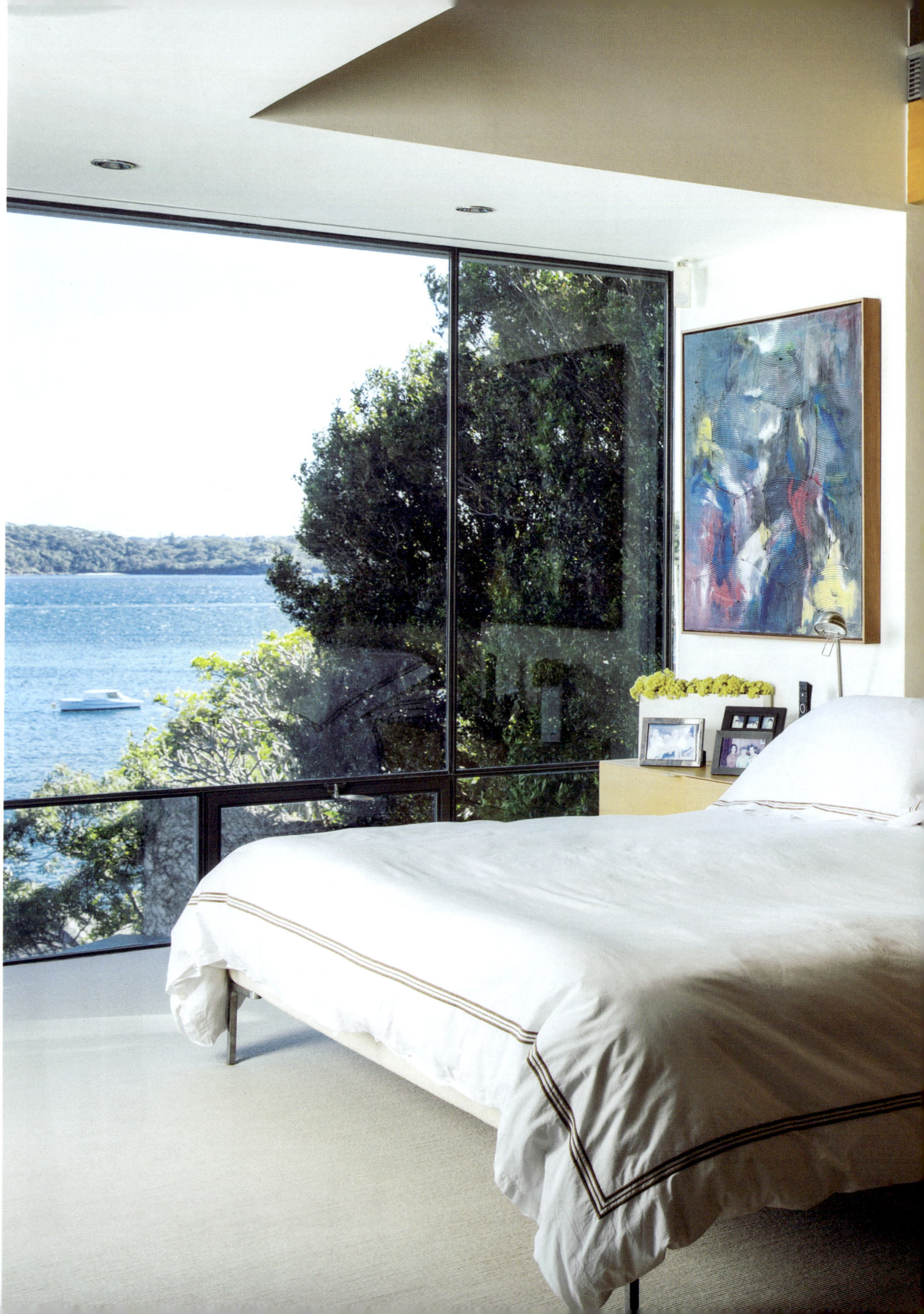

Intended Circulation, 2013–ongoing

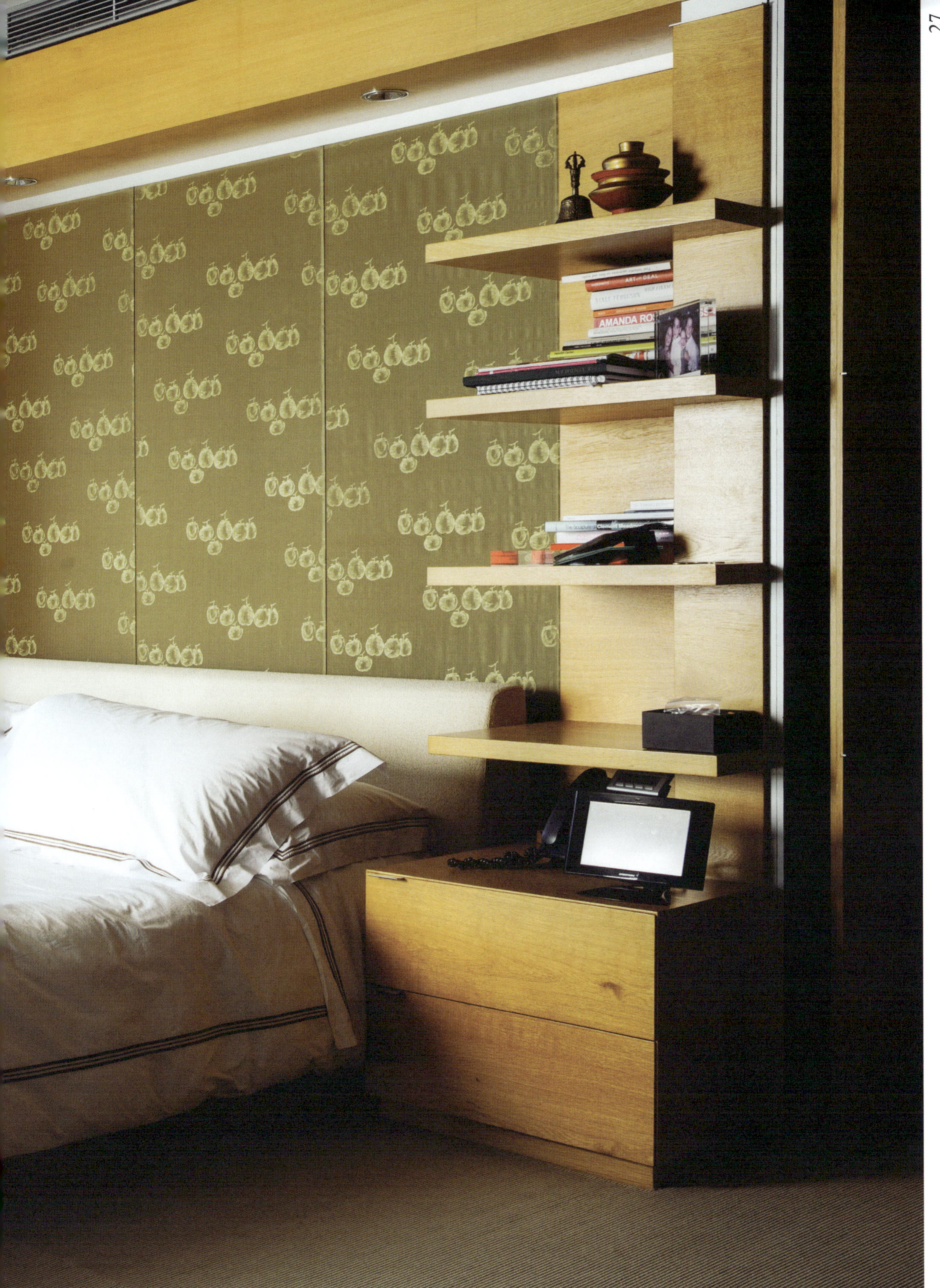

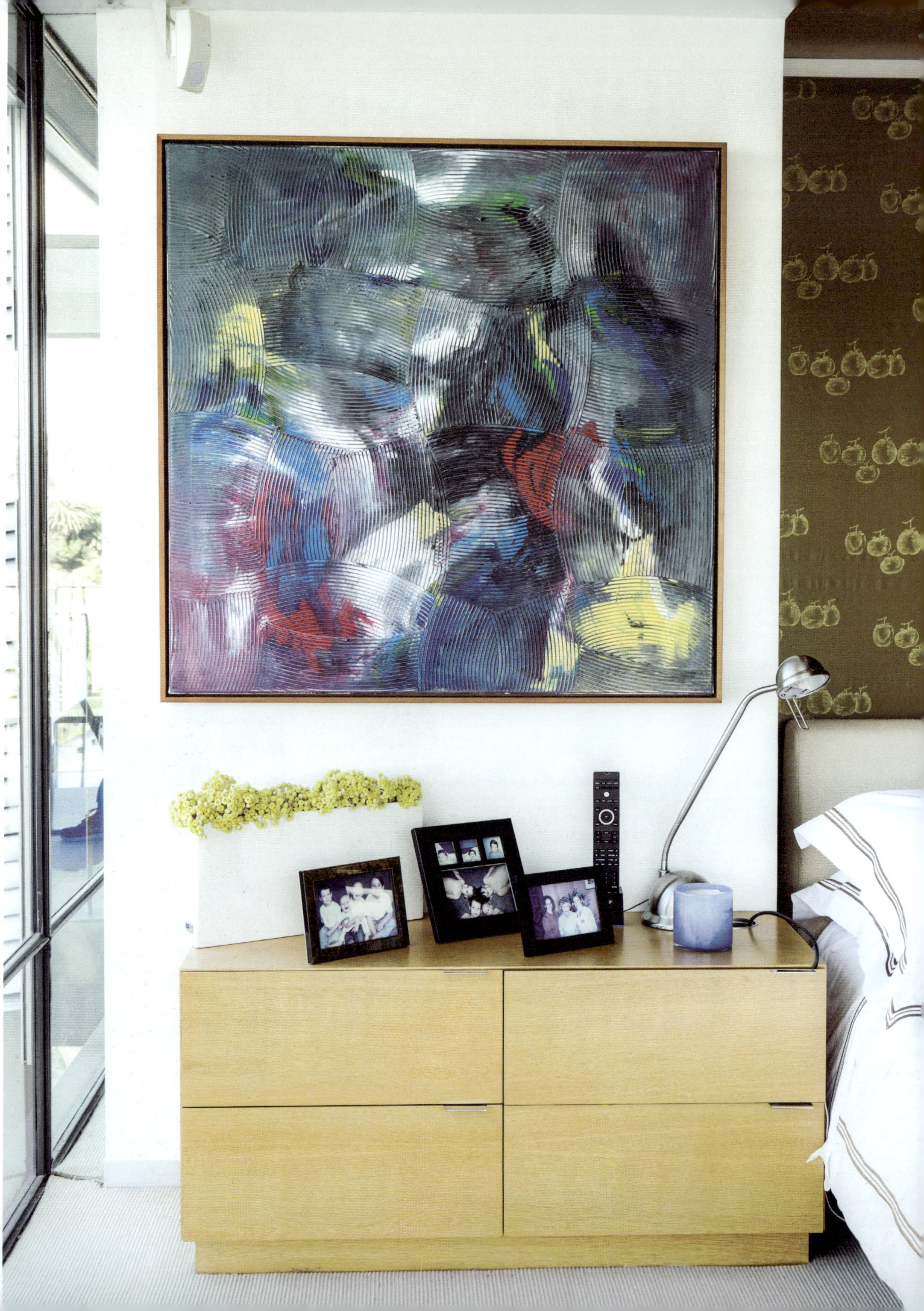

Intended Circulation, 2013–ongoing

Re: presentation   by Saim Demircan

> *A painting can be seen from the front and the wall can see it from the back and the artist can see it as the maker. When someone says to me, I have a painting of yours in my home, I say describe it to me and then I say, this picture I have not painted. Can't be mine. You don't have it in control.*
> —Martin Kippenberger, *Picture a Moon, Shining in the Sky: Conversation with Martin Kippenberger*, 3rd ed. (Berlin: Starship, 2013), 51.

I'm looking at a photo of a collector's living room. Clean, modern, tastefully decorated. On the wall hangs a painting, one of what are often referred to as Dan Rees's 'Artex paintings.' This is the same image Bank of America sent the artist, asking his permission to use it in a company advertisement. For Rees, this request at the time raised a pivotal question of control around the circumstances in which the Artex paintings are critically received. While it's fair to say that artists have to appreciate an inevitable detachment from their artwork once it enters a commercial system, it is unambiguous why, spurred by a marketing campaign in which the context of its destination had inadvertently changed, he would want to re-address these works. After turning down this unexpected request, the artist himself started to consider photographing the Artex paintings that reside in private homes. Rees originally conceived the paintings with respect to idea and medium, but not in terms of documenting them at their receiving end.

Bank of America's request may have been an impetus for Rees, yet the artist had already, when making the very first Artex painting, *imagined* an image of it in a domestic interior. Of course, as it turned out, forming a mental image of the work in its proposed surroundings was more prophetic than whimsical. Rees's incorporation of painting as a container for his ideas means that the works are more susceptible to changing conditions that affect the medium's specificity. As such, the artist's use of painting as a medium overturns the established notions of Conceptualism in which his practice is rooted. In this sense, Rees conflates a rigid distinction previously claimed between Conceptual art and its presentation as primary and secondary information.[1]

In thinking through such implications, which represent a loss of control over the work itself, it is worth taking a brief look at a prevalent contemporary condition heralded by the advent of online image circulation, which roughly corresponds, timewise, to the artist's reintroduction of painting into his practice. Considering the rate at which images of artworks flow through social media and aggregator websites, the ripple effect of their distribution has been said to disable 'the judgmental element of consensus in favour of collective attention.'[2] Looking back, Joseph Kosuth, for example, took it upon himself (vis-à-vis his writing alias, Arthur R. Rose) to control the criteria of judgment around his peer group of artists, and together with Seth Siegelaub publicised emerging Conceptual practices in the late 1960s. Fast forward forty-plus years, and what has 'become a process of simple visibility'[3] is comparatively uncontrollable through technocratic, user-generated forms of re-representation. The 'outside information'[4] Siegelaub pursued in print media, which at the time in part destabilised the role of the critic and shifted influence to that of the dealer, is extrapolated in today's reproducible image ad infinitum. A corresponding criteria of judgment around re-emergent trends and past tropes in painting simply cannot keep up with the pace of technologically enhanced image circulation, in some instances leading to reactionary texts on abstraction and its relationship with the market.[5] Painting has come to be seen as an obedient model, not least because the dimensions of the canvas are subservient to those of the screen. As Rosalind Krauss has noted, (photographic) reproduction rendered painting's previously 'resistant opacity' into a 'glitteringly transparent sign of its own subordination.'[6] The issue of control is therefore germane if one considers that artists can often find themselves 'controlled' by a particular image of their work, or the exhibition-as-image in which it might appear online.

By returning to the physical spaces in which the Artex paintings are sited, Rees reinserts himself as their maker into the circulation and reception of his work by systematically relocating the medium of painting within the frame of the photograph. Continuing an enduring acknowledgment of the latter's conceptual heritage, especially where it has been utilised as a recording device to document the finality of an action, the artist not only uses but has outsourced photography throughout his practice, from asking the artist Cerith Wyn Evans to select photographs of his Welsh birthplace for *One Afternoon And Evening In Llanelli; An Ode To Cerith Wyn Evans* (2007), to, more recently, mounting a show of large-scale chromogenic prints taken by his brother-in-law in Nicaragua, whom Rees briefed to document scenes of solidarity.[7] For the series *In The Ghetto It Gets Cold But We've Got Something To Warm Our Soles* (2012) Rees collaborated with the fashion photographer Michael Hemy on a photo shoot for an exhibition of the same name.[8] By stepping back in these cases, forfeiting the last subjective decision over the work's final actualisation, Rees further charges their predicament.

The Artex paintings in collectors' homes have been professionally photographed. In this instance, Rees decisively cedes control as a way of reconstituting a criterion of judgment around the work instead of letting any implied critique easily misconstrue the project. If the artist's initial concern was to restrain, or rein in, their reception for his own design, then it is important to reiterate that his decision to do so was not preemptively ideational, or premeditated in a manner or style of conceptual irony that already knows its endgame. By forging a path from painting to photography, Rees instead returns to an origin. Yet it is only since he has begun to exhibit these photographs alongside the actual paintings that their reception is problematised in public. Titling both the series as well as the individual images *Intended Circulation* serves as further vindication of the artist's original meaning for the work. Of course, the title also reinstates the exhibition as a site within this passage. Seeing the paintings through photography prolongs their stasis at their point of arrival in a collector's home.

It is helpful to read this movement between mediums in light of what David Joselit terms transitivity in painterly practices that 'offer a way out of a particularly enduring critical dead end: the reification trap. [...] The problem with the term "reification" is that it connotes the permanent arrest of an object's circulation within a network: it is halted, paid for, put on a wall, or sent to storage, therefore permanently crystallizing a particular social relation.'[9] Does Rees avoid what Joselit calls the 'reification trap' by having his paintings photographed in situ, and furthermore by re-exhibiting them via photographs? While they might currently exist in a state of 'permanent arrest' at their destinations, perhaps it was actually a corruption of the paintings' imagined potential when a corporate agency got mixed up with their acquisition, which Rees returns to with a conceptual sensibility rather than through a cynical replay of their materialism. Given that their transitivity from the studio to the collector's home is visualised quite explicitly through the transparency of the photographic image, then surely it would be disadvantageous to misjudge the Artex paintings as submissive to the market, or *Intended Circulation* as critically gestural towards it.

Apart from the subtle irony of displacing Artex (along with its class associations) from one interior to another, as well as from ceiling to wall, the Artex paintings themselves possess an aesthetic that puts distance between them and, let's say, a deskilled or more overtly conceptual approach to painting. Nor do they try to disrupt the *feng shui* of the homes they enter by calling out the tenacity of the market that led them there. If anything, their astuteness lies in parasiting painting itself, which ultimately becomes the host body for Rees's underlying conceptualism. For instance, two of the artist's earlier works explicitly deal with a displacement of their own circulation and reception, but through forms more obviously in debt to the tenets of Conceptual art. *The Postman's Decision Is Final* (2006) is a double-sided postcard upon which two different addresses can simultaneously be written, one always addressed to the gallery or site of exhibition, leaving it undetermined whether or not it will arrive at the show. The installation of 16mm films *Something To Fill That Empty Feeling* (2007) meanwhile depicts a corner of a gallery space, with each projection re-filmed and projected again, creating a Russian doll effect that embodies where it is shown with its own repeated image. Both of these works thrive on the systems within which they operate—whether postal or spatial— whereas Rees's paintings suggest a move away from materials normally associated with Conceptual art. More specifically they represent a dwindling interest in keeping the idea 'pure,' as has been propagated by some of its inheritors. One could say that whereas Martin Creed, for example, repeats a binary logic in his approach to painting, Rees has moved on from the instructional ideas of earlier series, such as applying paint to a canvas and then imprinting, or squashing, it directly onto the wall, or placing paintings in airtight clear bags, quite literally sealing the medium hermetically.

These somewhat irresolute attempts towards 'muddying the water' between painterly aesthetics and conceptualism arrive together in the Artex paintings precisely because they began to develop a 'life of their own' beyond the conceptual borders that might usually have defined their presentation as secondary information. In the artist's own self-admission, 'When [the Artex paintings] become beautiful, seductive objects they start to be awkward [...] betraying the concept.' This 'awkwardness' taints the purity of the idea with an aesthetic sensibility, a merging of the manual labour involved in interior decoration with the preparation and execution of abstract painting. As well as referencing the social context in which Artex was popularised, the Artex paintings were originally thought of as a meeting of a specific handicraft with the medium of painting. Yet the attention Rees gives to painterly *process*—he speaks about prepping the canvases with a concern for their material properties—is significant in that it moves the work away from the orthodoxy of hard-edged Conceptualism, where the idea remains the primary material.

'What do representations represent?' asks Helmut Draxler in his essay on Louise Lawler[10], who herself photographed artworks by other artists in spaces that contextualise them. 'The answer has to be: the social function of taste.'[11] At this stage it would be symptomatic to rethink Bank of America's request in context, because no doubt they imagined that the overall image—in which the artist's painting constitutes only a part—would appeal to their clientele. It is, after all, the context that represents the works in which they were 'intended,' or imagined, which led Rees to the idea for *Intended*

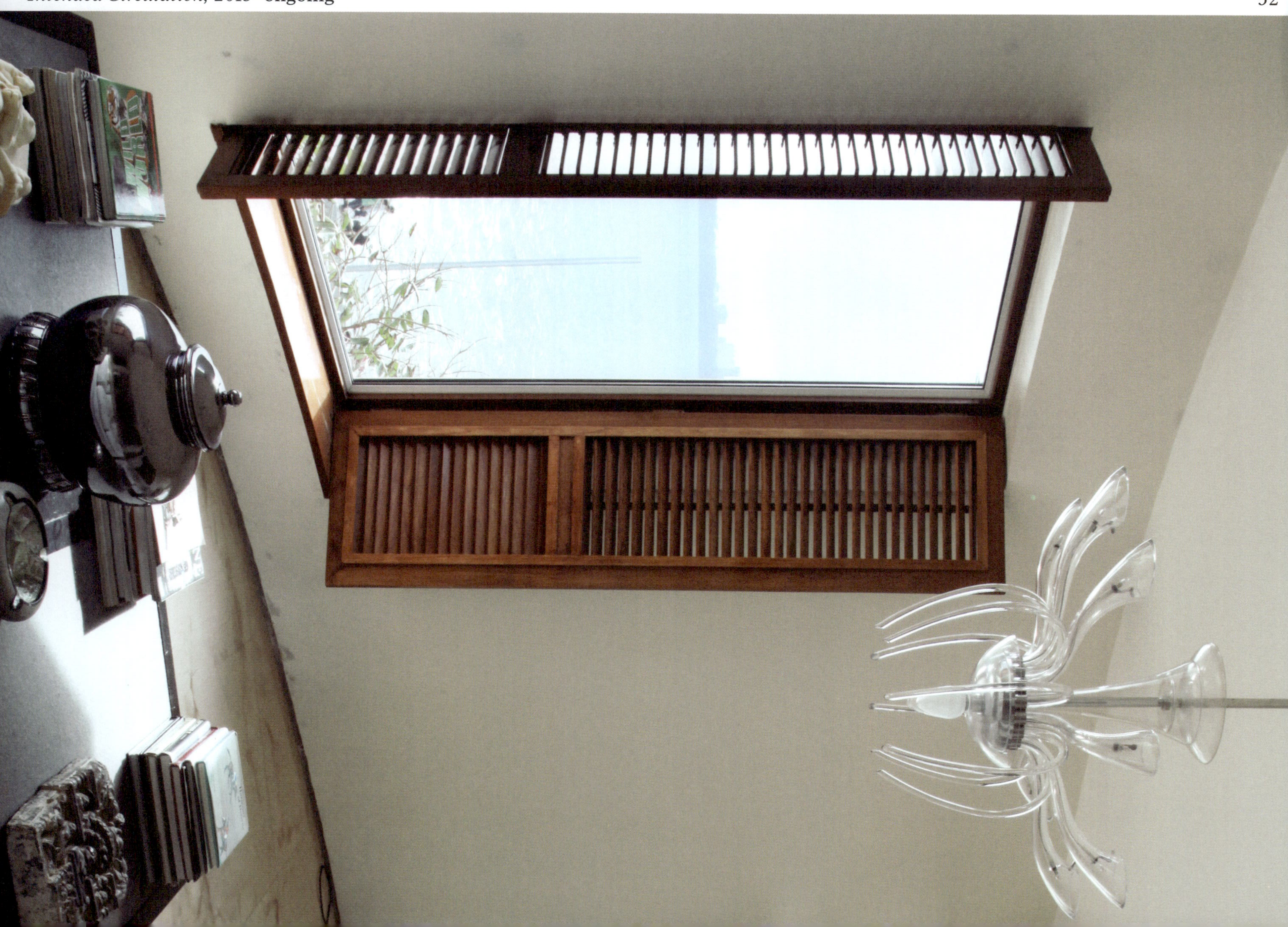

Circulation. However, to be at ease artistically with their context, the final representation of the Artex paintings requires the controlling interest of the artist himself. If art can be used to 'aestheticize the functions of power'[12] then maybe it needs an intervention in order to regulate such conditions. As such, Rees doesn't disrupt the system(s) in which his paintings operate but instead settles, even if just for himself, an issue of their circulation and reception by using 'strategies of representation' that call attention to their social function. In this respect, the Artex paintings find their point of arrival through photography with *Intended Circulation* the checkered flag in a figure-eight between cyclical discourses of painting and conceptualism.

1. Alexander Alberro, *Conceptual Art and the Politics of Publicity* (Cambridge, MA, and London: MIT Press, 2003), 56–57.

2. Michael Sanchez, 'Art and Transmission', *Artforum* (Summer 2013), 297.

3. Ivi.

4. Alexander Alberro, *Conceptual Art and the Politics of Publicity*, 57.

5. See Walter Robinson, 'Flipping and the Rise of Zombie Formalism', Artspace.com, http://www.artspace.com/magazine/contributors/see_here/the_rise_of_zombie_formalism-52184, or Jerry Saltz, 'Zombies on the Walls: Why Does So Much New Abstraction Look the Same?', Vulture.com, http://w\ww.vulture.com/2014/06/why-new-abstract-paintings-look-the-same.html.

6. Rosalind Krauss, 'Louise Lawler: Souvenir Memories', in *A Spot on the Wall*, ed. Hedwig Saxenhuber (Cologne: Oktagon Verlag, 1998), 36.

7. This was part of a larger research project about international solidarity campaigns between Wales and Nicaragua. The exhibition was *Dan Rees*, at Tanya Leighton, Berlin, 2013.

8. *In The Ghetto It Gets Cold But We've Got Something To Warm Our Soles* showed at Baronian-Francey, Brussels, in 2012.

9. David Joselit, 'Painting Beside Itself', *October* 130 (Fall 2009), 125–34.

10. Helmut Draxler, 'Art Into Culture Exhibition as Social Intervention', in *A Spot On The Wall*, 70.

11. Ivi.

12. Ibid., 72.

Ri: presentazione *di Saim Demircan*

Un dipinto può essere visto da davanti, il muro può vederlo da dietro e l'artista può vederlo in quanto l'ha creato. Quando qualcuno mi dice: "Ho un suo dipinto a casa", chiedo di descrivermelo e poi rispondo: "Non ho dipinto quest'immagine. Non può essere mia. Lei non la controlla".
—Martin Kippenberger, *Picture a Moon, Shining in the Sky: Conversation with Martin Kippenberger*, terza edizione, Starship, Berlino 2013, p. 51.

Sto osservando la foto del salotto di un collezionista: pulito, moderno, decorato con gusto. Al muro è appeso un dipinto, uno di quelli che spesso vengono definiti i "dipinti Artex" di Dan Rees. È la stessa foto che la Bank of America ha spedito all'artista, chiedendogli il permesso di usarla per una pubblicità aziendale. Allora, la richiesta ha posto Rees davanti al fondamentale problema del controllo delle circostanze in cui i dipinti Artex vengono accolti a livello critico. Se è corretto dire che gli artisti devono accettare un inevitabile distacco dalla propria opera quando viene immessa in un sistema commerciale, è evidente perché Rees – spinto da una campagna marketing in cui il contesto di destinazione era cambiato – abbia voluto rivisitare questi dipinti. Dopo aver rifiutato l'inaspettata proposta, l'artista ha cominciato a pensare di fotografare i dipinti Artex che si trovano all'interno di residenze private. In origine li ha concepiti pensando all'idea e al medium, ma non per documentarli nel luogo di destinazione.

Forse la richiesta della Bank of America è stata uno stimolo per Rees, che però, realizzando il primo dipinto Artex, ne aveva già *immaginato* un'immagine all'interno di una casa. Com'è naturale, e come hanno dimostrato i fatti, la creazione di un'immagine mentale dell'opera nell'ambiente proposto si

è rivelata più profetica che eccentrica. Rees incorpora il dipinto come contenitore per le proprie idee, e ciò significa che le opere sono più soggette alle condizioni mutevoli che influenzano la specificità del medium. L'uso che l'artista fa del dipinto come medium capovolge così il principio consolidato del concettualismo, nel quale la sua pratica affonda le radici. In questo senso, Rees fonde l'attestata e rigida distinzione tra l'arte concettuale e la sua presentazione, viste come informazione primaria e secondaria.[1]

Se si riflette su tali implicazioni, che rappresentano una perdita di controllo sull'opera stessa, vale la pena esaminare rapidamente una condizione contemporanea dominante annunciata dall'avvento della circolazione online delle immagini, che a livello temporale corrisponde grossomodo al momento in cui l'artista ha reintrodotto la pittura nella propria pratica. Se si considera il ritmo con cui le immagini delle opere d'arte scorrono attraverso i social media e gli aggregatori, è stato detto che l'effetto domino della loro distribuzione "invalida l'elemento critico del consenso a favore dell'attenzione collettiva".[2] Pensiamo al passato: Joseph Kosuth, per esempio, si è assunto (*vis-à-vis* con il suo pseudonimo letterario, Arthur R. Rose) la responsabilità di controllare i criteri di giudizio nel suo gruppo di artisti; e alla fine degli anni Sessanta, insieme a Seth Siegelaub, ha reclamizzato pratiche concettuali emergenti. *Fast forward*: oltre quarant'anni dopo, ciò che è "diventato un processo di semplice visibilità"[3] è ormai relativamente incontrollabile per via delle forme di ri-rappresentazione tecnocratiche e *user-generated*. L'"informazione esterna"[4] ricercata da Siegelaub nella stampa, che all'epoca ha in parte destabilizzato il ruolo del critico spostandone l'influenza su quello del mercante, è estrapolata nell'odierna immagine riproducibile all'infinito. Simili criteri di giudizio riguardanti tendenze riemergenti e tropi del passato in pittura non riescono a stare al passo con la circolazione dell'immagine potenziata dalla tecnologia, e in alcuni casi portano a testi reazionari sull'astrazione e sul suo rapporto con il mercato.[5] La pittura è ormai vista come un modello obbediente, anche perché le dimensioni della tela sono sottomesse a quelle dello schermo. Come ha osservato Rosalind Krauss, la riproduzione (fotografica) ha trasformato la precedente "opacità resistente" dei dipinti in un "segno trasparente e sfavillante della sua stessa subordinazione".[6] Il problema del controllo è quindi pertinente, se si pensa che spesso gli artisti sono "controllati" da una particolare immagine della propria opera, o dalla "mostra-come-immagine" in cui può comparire online.

Tornando agli spazi fisici in cui si trovano i dipinti Artex, Rees si reinserisce come creatore nella circolazione e nella ricezione della propria opera, trasferendo sistematicamente il medium della pittura nella cornice della fotografia. Portando avanti un riconoscimento duraturo dell'eredità concettuale della seconda – soprattutto laddove è stata usata come strumento di registrazione per documentare la finalità di un'azione –, l'artista non solo usa, ma subappalta la fotografia attraverso la propria pratica. Dalla richiesta fatta all'artista Cerith Wyn Evans di selezionare delle foto del luogo in cui è nato, nel Galles, per *One Afternoon and Evening In Llanelli; An Ode To Cerith Wyn Evans* (2007), fino all'allestimento, in tempi più recenti, di una mostra di stampe cromogeniche di grande formato scattate dal cognato di Rees in Nicaragua, cui l'artista ha chiesto di documentare scene di solidarietà.[7] Per la serie *In The Ghetto It Gets Cold But We've Got Something To Warm Our Soles* (2012), Rees ha collaborato con il fotografo di moda Michael Hemy in un servizio per una mostra omonima.[8] In queste occasioni Rees ha fatto un passo indietro, ha rinunciato all'ultima decisione soggettiva sull'attuazione finale dell'opera, caricandole così di ulteriore significato.

I dipinti Artex nelle case dei collezionisti sono fotografie professionali. In questo caso, Rees cede in modo definitivo il controllo per ricostituire un criterio di giudizio sull'opera anziché permettere a una qualche critica sottintesa di fraintendere il progetto. Se la preoccupazione iniziale dell'artista era di frenarne o di controllarne la ricezione per i propri scopi, è importante ripetere che la decisione di farlo non è stata preventivamente ideativa né premeditata con una modalità o uno stile di ironia concettuale consapevoli fin dall'inizio della propria conclusione. Creando un percorso che va dalla pittura alla fotografia, Rees torna invece a un'origine. Eppure è solo da quando ha cominciato a esporre queste fotografie insieme ai dipinti che la loro ricezione è stata problematizzata a livello pubblico. Intitolare sia la serie sia le singole immagini *Intended Circulation* è un'ulteriore rivendicazione del significato originario che l'artista ha immaginato per l'opera. Naturalmente, il titolo ripristina anche il ruolo della mostra come un luogo all'interno di questo passaggio. Vedere i dipinti attraverso la fotografia ne prolunga la stasi al punto di arrivo nella casa di un collezionista.

È utile interpretare questo movimento tra medium alla luce di ciò che David Joselit definisce transitività nelle pratiche pittoriche "che offrono una via d'uscita da un vicolo cieco critico particolarmente duraturo: la trappola della reificazione. [...] Il problema del termine "reificazione" è che determina l'arresto permanente della circolazione di un oggetto all'interno di una rete: è sospeso, pagato, appeso a un muro o riposto in un magazzino, e quindi cristallizza in modo permanente un particolare rapporto sociale".[9] Rees, facendo fotografare i propri dipinti sul posto e, oltretutto, rimettendoli in mostra attraverso le fotografie, evita ciò che Joselit chiama la "trappola della reificazione"? Benché ora possano esistere in uno stato di "arresto permanente" nel loro luogo di destinazione, forse si è verificata una corruzione del potenziale immaginato dei dipinti quando l'istituzione aziendale si è inserita nella loro acquisizione, su cui Rees torna con una sensibilità concettuale anziché attraverso una cinica ripetizione del loro materialismo. Dato che la transitività dall'atelier alla casa del collezionista è raffigurata apertamente dalla trasparenza dell'immagine fotografica, sarebbe di certo sfavorevole pensare – erroneamente – che i dipinti Artex siano sottomessi al mercato o che *Intended Circulation* sia un gesto critico nei suoi confronti.

Al di là della sottile ironia dello spostamento dell'Artex (e delle sue associazioni di classe) da un interno all'altro, così come dal soffitto alla parete, gli stessi dipinti Artex possiedono un'estetica che pone una distanza tra loro e, diciamo, un approccio alla pittura dequalificato o più apertamente concettuale. Non tentano nemmeno di sovvertire il *feng shui* delle case in cui penetrano, sfidando la tenacia del mercato che li ha condotti fin lì. Al contrario, la loro astuzia risiede nel diventare parassiti della pittura stessa, che in definitiva diventa il corpo ospite per il concettualismo implicito di Rees. Due delle prime opere dell'artista, per esempio, trattano apertamente lo spostamento della propria circolazione e ricezione, ma attraverso forme più chiaramente in debito con i principi dell'arte concettuale. *The Postman's Decision Is Final* (2006) è una cartolina doppia su cui è possibile scrivere due indirizzi insieme; uno è sempre quello della galleria o del luogo in cui si tiene la mostra, senza chiarire se la cartolina vi arriverà. L'installazione di pellicole 16mm *Something To Fill That Empty Feeling* (2007), invece, rappresenta un angolo di una galleria, in cui ogni proiezione è ri-filmata e ri-proiettata, creando un effetto matrioska che incarna il luogo espositivo attraverso la ripetizione della sua immagine. Entrambe le opere prosperano nei sistemi in cui agiscono – siano essi postali o spaziali –, mentre i dipinti di Rees suggeriscono un allontanamento dai materiali di norma associati all'arte concettuale. Più specificamente, rappresentano un interesse sempre più debole verso il

mantenimento del concetto "puro" che è stato diffuso da alcuni dei suoi eredi. Si potrebbe dire per esempio che, laddove Martin Creed ripete una logica binaria nel suo approccio alla pittura, Rees ha superato i concetti informativi delle prime serie, dove applicava la pittura sulla tela per poi fissarla o schiacciarla direttamente sul muro, o metteva i dipinti in sacchetti ermetici trasparenti, sigillando ermeticamente il medium in modo letterale.

Questi tentativi, in una certa misura indecisi, di "confondere le acque" tra l'estetica pittorica e il concettualismo, si ritrovano insieme nei dipinti Artex proprio perché essi hanno cominciato a sviluppare una "vita propria" al di là dei confini concettuali che di norma possono averne definito la presentazione come informazione secondaria. Come ammette l'artista stesso, "quando diventano oggetti belli e seducenti [i dipinti Artex] iniziano a essere goffi […], tradiscono il concetto". Questa "goffaggine" contamina la purezza del concetto con una sensibilità estetica, una fusione tra il lavoro manuale richiesto dalla decorazione di interni e la preparazione e l'esecuzione della pittura astratta. Oltre a rimandare al contesto sociale in cui l'Artex è stato diffuso, in origine i dipinti Artex sono stati concepiti come l'incontro tra una specifica abilità manuale e il medium pittorico. Eppure l'attenzione che Rees dedica al *processo* pittorico – racconta di preparare le tele facendo attenzione alle caratteristiche materiali – è significativa in quanto sposta l'opera dall'ortodossia del rigido concettualismo in cui il concetto resta il materiale primario.

"Cosa rappresentano le rappresentazioni?" chiede Helmut Draxler nel suo saggio su Louise Lawler,[10] che ha fotografato le opere di altri artisti nei luoghi che li contestualizzano. "La risposta dev'essere: la funzione sociale del gusto"[11]. A questo punto sarebbe sintomatico ripensare alla richiesta della Bank of America in questo contesto, perché non c'è dubbio che l'azienda abbia immaginato che l'immagine complessiva – di cui il dipinto dell'artista costituisce solo una parte – avrebbe attirato la propria clientela. Dopotutto è il contesto che rappresenta le opere, nel quale erano "previste" o immaginate, che ha dato a Rees l'idea per *Intended Circulation*. In ogni caso, affinché i dipinti Artex siano artisticamente a proprio agio con il contesto, la loro rappresentazione finale esige che l'artista stesso abbia un interesse per il controllo. Se l'arte può essere usata per "estetizzare le funzioni del potere",[12] forse necessita di un intervento che regoli tali condizioni. Così, Rees non sovverte il sistema (o i sistemi) in cui i suoi dipinti agiscono, ma anzi risolve – anche se forse solo per se stesso – un problema che riguarda la loro circolazione e ricezione utilizzando "strategie di rappresentazione" che richiamano l'attenzione sulla loro funzione sociale. A tale riguardo, i dipinti Artex trovano il loro punto d'arrivo attraverso la fotografia con *Intended Circulation*, come la bandiera a scacchi che sventola tra discorsi ciclici su pittura e concettualismo.

1. Alexander Alberro, *Arte concettuale e strategie pubblicitarie*, Johan & Levi, Truccazzano (Milano) 2011, p. 60.

2. Michael Sanchez, "Art and Transmission", *Artforum*, estate 2013, p. 297.

3. Ivi.

4. Alexander Alberro, *Arte concettuale e strategie pubblicitarie*, cit., p. 60.

5. Si vedano Walter Robinson, "Flipping and the Rise of Zombie Formalism", Artspace. com, http://www.artspace.com/ magazine/contributors/see_here/ the_rise_of_zombie_formalism-52184, o Jerry Saltz, "Zombies on the Walls: Why Does So Much New Abstraction Look the Same?", Vulture.com, http://www.vulture. com/2014/06/why-new-abstract-paintings-look-the-same.html.

6. Rosalind Krauss, "Louise Lawler: Souvenir Memories", in *A Spot on the Wall*, a cura di Hedwig Saxenhuber, Oktagon Verlag, Colonia, 1998, p. 36.

7. Era parte di un progetto di ricerca più ampio sulle campagne internazionali di solidarietà tra il Galles e il Nicaragua. Il titolo della mostra era "Dan Rees", e si è svolta presso Tanya Leighton, Berlino 2013.

8. "In the Ghetto It Gets Cold But We've Got Something To Warm Our Soles", presso la galleria Baronian-Francey, Bruxelles, 2012.

9. David Joselit, "Painting Beside Itself", *October* 130, autunno 2009, pp. 125–34.

10. Helmut Draxler, "Art Into Culture Exhibition as Social Intervention", in *A Spot on the Wall*, cit., p. 70.

11. Ivi.

12. Ibid., p. 72.

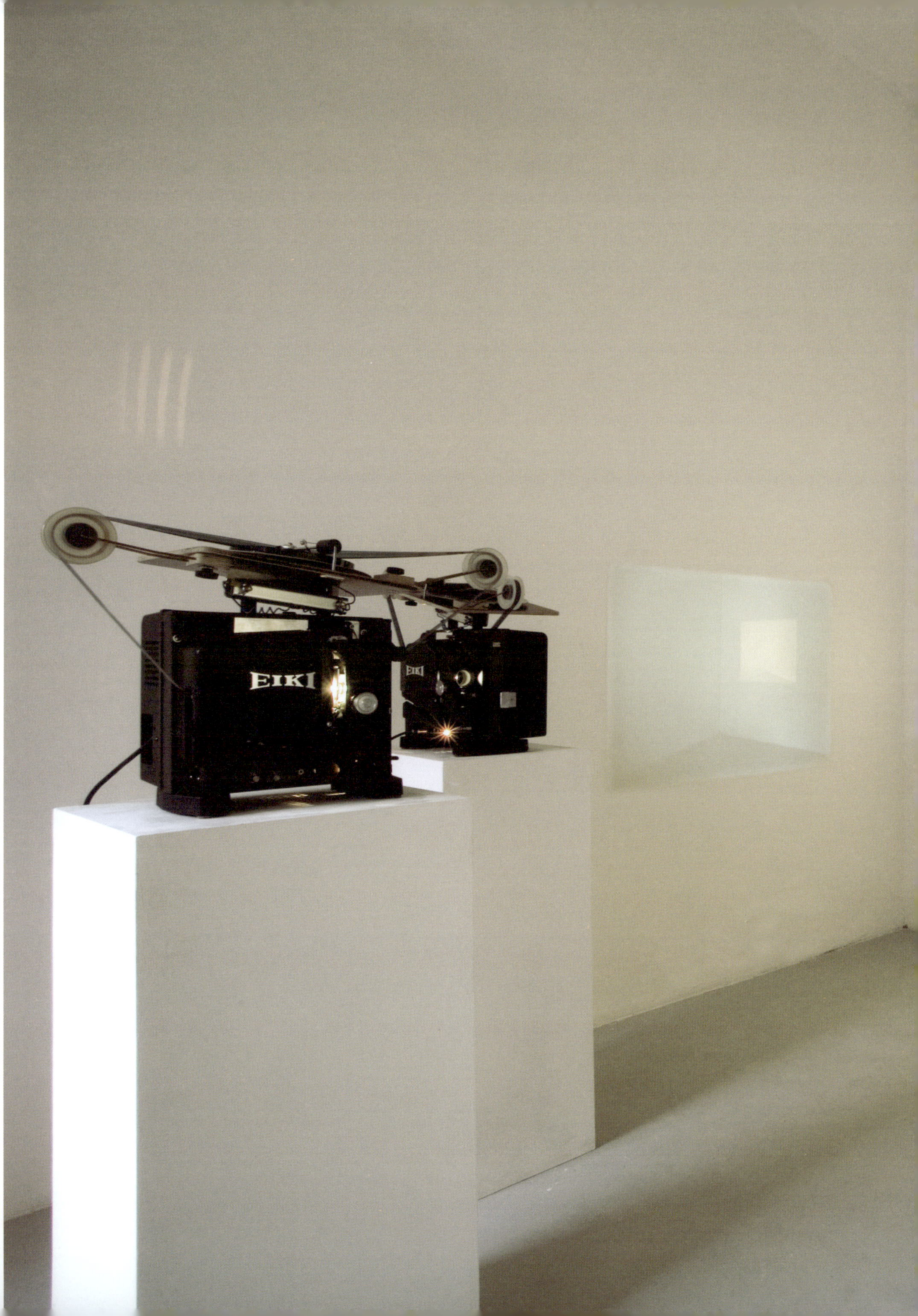

Something To Fill That Empty Feeling, 2007, T293, Naples

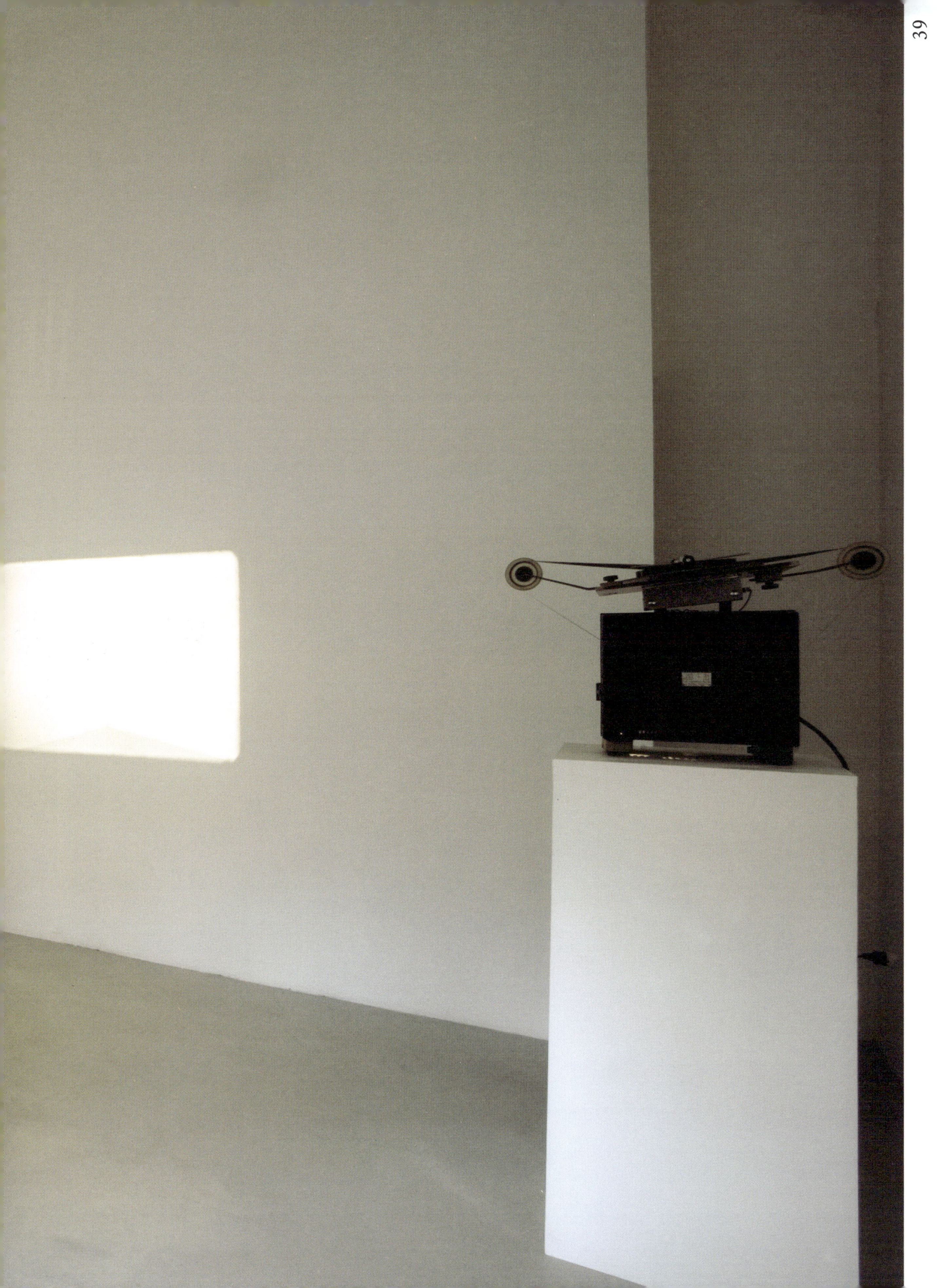

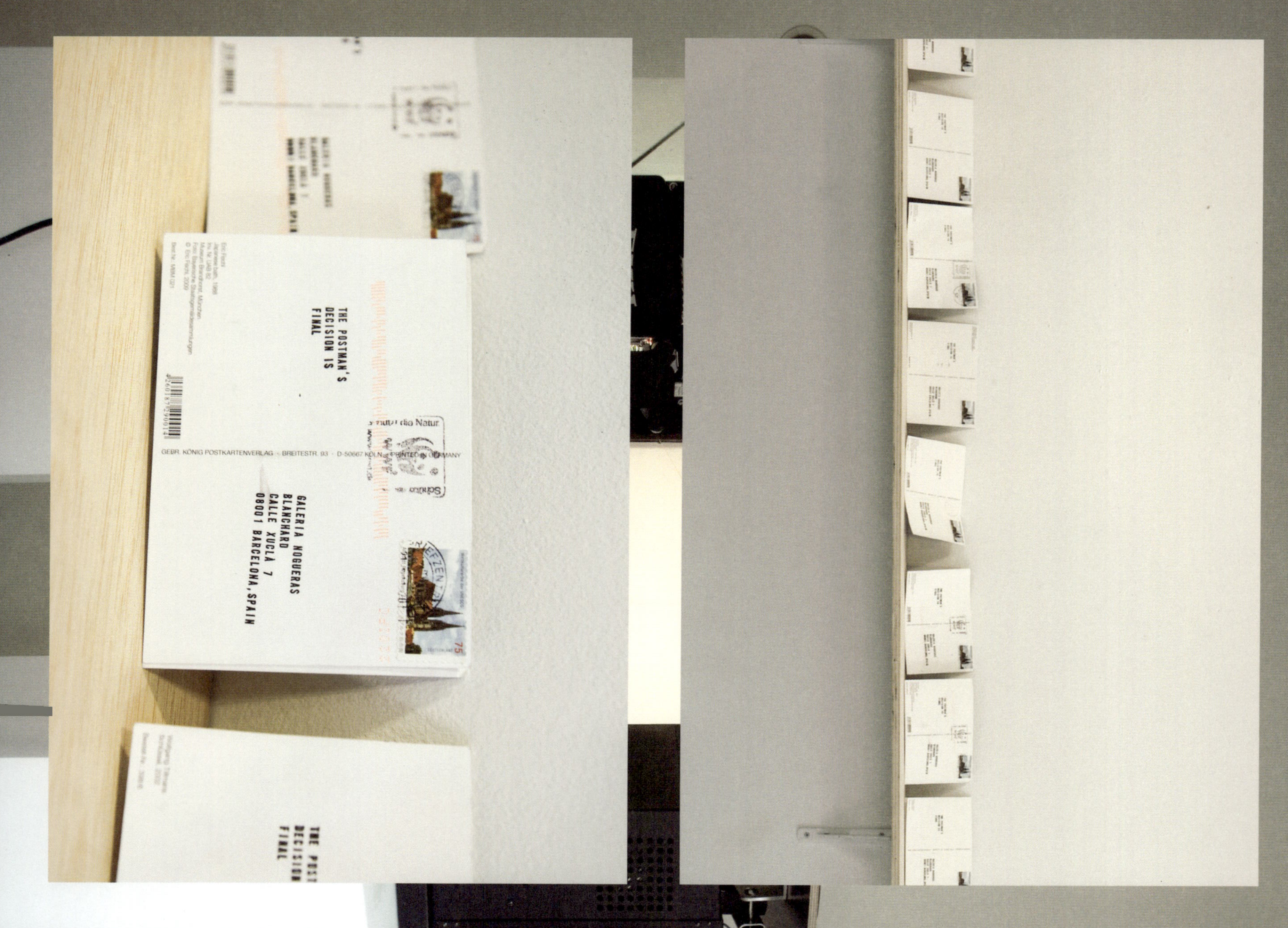

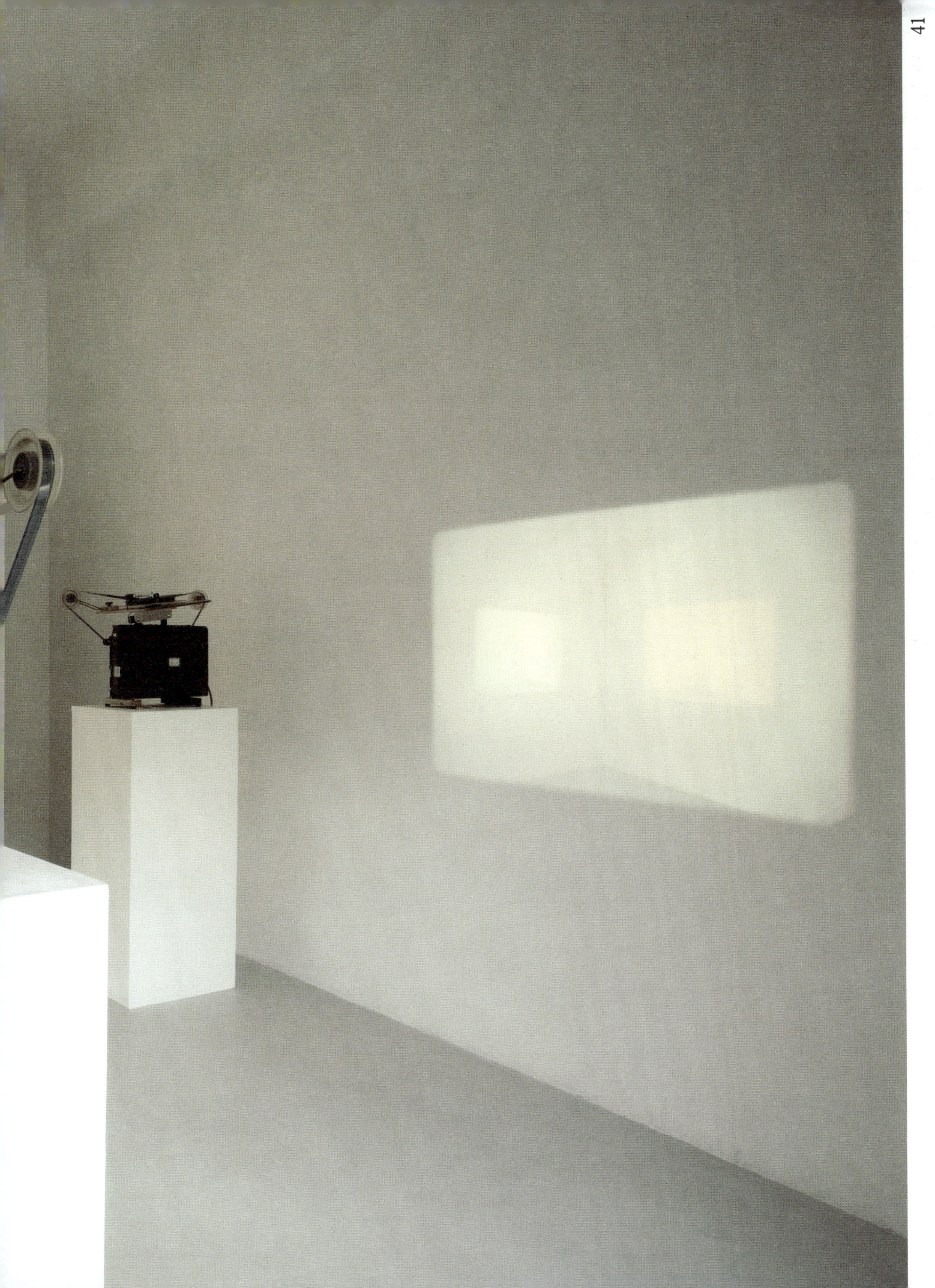

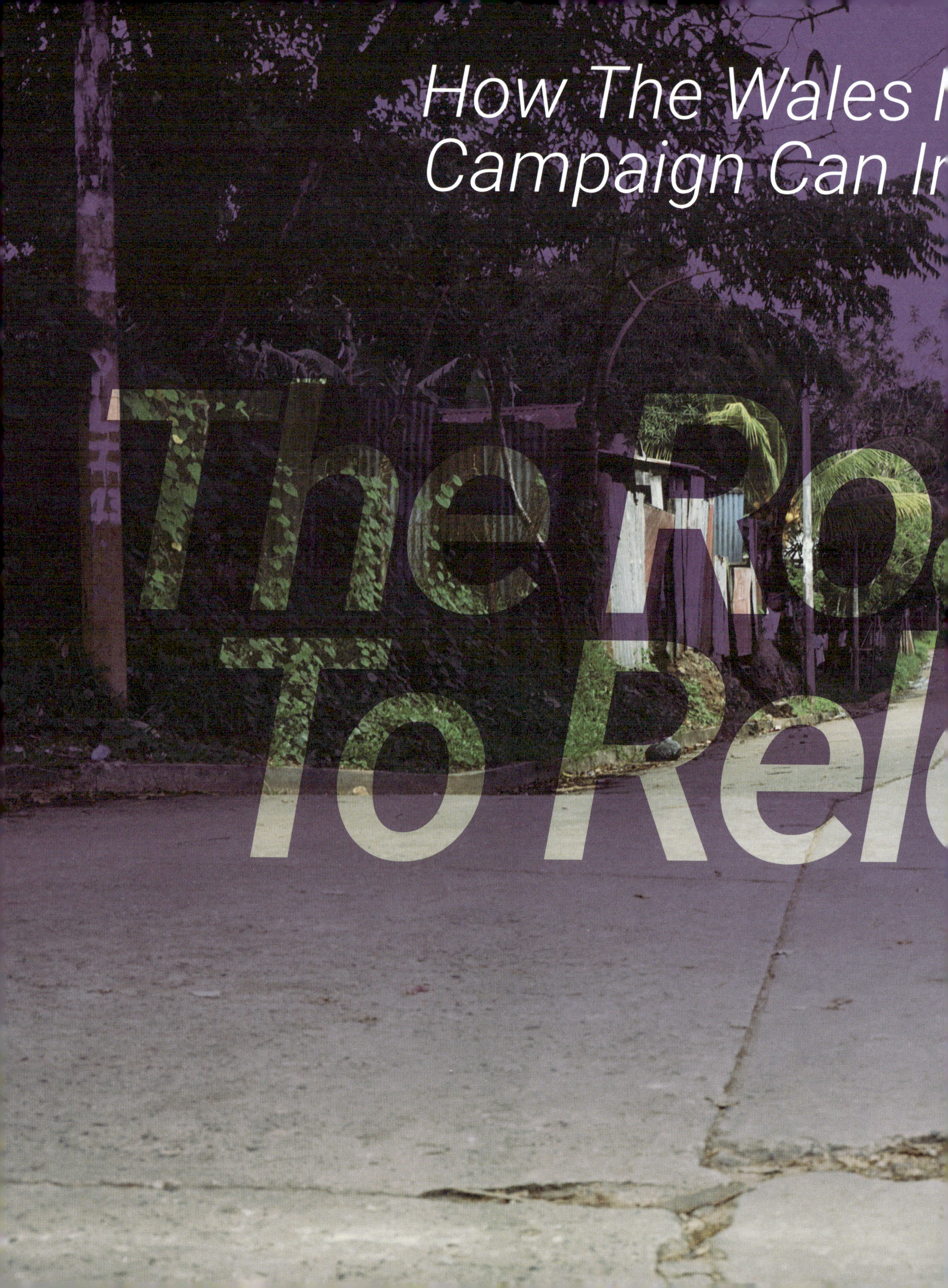

How The Wales N
Campaign Can In
The Ro
To Rel

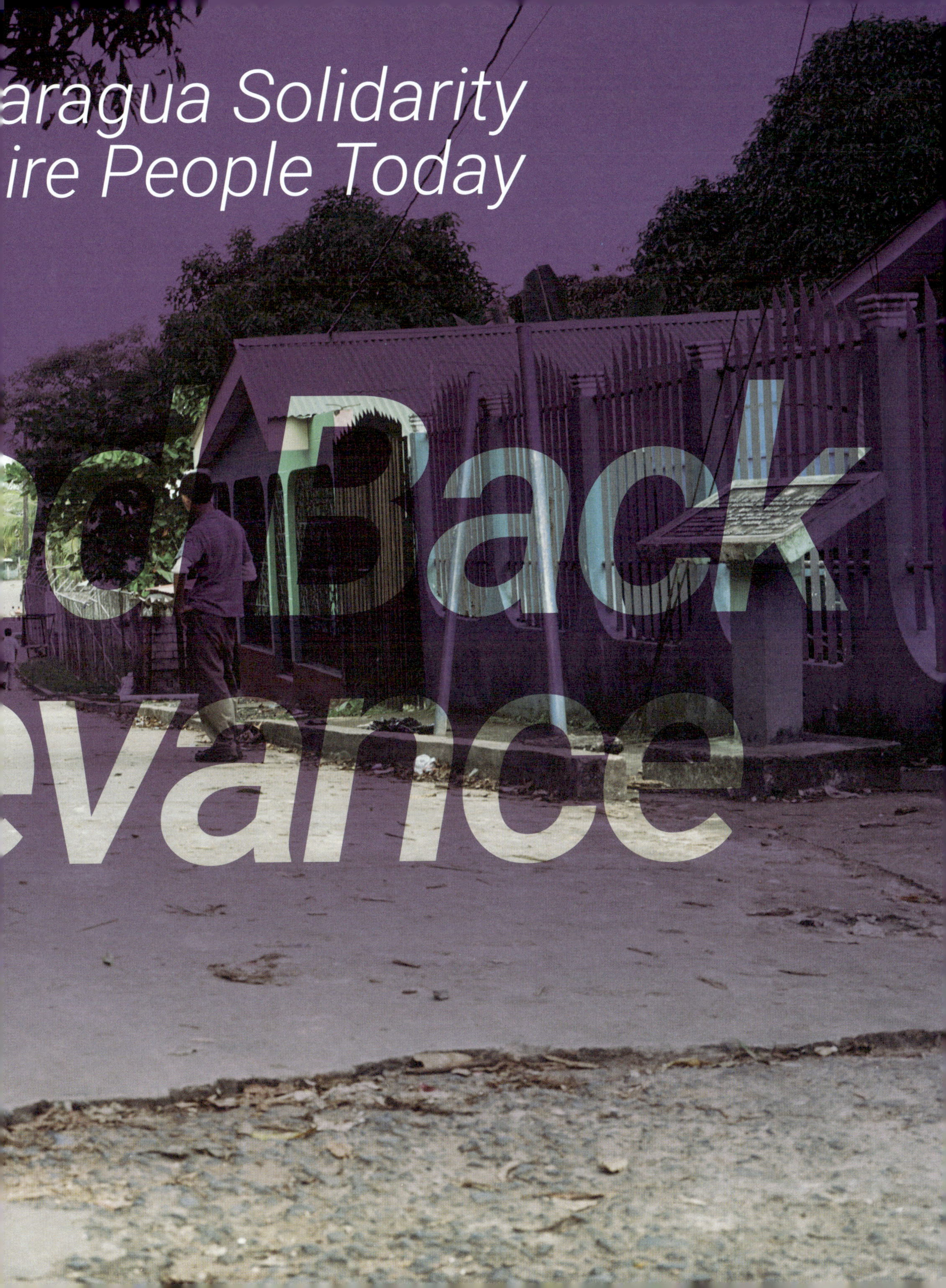

aragua Solidarity
ire People Today
Back
evance

The Wales Nicaragua Solidarity Campaign (NSC) was born in 1986 in the aftermath of the National Union of Miners' crushing defeat at the hands of Margaret Thatcher's government.

Entire communities had their hearts torn out, their hopes and aspirations turned to despair.

Campaigns were formed across the world to support the Nicaraguan people against the tyranny they faced.

Campaigning in Wales was tireless. The emphasis was on getting delegates to Nicaragua to offer practical advice to workers and on setting up co-operatives and education programmes.

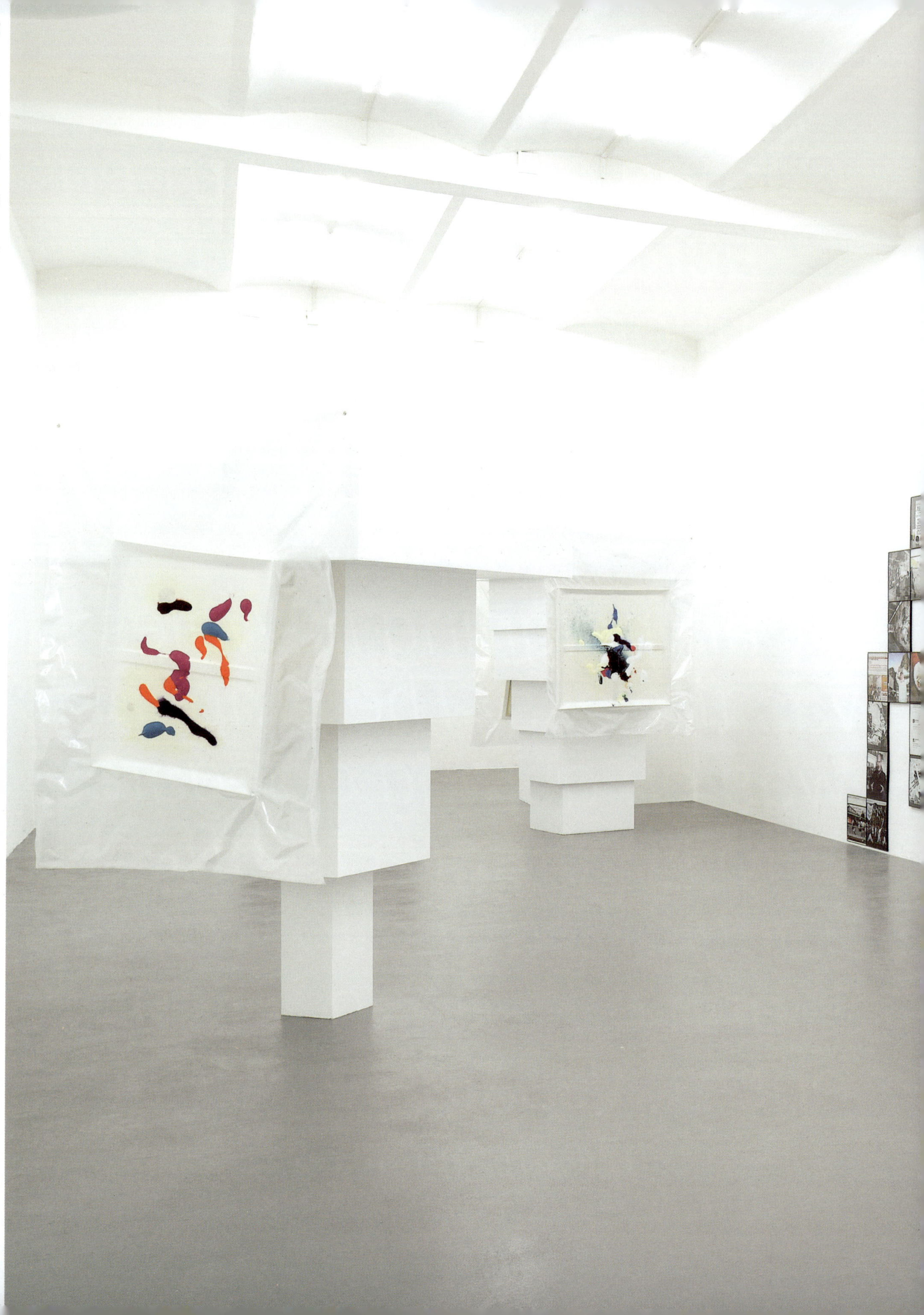

Top Heavy, 2013, T293, Rome

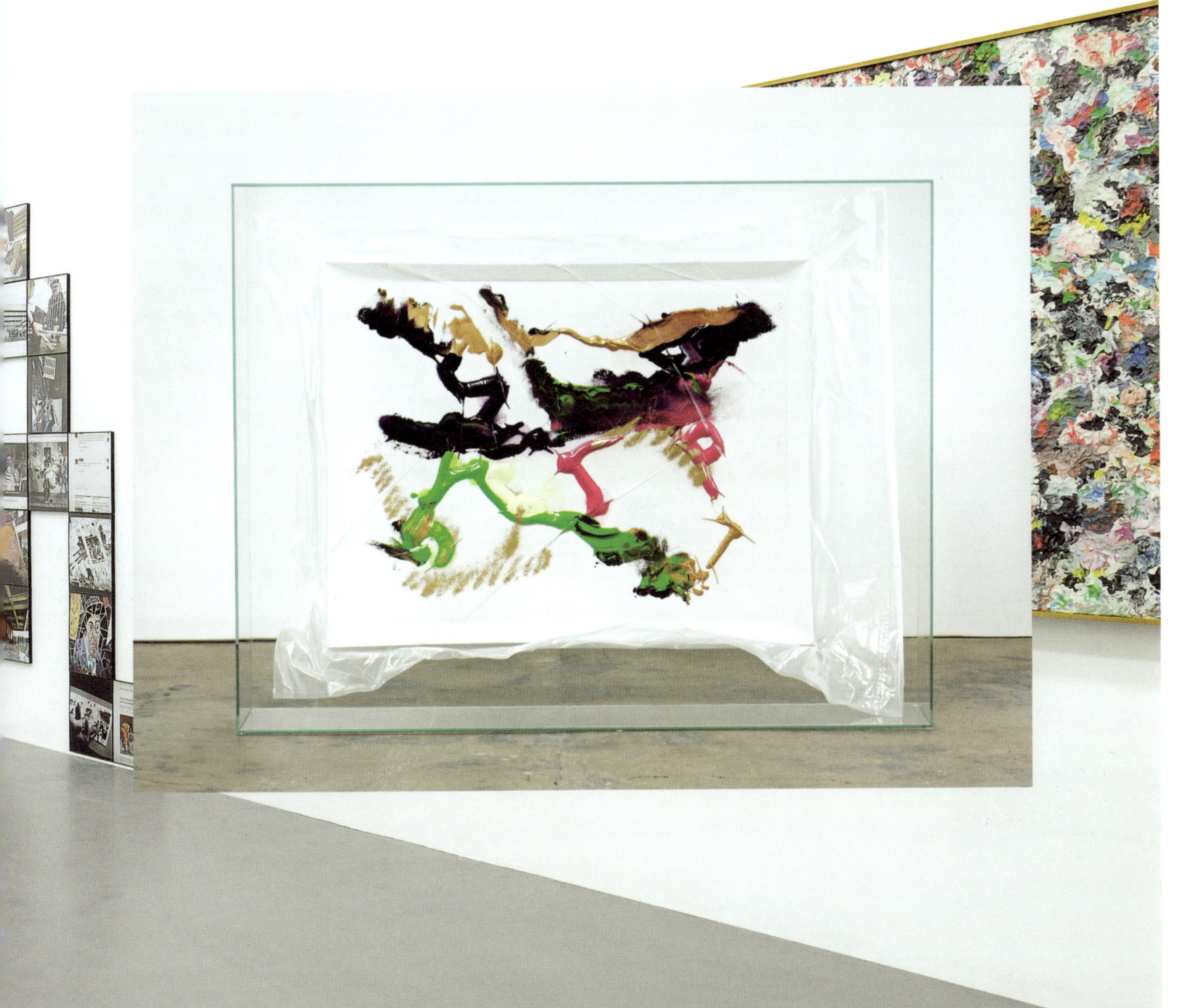

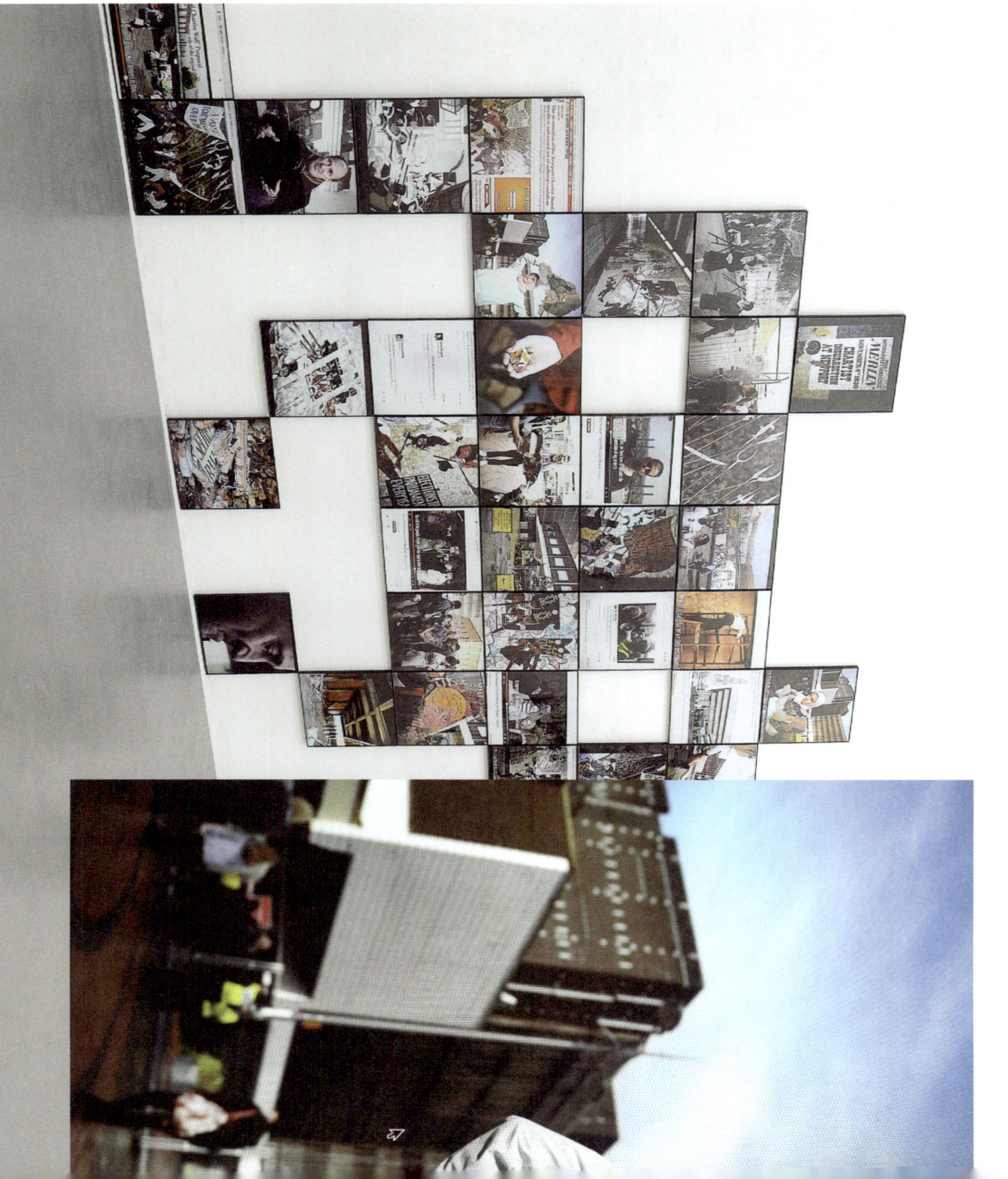

Space Invader (*Chartist Mural*) (detail), 2013

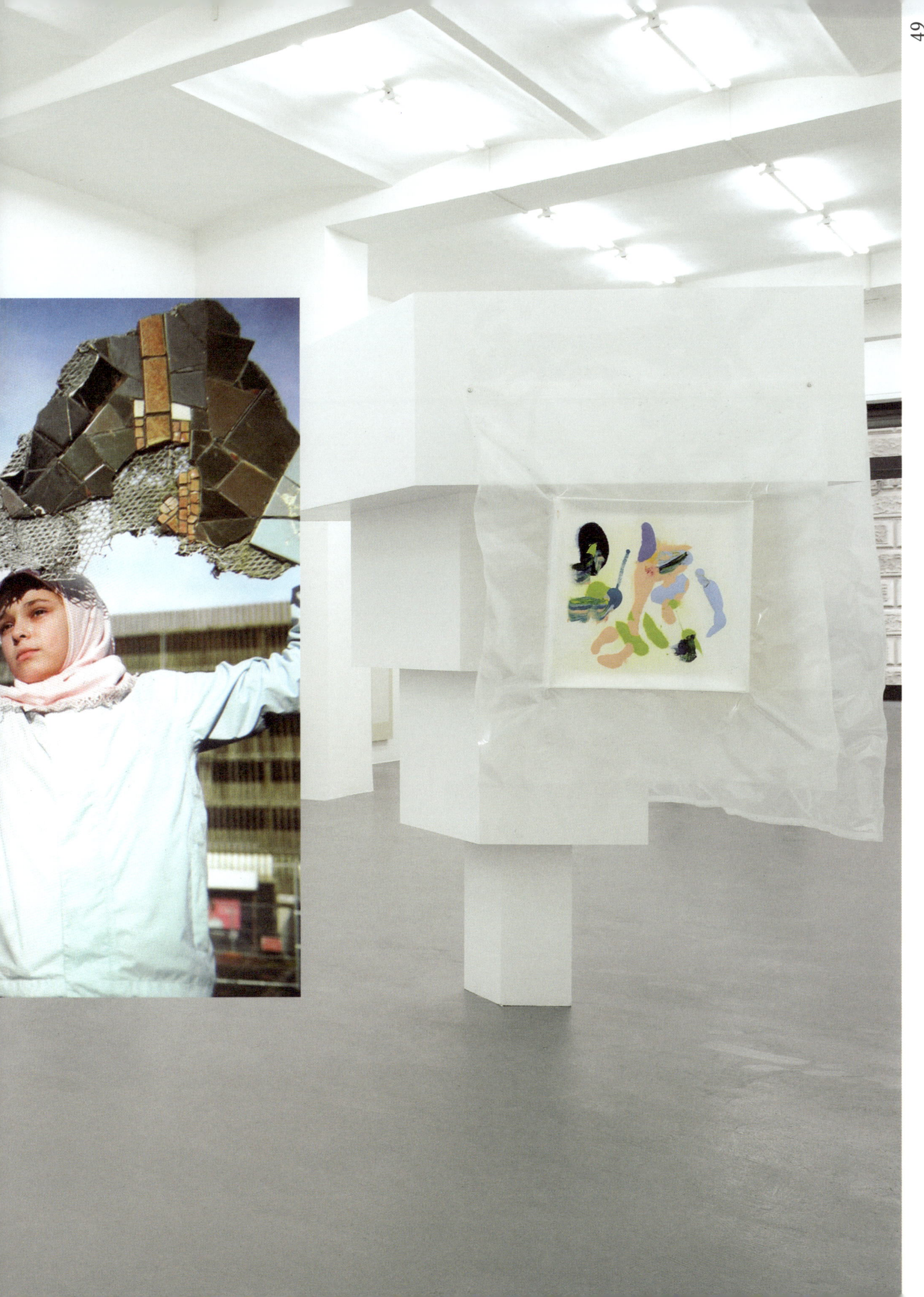

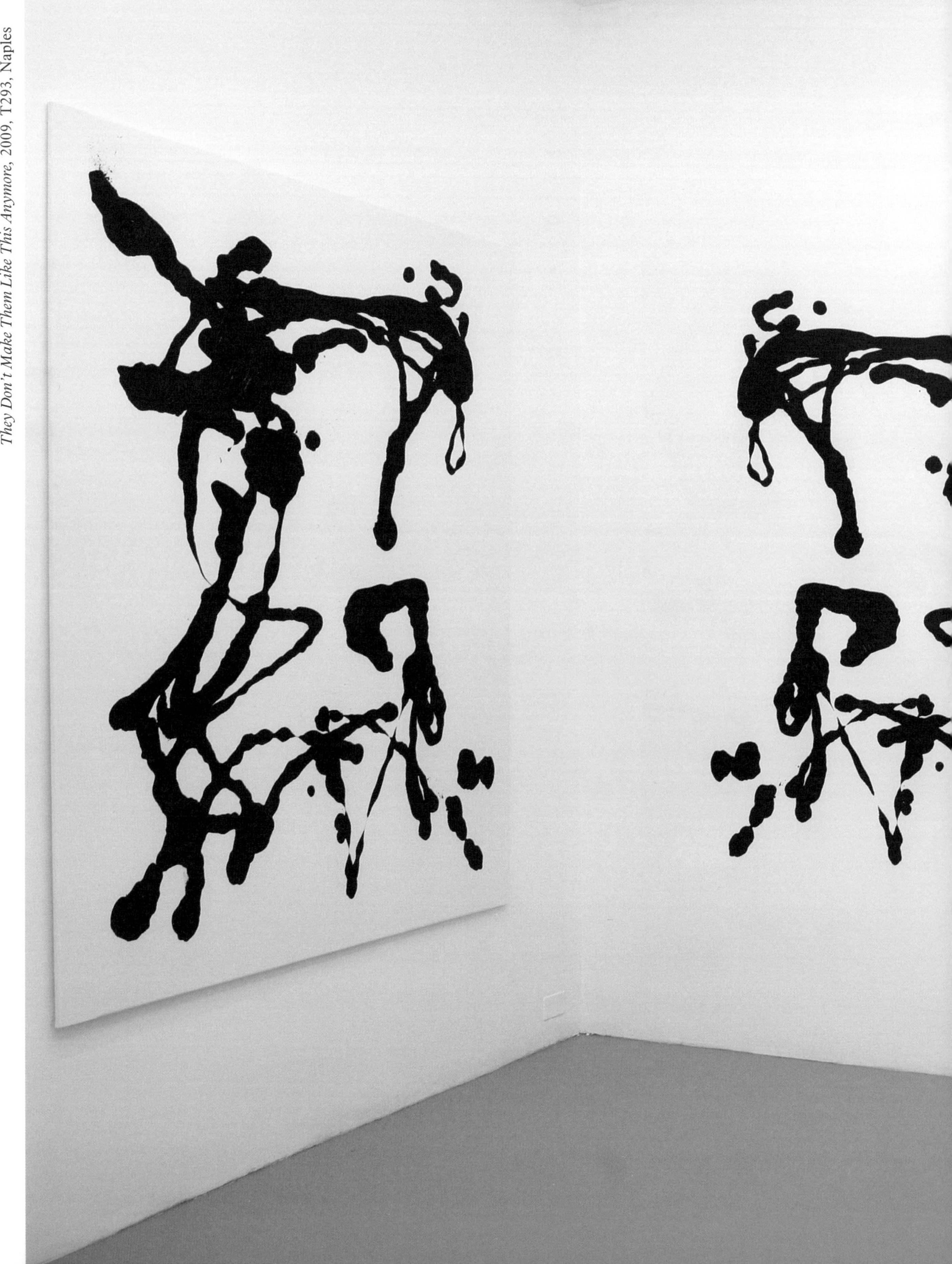

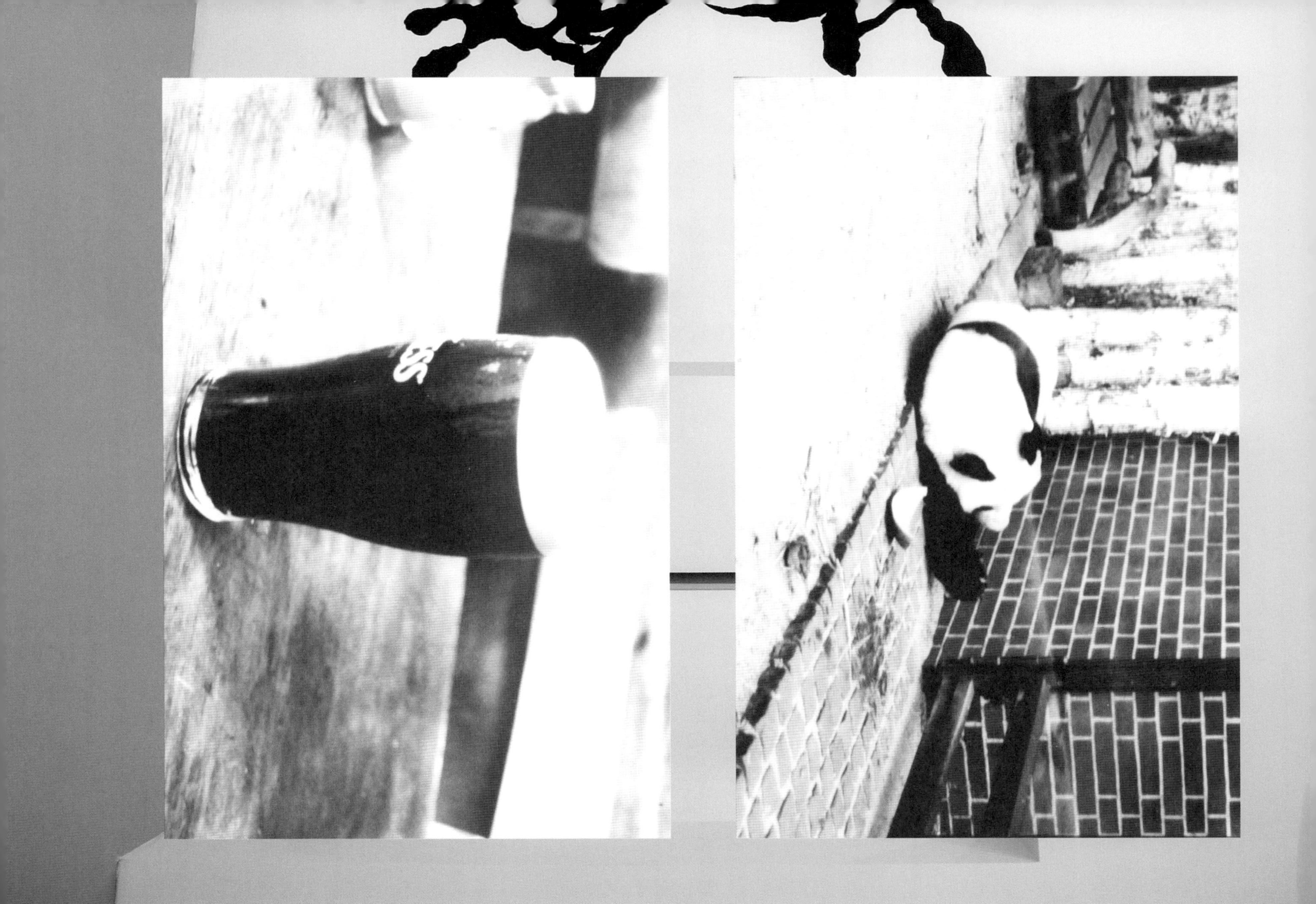

Black And White Things In Black And White (Panda), (Guinness), 2006

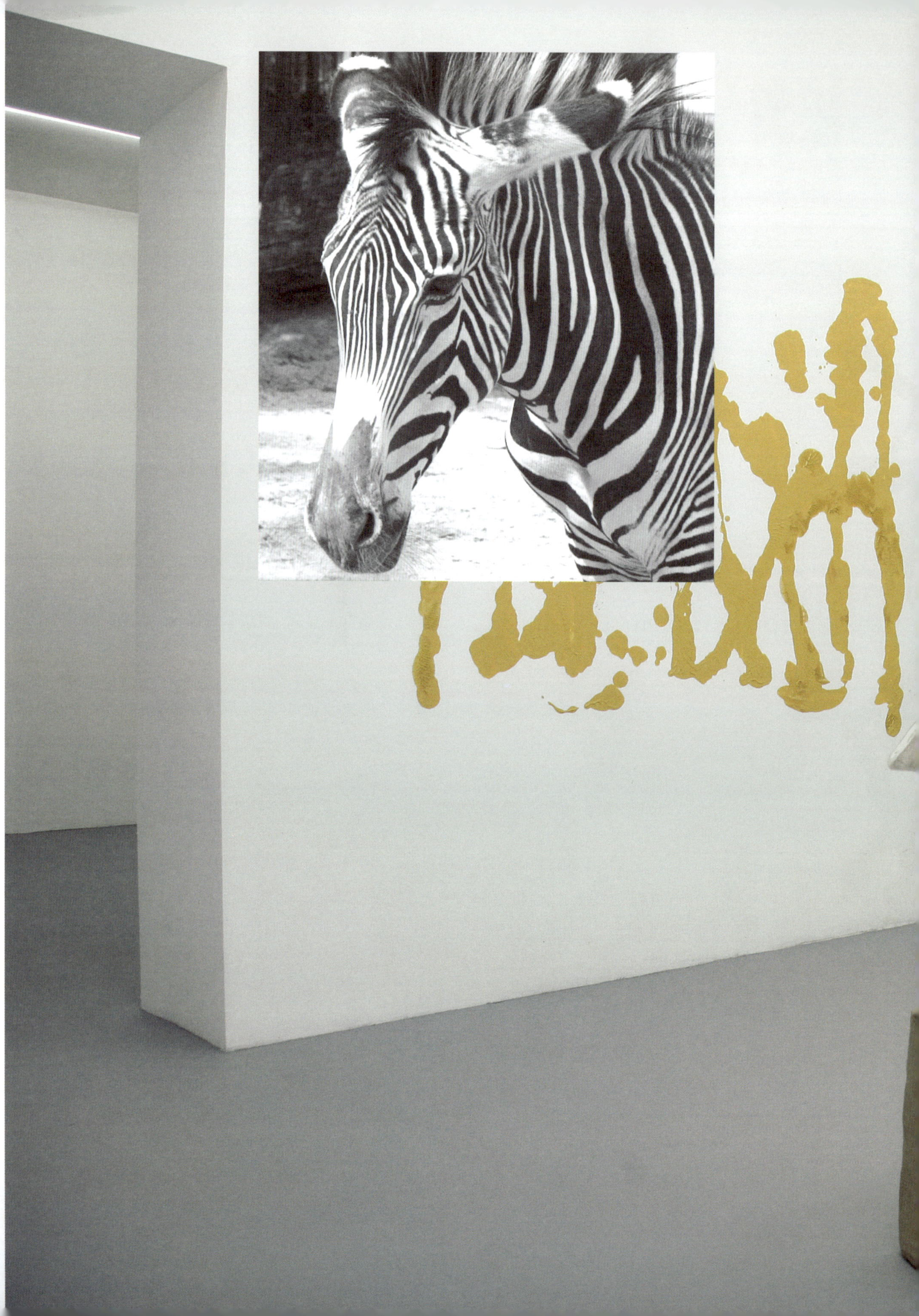

They Don't Make Them Like This Anymore, 2009, T293, Naples

Black And White Things In Black And White (Zebra), 2006

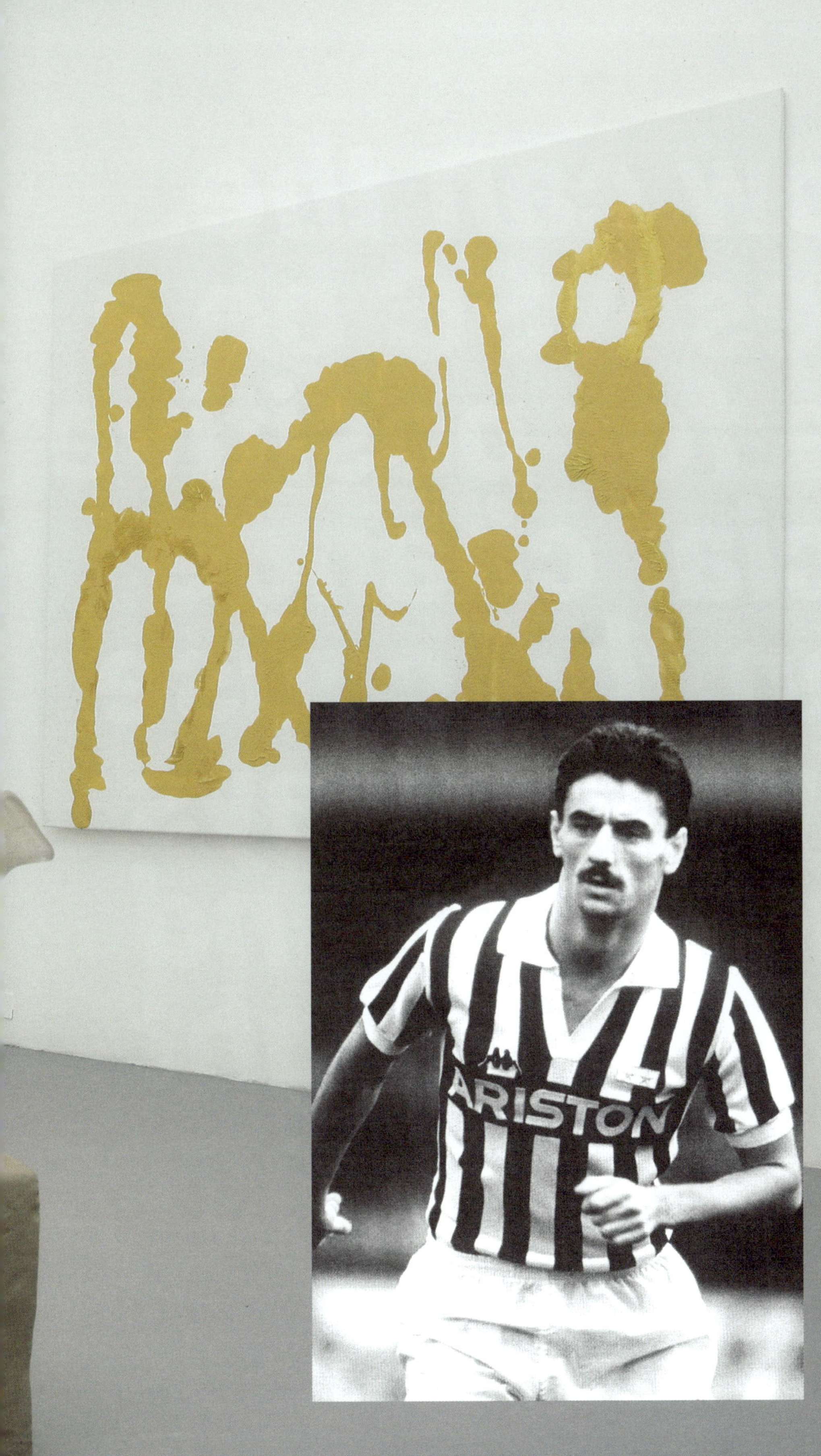

Black And White Things In Black And White (Rush), 2006

How can the Wales NSC be a force for positive social change when the cause they've always fought for and how they fight appear no longer relevant?

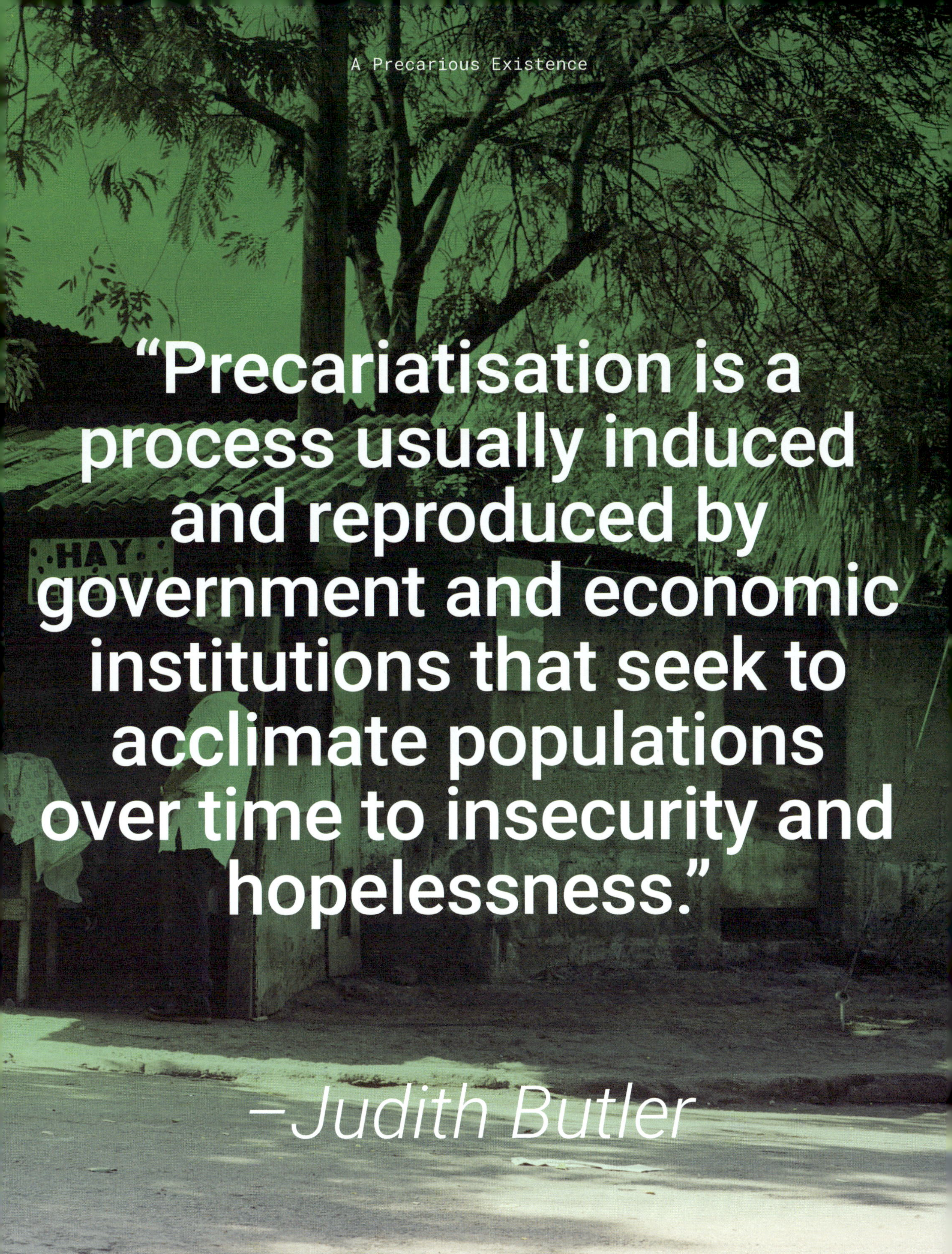
"Precariatisation is a process usually induced and reproduced by government and economic institutions that seek to acclimate populations over time to insecurity and hopelessness."

– Judith Butler

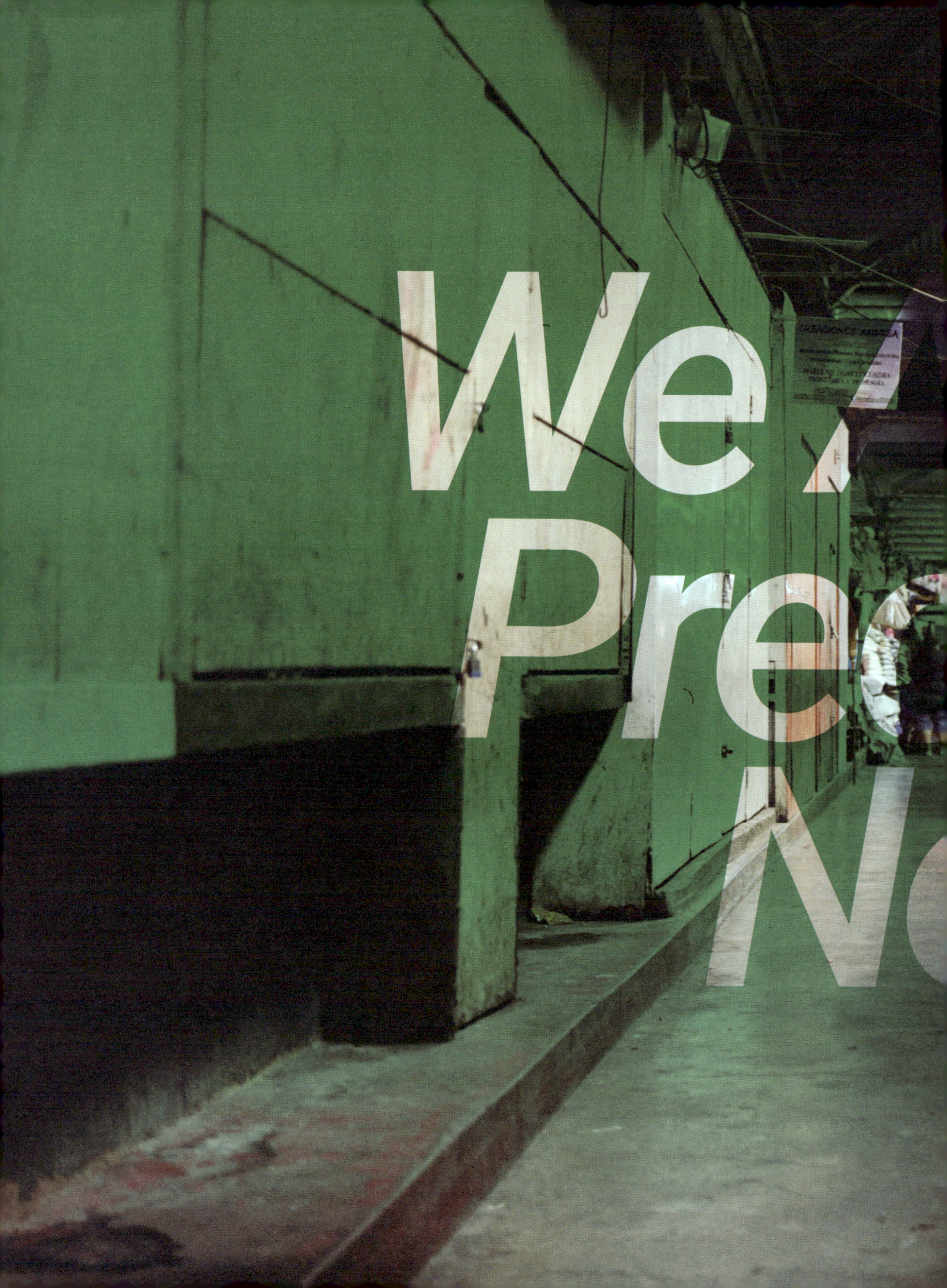

We/
Prec
No

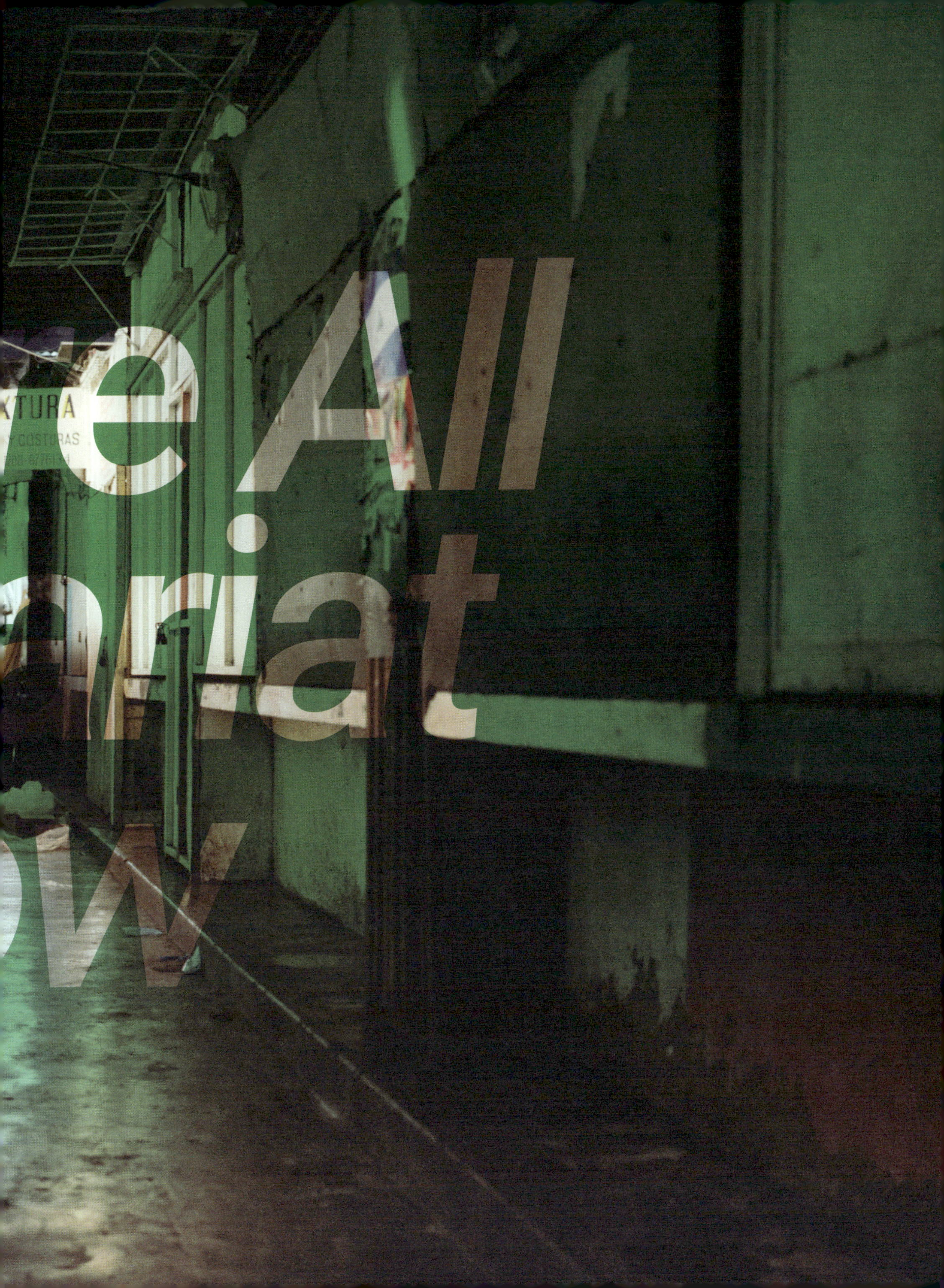
TURA
COSTURAS
e All
oriat
ow

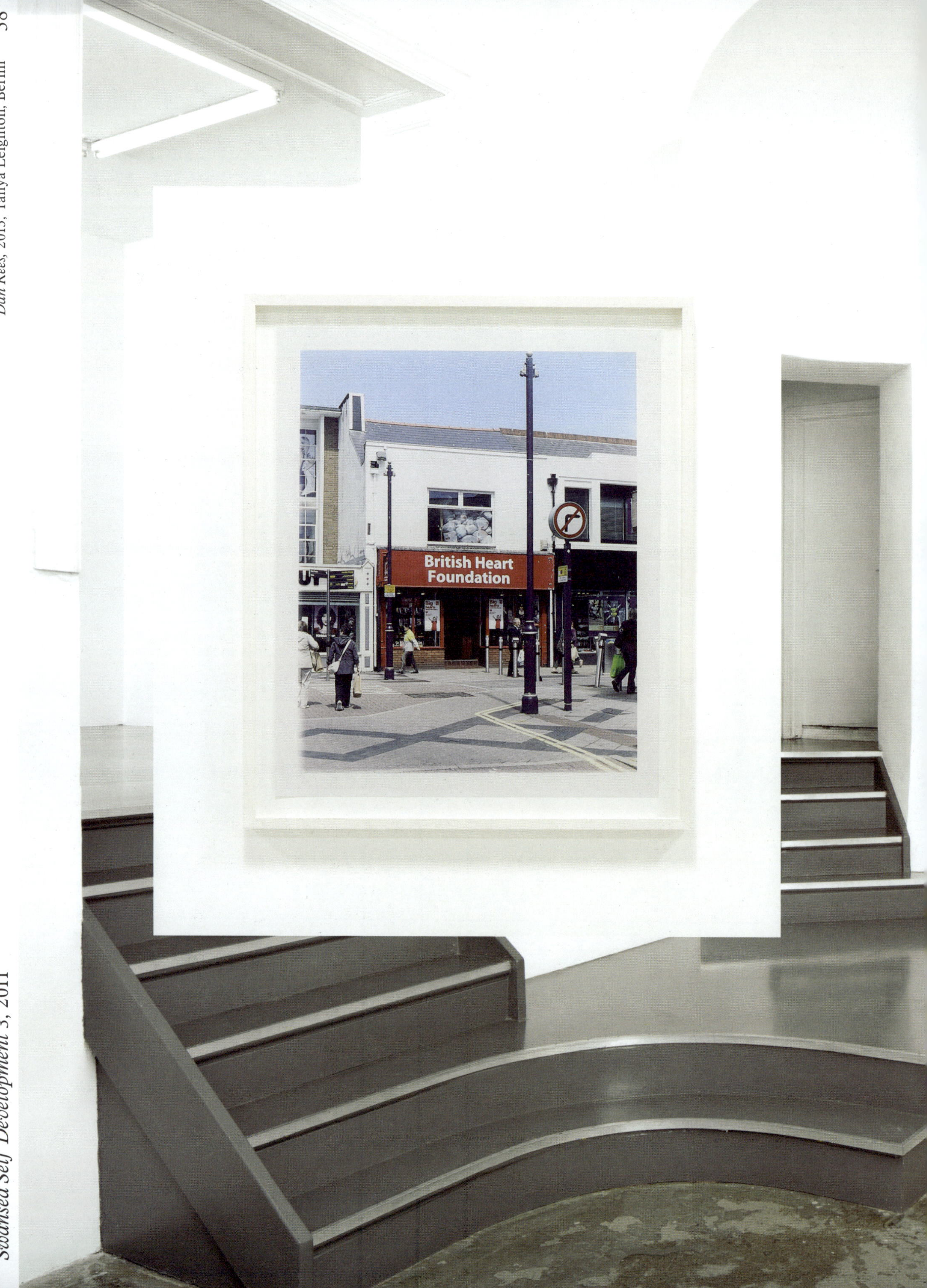

Swansea Self Development 3, 2011

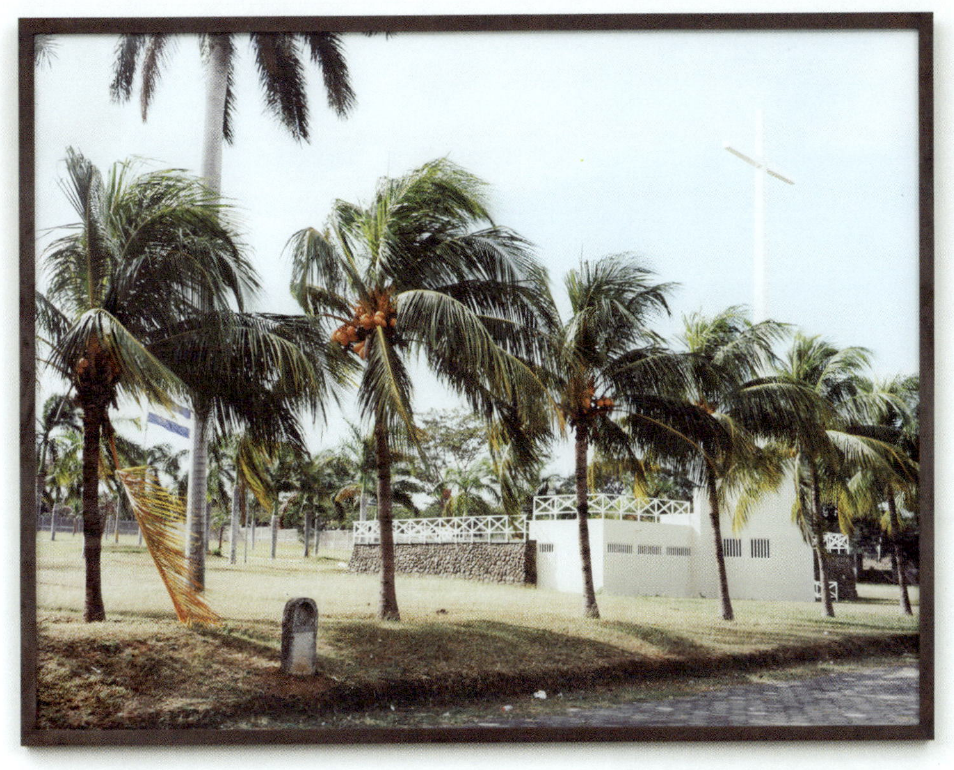

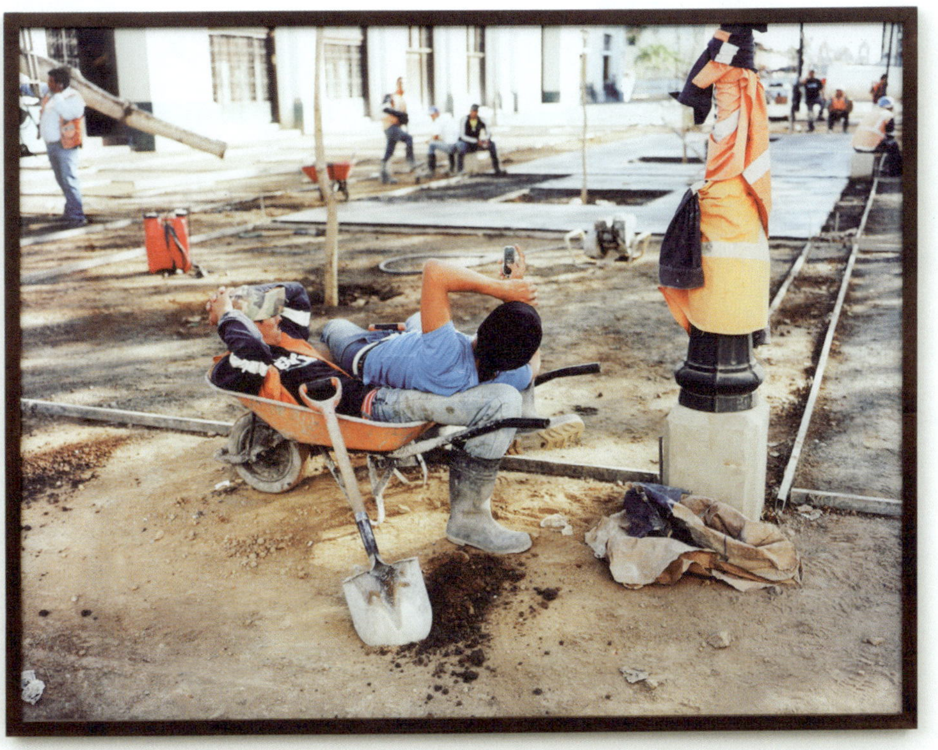

Opposite The Church, 2013 Workers In A Wheelbarrow, 2013

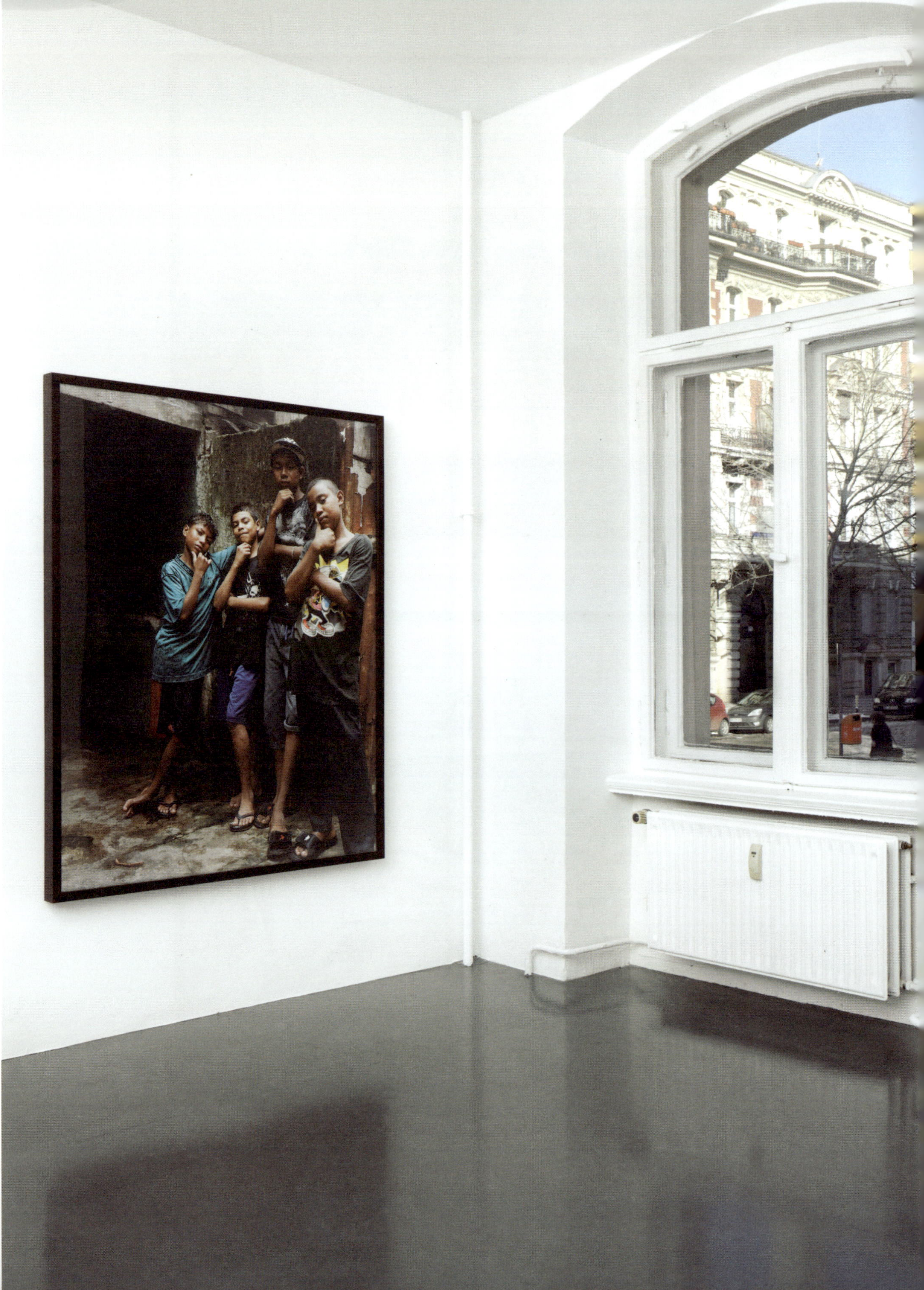

Boys Sharing Flip-Flops, 2013

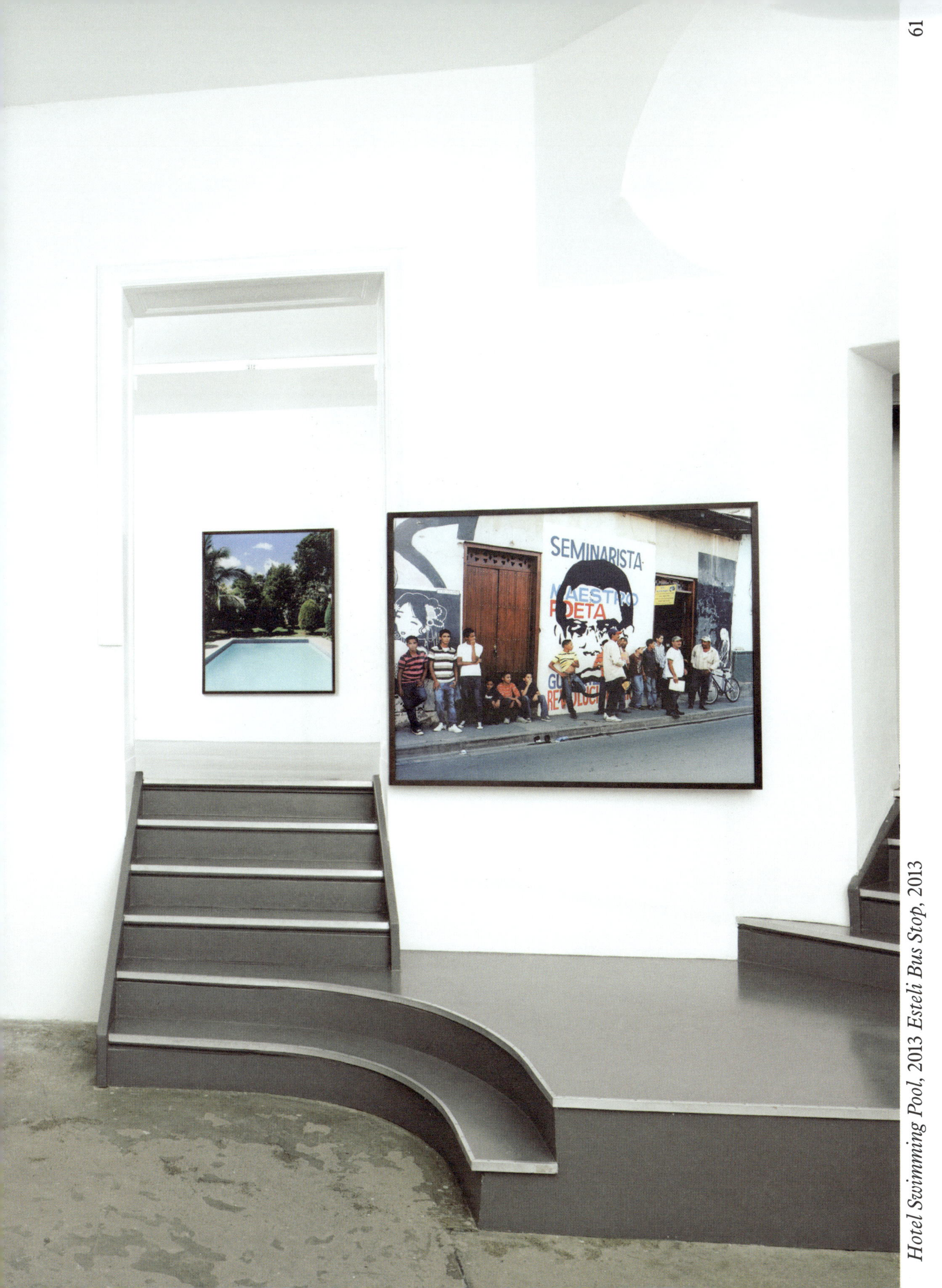

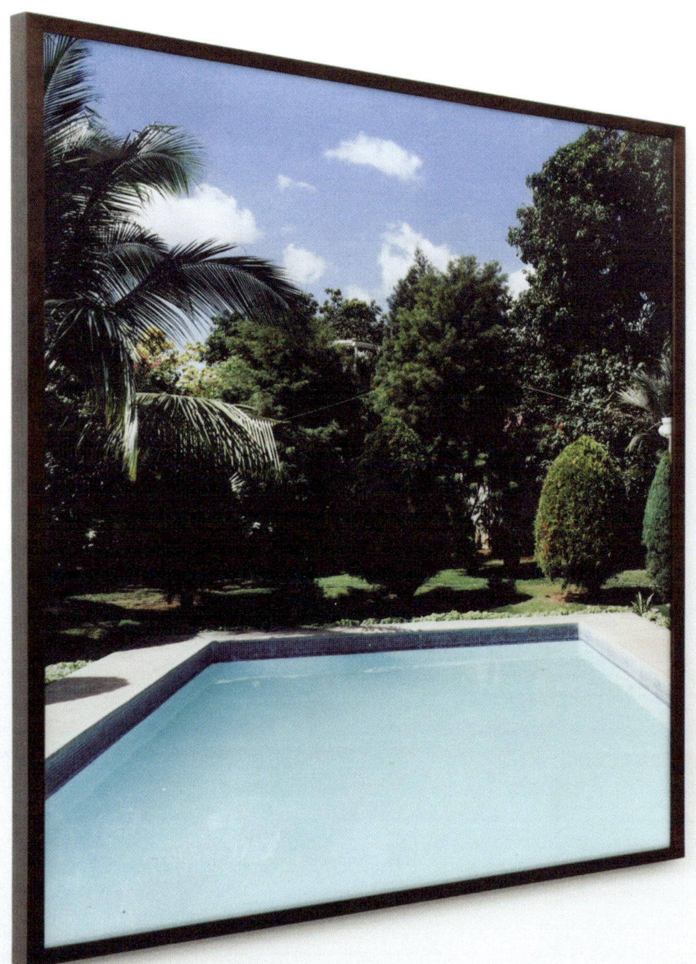

Hotel Swimming Pool, 2013

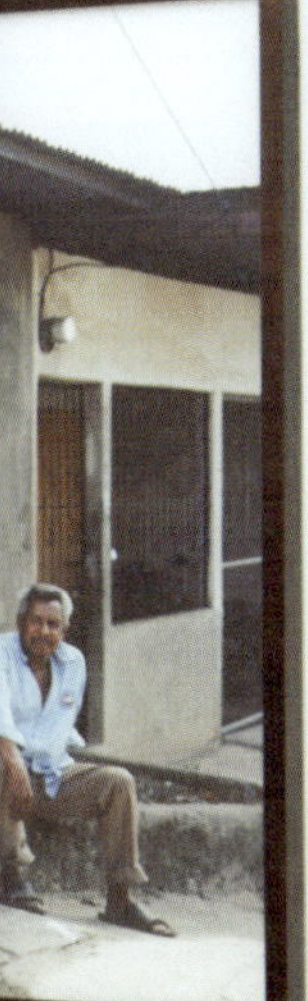

Solidarity by Ben Gregory

I write this an hour after the Scottish referendum result. Like much of the UK, I was transfixed in front of the television screen for most of the night. Three months ago I joined a Welsh delegation to meet independence campaigners in Scotland. As well as representatives of the official Yes campaign, we met with Green Yes, Women for Independence, Labour for Independence, the National Collective, the Radical Independence Campaign, and others. Their political and cultural activities have transformed Scotland, creating a social movement out of a diversity of organisations. The other striking thing about the visit was that the majority of people in the group had also been part of the last Wales Nicaragua Solidarity Campaign delegation, to Nicaragua, in 2013. In the eyes of the participants, this trip, too, was a solidarity visit.

The Nicaraguan solidarity movement grew out of the support for the revolution in the 1980s, and continued as the Nicaraguan people, like peoples all over the globe, struggled against neoliberalism. The revolution was led by the Frente Sandinista de Liberación Nacional. Like other Latin American revolutions, it was first and foremost a struggle for national liberation, as were many of the anticolonial wars of the twentieth century. Edward Said, the great Palestinian academic, once argued that despite the success of many of these fights for national liberation, their emphasis had been wrong:

> I would like to suggest that *liberation*, not nationalist independence, is the new alternative, liberation which by its very nature involves, in Fanon's words, a transformation of social consciousness beyond national consciousness.[1]

So were we mistaken to go to Scotland to learn about its independence movement? The Scottish First Minister and SNP leader Alex Salmond stated in the referendum consultation document: 'Scotland is not oppressed and we have no need to be liberated. Independence matters because we do not have the power to reach our potential.'

The groups we met would disagree. They saw the need to be liberated, from neoliberalism and the power of big business. They were fighting for social justice. Their view would seem to be borne out by events. Presidents and prime ministers queued up to warn against independence. The president of the European Commission joined the line. The Secretary General of NATO and the heads of the British Armed Forces warned of dire consequences for 'the global war on terror.' British banks warned of capital flight and dwindling pensions, whilst the Deutsche Bank even predicted that Scottish independence would trigger a 1930s-style world depression.

These are the same warnings that countries such as Nicaragua have endured for the past two decades and more. Any moves toward genuine liberation are met with ominous warnings, and worse actions when the warnings do not work. The language of the Nicaraguan people and organisations we met during the 1990s and early 2000s was little different from that of the Scottish organisations we talked to.

Most of the time the status quo is easily maintained, inculcated as it is by the education system, corporate media, and the entertainment industry. More than thirty years ago, the Uruguayan writer Eduardo Galeano described how this works:

The majority must resign itself to the consumption of fantasy. Illusions of wealth are sold to the poor, illusions of freedom to the oppressed, dreams of victory to the defeated and of power to the weak.[2]

Raymond Williams, at the end of the 1950s, believed that culture is ordinary. We create meaning of the world around us from the ideas and artifacts we produce and reproduce:

Culture is ordinary: that is the first fact. Every human society has its own shape, its own purposes, its own meanings. Every human society expresses these, in institutions, and in arts and learning. The making of a society is the finding of common meanings and direction, and its growth is an active debate and amendment in the process of experience, contact and discovery, writing themselves onto the land [...]. A culture has two aspects: the known meanings and directions its members are trained to; the new observations and meanings, which are offered and tested.[3]

When I was growing up in Tredegar in the south Wales valleys it seemed natural for my family to talk about Paul Robeson, the black American activist, actor, and singer. I was vaguely aware of his connections with the miners' union. This led me to learn more about his life and his part in the civil rights movement. The first Nicaraguan solidarity group I belonged to was in the neighbouring town of Merthyr. There didn't seem anything unusual about their programming a series of films to raise money for Nicaragua, including the 1986 German film *Rosa*, the story of Rosa Luxemburg, the Polish/German revolutionary. It was also natural enough to show the Welsh-language film *Milwr Bychan* (Boy Soldier, 1986), which is about a soldier serving in Northern Ireland, and not to blink when you learned that the Welsh director of the film was named after Karl Liebknecht, the German revolutionary murdered with Rosa Luxemburg in 1919.

Looking back, I can now see these connections clearly: why they were made, and why they seemed so natural. It was part of the outward-looking culture these Welsh communities by and large created for themselves without depending on corporations or arts councils to do it for them.

David Featherstone, in his recent book *Solidarity: Hidden Histories and Geographies of Internationalism*, argues persuasively that solidarity is not necessarily innate (though this is undoubtedly true), but can be based on the nurturing of relations:

This relational approach is a condition for asserting a politics of solidarity. It shapes different ways of understanding how relations are made political and the terms on which political communities are shaped and constituted [...]. It is not a case of just connecting pre-existing communities in already fixed relationships. This also highlights the problem of any group which diverges from these, which is seen as undermining left politics.[4]

Solidarity is not immune from following received wisdom, or even following the party line. But there are enough examples that support Featherstone's argument close to home. Two things come to mind from the miners' strike. The first was the support from Cymdeithas yr Iaith (the Welsh Language Society) for the striking miners. Language activists weren't supposed to be interested in industrial disputes. But the links they chose to forge were created around communities, in a shared struggle for the right to exist.

The second was an even stronger example of what Featherstone describes as 'the importance of solidarities in constructing relations between places, activists, diverse groups.'5 In a fortnight I'll be going to see *Pride*. It describes the links made between the London-based Lesbians and Gays Support the Miners group and the striking miners in the Dulais Valley in south Wales. The film seeks to answer the question posed by one gay activist in the film: 'The miners' strike? What's it got to do with us?'

With solidarity the answer to this question is twofold: 'everything' and 'whatever we want.' This second answer also points us in the direction of the campaigning that follows. The posters produced, the T-shirts worn, the mugs drunk out of, the protests organised, even how meetings are run—they all help create meaning for activists and for the wider public. The form they take is as important to helping people understand as the result they produce.

Cyfarthfa Castle Museum and Gallery is a special place. Two-thirds of the visitors are schoolchildren, and I would guess that more than 90 percent of visitors are local. What does the museum do? It helps people in Merthyr make sense of their place in the world, their past and their present.

In one corner is a display given over to Merthyr's rich history of political and social protest. In the display is a small poster advertising a public meeting in 1986 where Paul Robeson's son, Paul Robeson Jr., was to speak about Central America. His talk there led to the founding of the Nicaragua Support Group in Merthyr. It was from Paul Robeson Jr. that I first heard some of the history of Nicaragua and the Sandinista Revolution. Do Merthyr schoolchildren today look at the poster and understand why such a thing happened in Merthyr at such a time, like the other social movements that are celebrated in the display? It's part of their culture. It's ordinary.

1. Edward W. Said, *Culture and Imperialism* (London: Vintage, 1994), 278.

2. Eduardo Galeano, quoted in Noam Chomsky, *Deterring Democracy* (London: Vintage, 1992), 370.

3. Raymond Williams, 'Culture Is Ordinary', in *Resources of Hope* (London: Verso, 1989), 4.

4. David Featherstone, *Solidarity: Hidden Histories and Geographies of Internationalism* (London: Zed Books Ltd., 2014), 245–46.

5. Ibid., 5.

Lesbians & Gays Support the Miners in 1985

Solidarietà

di Ben Gregory

Scrivo queste parole un'ora dopo l'esito del referendum sull'indipendenza della Scozia. Come gran parte del Regno Unito, sono rimasto immobile davanti allo schermo della tv per quasi tutta la notte. Tre mesi fa mi sono unito a una delegazione gallese per incontrare gli attivisti per l'indipendenza scozzese. Oltre ai rappresentanti della campagna ufficiale Yes, abbiamo parlato con Green Yes, Women for Independence, Labour for Independence, il National Collective, la Radical Independence Campaign e altri ancora. Le loro attività politiche e culturali hanno trasformato la Scozia, dando vita a un movimento sociale nato da una varietà di organizzazioni. L'altro aspetto della visita che mi ha colpito è stato che la maggioranza delle persone del gruppo aveva fatto parte anche dell'ultima delegazione della Wales Nicaragua Solidarity Campaign, che era stata in Nicaragua nel 2013. Agli occhi dei partecipanti anche questo viaggio era una visita di solidarietà.

Il movimento di solidarietà con il Nicaragua è nato dal sostegno alla rivoluzione negli anni Ottanta, e ha continuato a esistere mentre il popolo nicaraguense, come quelli di tutto il mondo, lottava contro il neoliberismo. La rivoluzione era guidata dal Fronte Sandinista di Liberazione Nazionale. Al pari di altre rivoluzioni dell'America Latina, è stata innanzitutto una lotta per la liberazione nazionale, come d'altronde molte guerre anticoloniali del ventesimo secolo. Edward Said, il grande teorico palestinese, ha affermato che, malgrado il successo di molte di esse, queste lotte per la liberazione nazionale si concentravano sull'aspetto sbagliato:

> È la *liberazione*, e non l'indipendenza nazionalista, la nuova alternativa: una liberazione che per sua stessa natura implica, per usare le parole di Fanon, lo sviluppo di una coscienza sociale che vada oltre il semplice orizzonte del nazionalismo.[1]

Era quindi un errore recarci in Scozia per scoprire qualcosa sul suo movimento indipendentista? Alex Salmond, primo ministro e leader del Partito Nazionale Scozzese, nel documento di consultazione del referendum, ha dichiarato che "la Scozia non è oppressa e non abbiamo alcun bisogno di essere liberati. L'indipendenza è importante perché non abbiamo il potere di sfruttare appieno le nostre potenzialità".

I gruppi che abbiamo incontrato non sarebbero d'accordo: per loro, invece, il bisogno di essere liberati dal neoliberismo e dal potere delle grandi imprese esisteva, lottavano in nome della giustizia sociale. E la loro visione sembrava confermata dagli eventi: presidenti e primi ministri hanno fatto la fila per mettere in guardia dai rischi dell'indipendenza. Il presidente della Commissione europea si è unito al coro, il segretario generale della NATO e i capi delle Forze armate britanniche hanno previsto conseguenze terribili per la "guerra globale al terrorismo". Le banche inglesi hanno parlato di fuga di capitali e di riduzione delle pensioni, mentre la Deutsche Bank ha addirittura ipotizzato che l'indipendenza della Scozia avrebbe innescato una depressione a livello mondiale paragonabile a quella degli anni Trenta.

Sono gli stessi moniti che paesi come il Nicaragua subiscono da oltre vent'anni. Qualsiasi passo verso un'autentica liberazione si scontra con minacciosi avvertimenti e atti ancora peggiori quando i primi non funzionano. Il linguaggio del popolo nicaraguense e delle organizzazioni che abbiamo incontrato negli anni Novanta e nei primi Duemila non era molto diverso da quello delle organizzazioni scozzesi con cui abbiamo parlato.

Nella maggior parte dei casi lo *status quo* viene mantenuto con facilità, dato che viene inculcato dal sistema scolastico, dai *corporate media* e dal mondo dello spettacolo. Più di trent'anni fa, lo scrittore uruguayano Eduardo Galeano ha descritto il funzionamento di tutto ciò:

> La maggioranza deve rassegnarsi a consumare fantasia. Si vendono illusioni di ricchezza ai poveri, illusioni di libertà agli oppressi, sogni di vittoria agli sconfitti e di potere ai deboli.[2]

Alla fine degli anni Cinquanta, Raymond Williams riteneva che la cultura fosse ordinaria. Creiamo un significato per il mondo che ci circonda partendo dai concetti e dagli artefatti che produciamo e riproduciamo:

> La cultura è ordinaria: questo è il primo fatto. Ogni società umana ha la propria forma, i propri obiettivi, i propri significati. Ogni società umana li esprime nelle istituzioni, nelle arti e nell'apprendimento. La costituzione di una società è la scoperta di significati e di una direzione comuni, e la sua crescita è un dibattere e un emendare attivamente nel processo dell'esperienza, del contatto e della scoperta, che si imprimono sul territorio [...]. Una cultura ha due aspetti: i significati e le direzioni noti cui i suoi membri vengono addestrati; le osservazioni e i significati nuovi, che vengono proposti e messi alla prova.[3]

Sono cresciuto a Tredegar, nelle valli del Galles meridionale, e alla mia famiglia sembrava naturale parlare di Paul Robeson, l'attivista, attore e cantante americano di colore. Avevo una vaga idea del suo legame con il sindacato dei minatori, e questo mi ha spinto a informarmi sulla sua vita e sul suo ruolo nella lotta per i diritti civili. Il primo gruppo di solidarietà con il Nicaragua di cui ho fatto parte aveva sede nella vicina città di Merthyr. Era stata organizzata la proiezione di una serie di film per raccogliere fondi per il Nicaragua, tra cui la pellicola tedesca *Rosa L.* (1986), sulla rivoluzionaria polacca naturalizzata tedesca, e la selezione non sembrava affatto strana. Era inoltre naturale proiettare il film in gallese *Milwr Bychan* ("Ragazzo soldato", 1986), che racconta la storia di un soldato che presta servizio nell'Irlanda del Nord, e non battere ciglio quando si scopriva che il regista, gallese, doveva il proprio nome a Karl Liebknecht, il rivoluzionario tedesco ucciso con Rosa Luxemburg nel 1919.

A posteriori, vedo chiaramente questi legami: perché sono nati e perché apparivano tanto naturali. Fa tutto parte della cultura proiettata verso l'esterno che in generale queste comunità gallesi si sono create, senza affidarsi a enti o comitati per le arti che lo facessero al posto loro.

David Featherstone, nel suo recente libro *Solidarity: Hidden Histories and Geographies of Internationalism*, sostiene in modo convincente che la solidarietà non è per forza innata (benché ciò sia innegabilmente vero), ma che può fondarsi sulla coltivazione delle relazioni:

> Tale approccio relazionale è un requisito per poter affermare una politica di solidarietà. Modella diversi modi di comprendere come le relazioni vengono rese politiche e i termini in cui le comunità politiche vengono plasmate e costituite. [...] Non si tratta semplicemente di collegare comunità preesistenti in rapporti prefissati. Ciò sottolinea inoltre il problema di qualsiasi gruppo che si allontani da essi, un allontanamento che viene interpretato come un indebolimento delle politiche di sinistra.[4]

La solidarietà non è immune dal seguire le credenze comuni o persino la linea di partito. Ma a favore della tesi di Featherstone ci sono esempi sufficienti che ci toccano da vicino. Lo sciopero dei minatori britannici rievoca due cose. La prima è il sostegno ai minatori offerto dalla Cymdeithas yr Iaith (la Società della lingua gallese): in teoria, gli attivisti di quell'ambito non avrebbero dovuto interessarsi a controversie industriali, eppure i legami che scelsero di stabilire furono creati attorno alle comunità, in una lotta condivisa per il diritto a esistere.

La seconda è un esempio ancora più forte di ciò che Featherstone descrive come "l'importanza delle solidarietà nella costruzione di relazioni tra luoghi, attivisti e gruppi diversi".[5] Tra un paio di settimane andrò a vedere *Pride*, che descrive i legami tra il gruppo londinese Lesbians and Gays Support the Miners e i minatori in sciopero nella Dulais Valley, nel sud del Galles. Il film tenta di rispondere alla domanda posta da uno degli attivisti gay nella pellicola stessa: "Lo sciopero dei minatori? Che c'entra con noi?"

La risposta a questa domanda, nell'ottica della solidarietà, è duplice: "Tutto" e: "Qualsiasi cosa vogliamo". La seconda ci indirizza anche verso la campagna che ne deriva; i poster stampati, le magliette indossate, le tazze da cui si beve, le proteste organizzate, persino il modo in cui vengono condotte le riunioni: tutto ciò contribuisce a creare un significato per gli attivisti e il pubblico in generale. Per aiutare la gente a capire, la forma che queste cose assumono ha la stessa importanza del risultato che generano.

Il Cyfarthfa Castle Museum and Gallery è un luogo speciale. Due terzi dei visitatori sono composti da scolaresche, e direi che più del 90 per cento di essi è gente della zona. Qual è il ruolo del museo? Aiutare la popolazione di Merthyr a dare un senso al proprio posto nel mondo, al proprio passato e presente.

In un angolo si trova una teca dedicata alla ricca storia di protesta politica e sociale di Merthyr. All'interno c'è un volantino che annuncia un incontro pubblico del 1986, in cui il figlio di Paul Robeson, Paul Robeson Jr., avrebbe parlato dell'America Centrale. Quel suo intervento ha portato alla fondazione del Nicaragua Support Group di Merthyr. È stato dalla voce di Paul Robeson Jr. che ho sentito parlare per la prima volta della storia del Nicaragua e della Rivoluzione Sandinista. Le scolaresche di Merthyr osservano il volantino e capiscono perché una cosa del genere è successa proprio a Merthyr e proprio in quel periodo, al pari degli altri movimenti sociali ricordati nella teca? È parte della loro cultura. È ordinario.

1. Edward W. Said, *Cultura e imperialismo*, Gamberetti, Roma 1998, p. 258.

2. Eduardo Galeano, citato in Noam Chomsky, *Anarchismo*, Marco Tropea Editore, Milano 2008, p. 205.

3. Raymond Williams, *Resources of Hope*, Verso, Londra 1989, p. 4.

4. David Featherstone, *Solidarity: Hidden Histories and Geographies of Internationalism*, Zed Books Ltd, Londra 2014, pp. 245–46.

5. Ibid., p. 5.

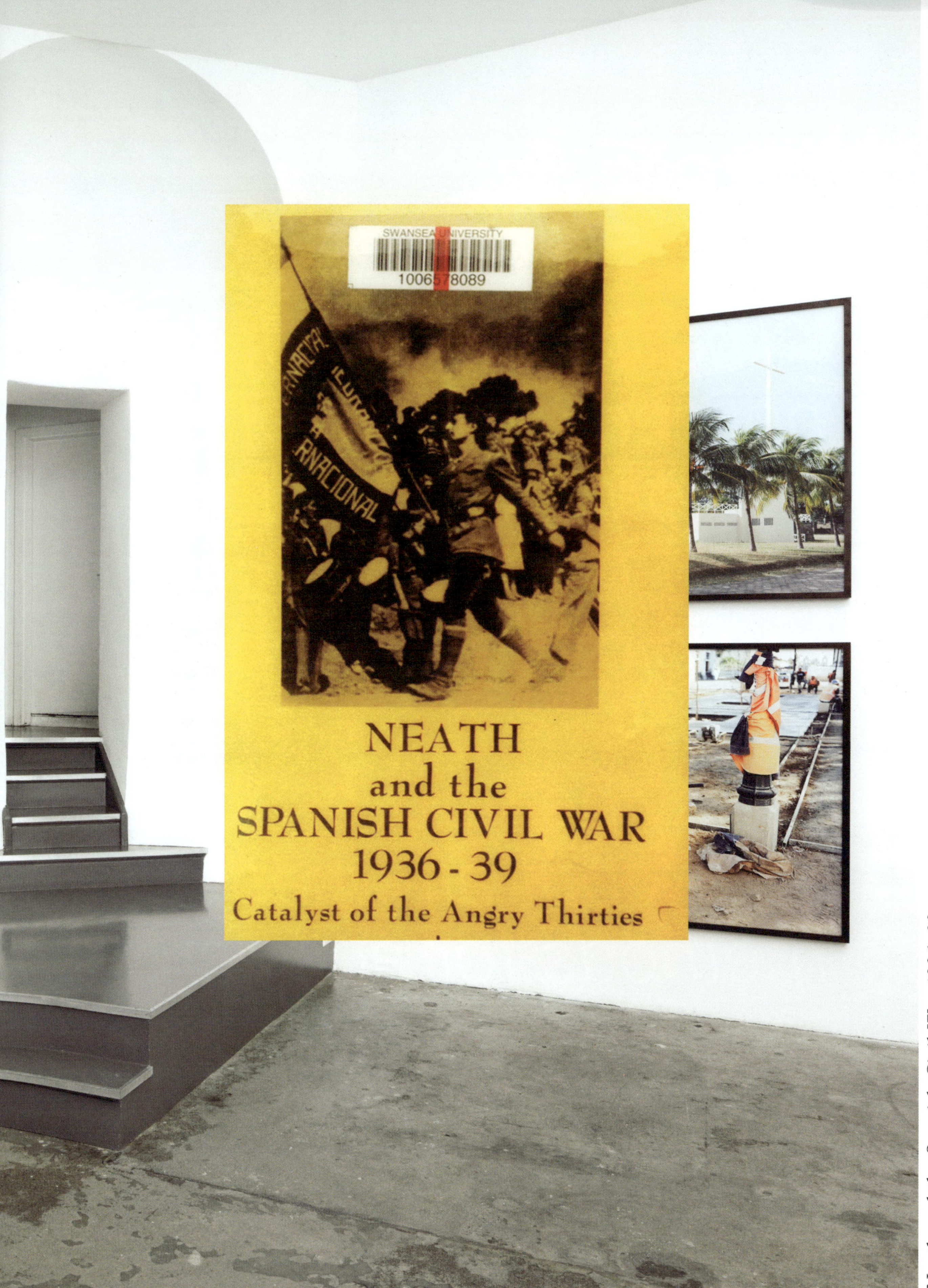
SWANSEA UNIVERSITY
1006578089
NEATH
and the
SPANISH CIVIL WAR
1936 - 39
Catalyst of the Angry Thirties

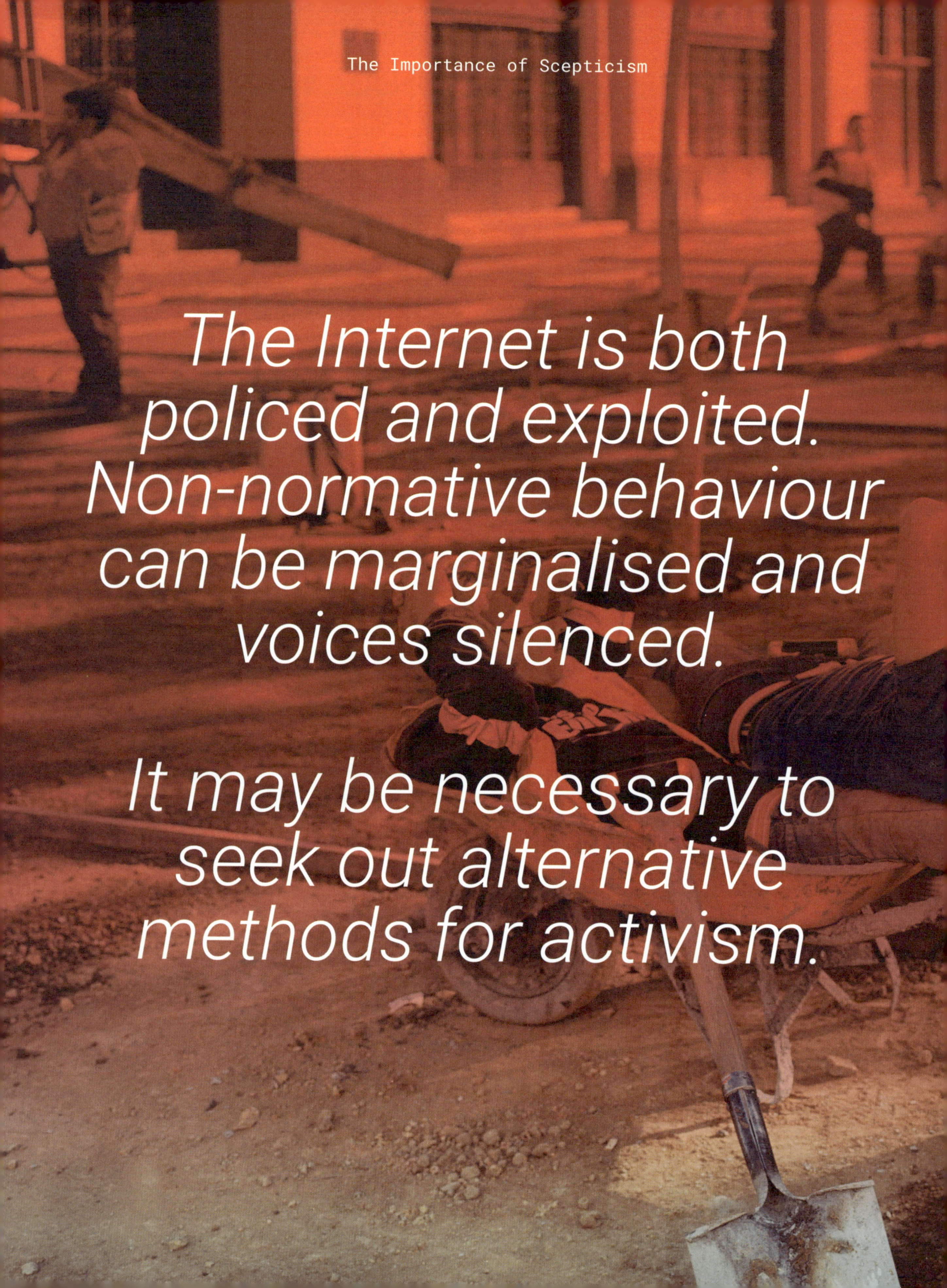
The Internet is both policed and exploited. Non-normative behaviour can be marginalised and voices silenced.

It may be necessary to seek out alternative methods for activism.

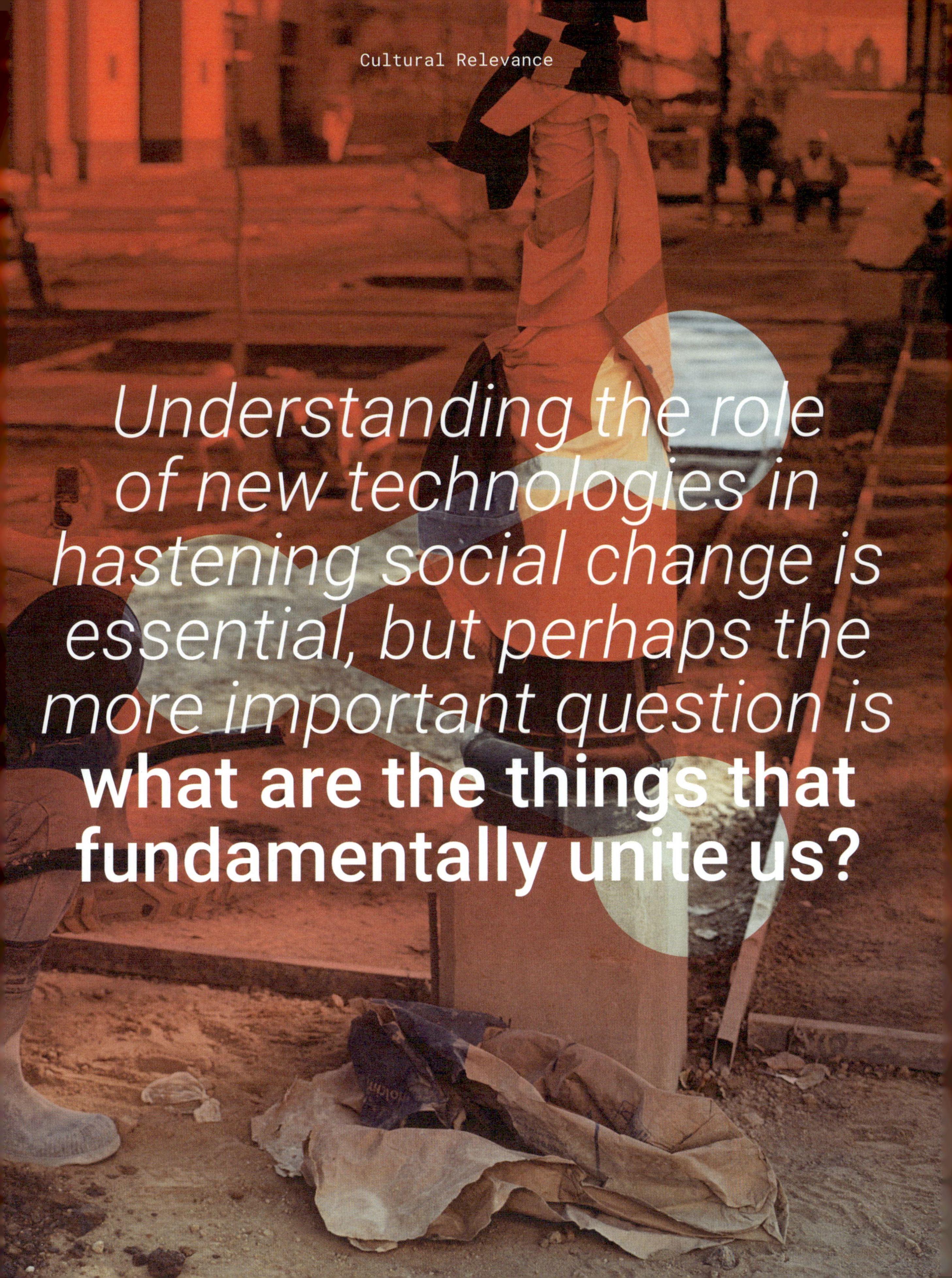

Cultural Relevance
Understanding the role of new technologies in hastening social change is essential, but perhaps the more important question is what are the things that fundamentally unite us?

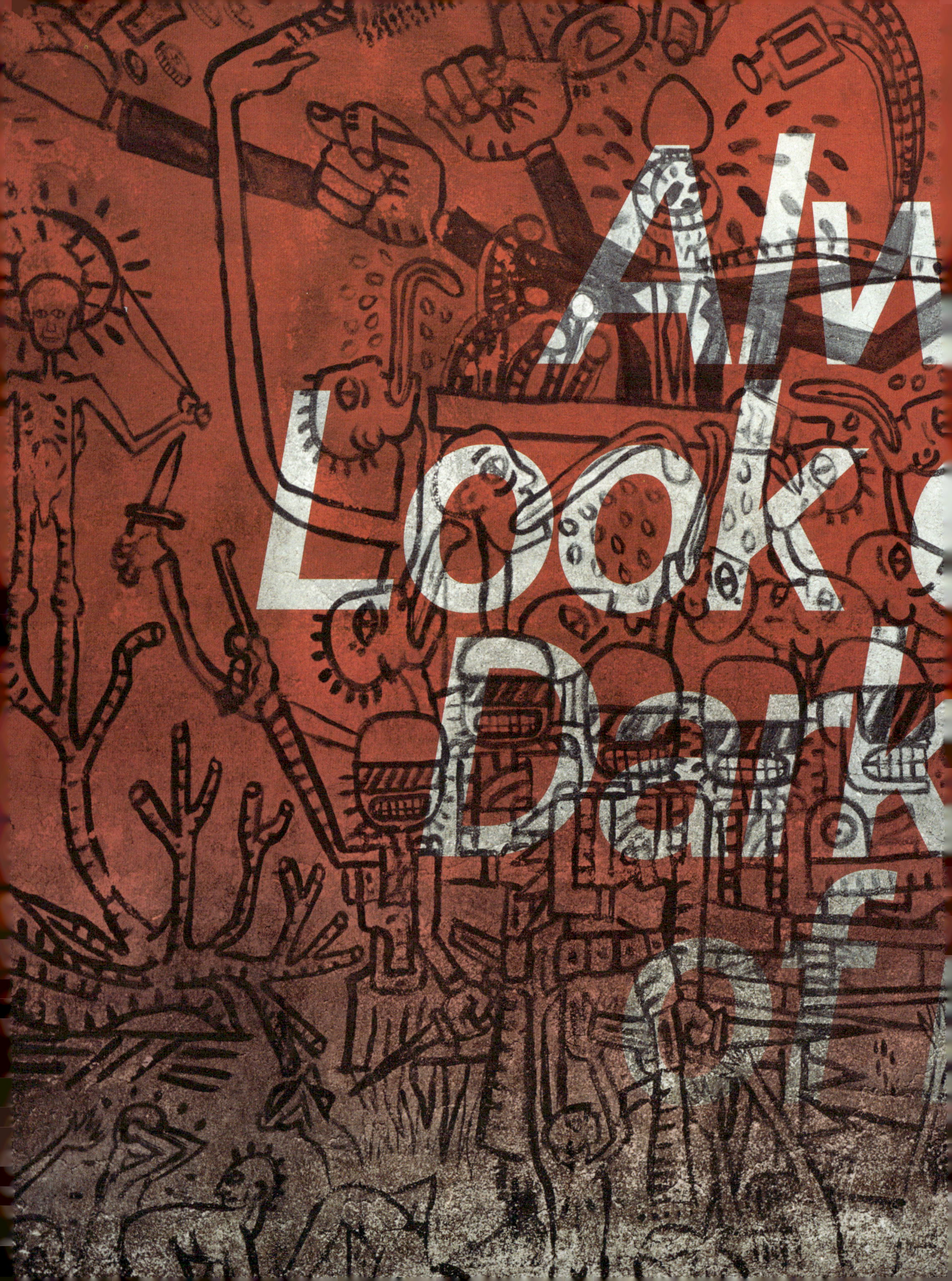
I AM
Looks
Dark

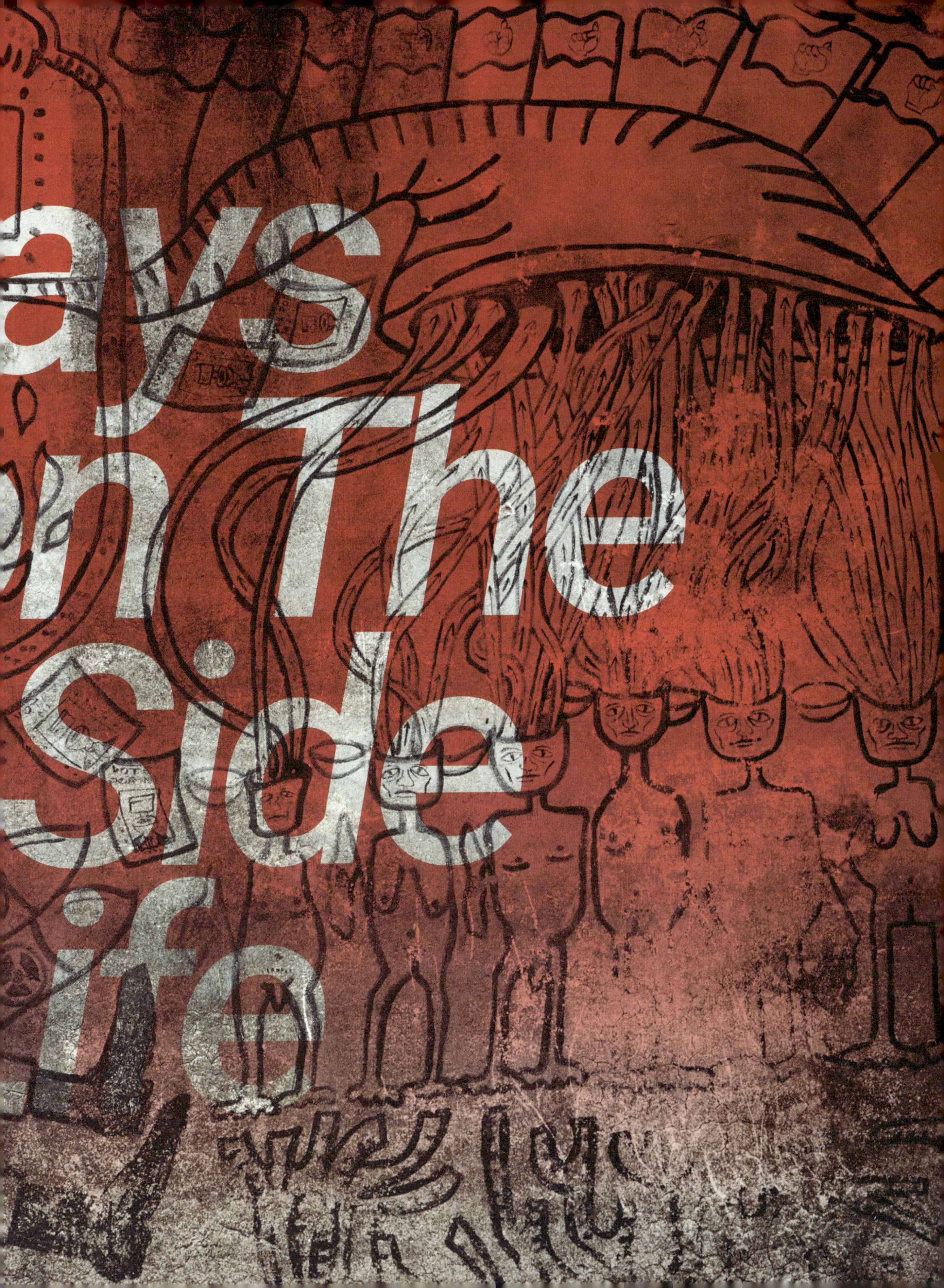

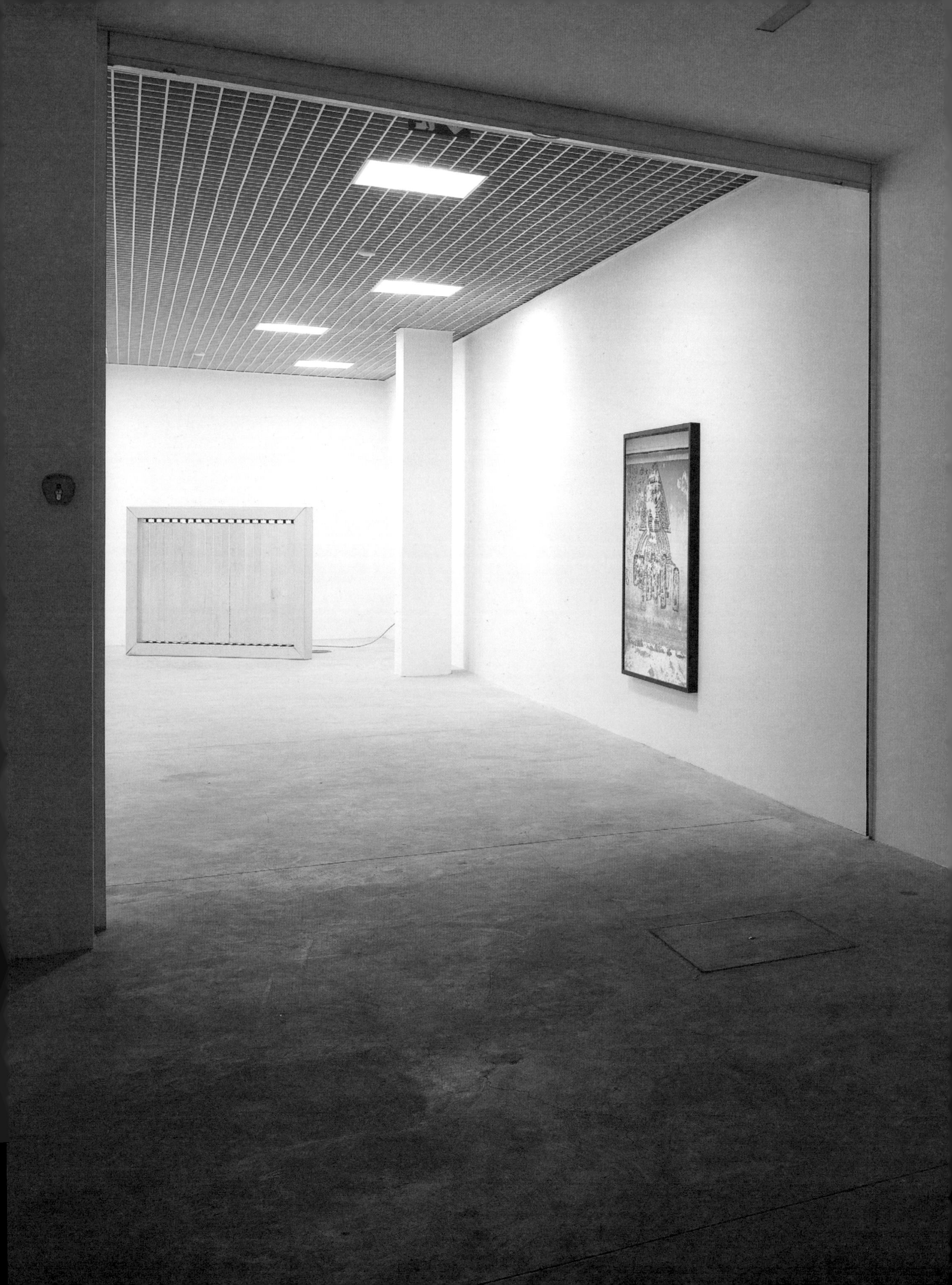

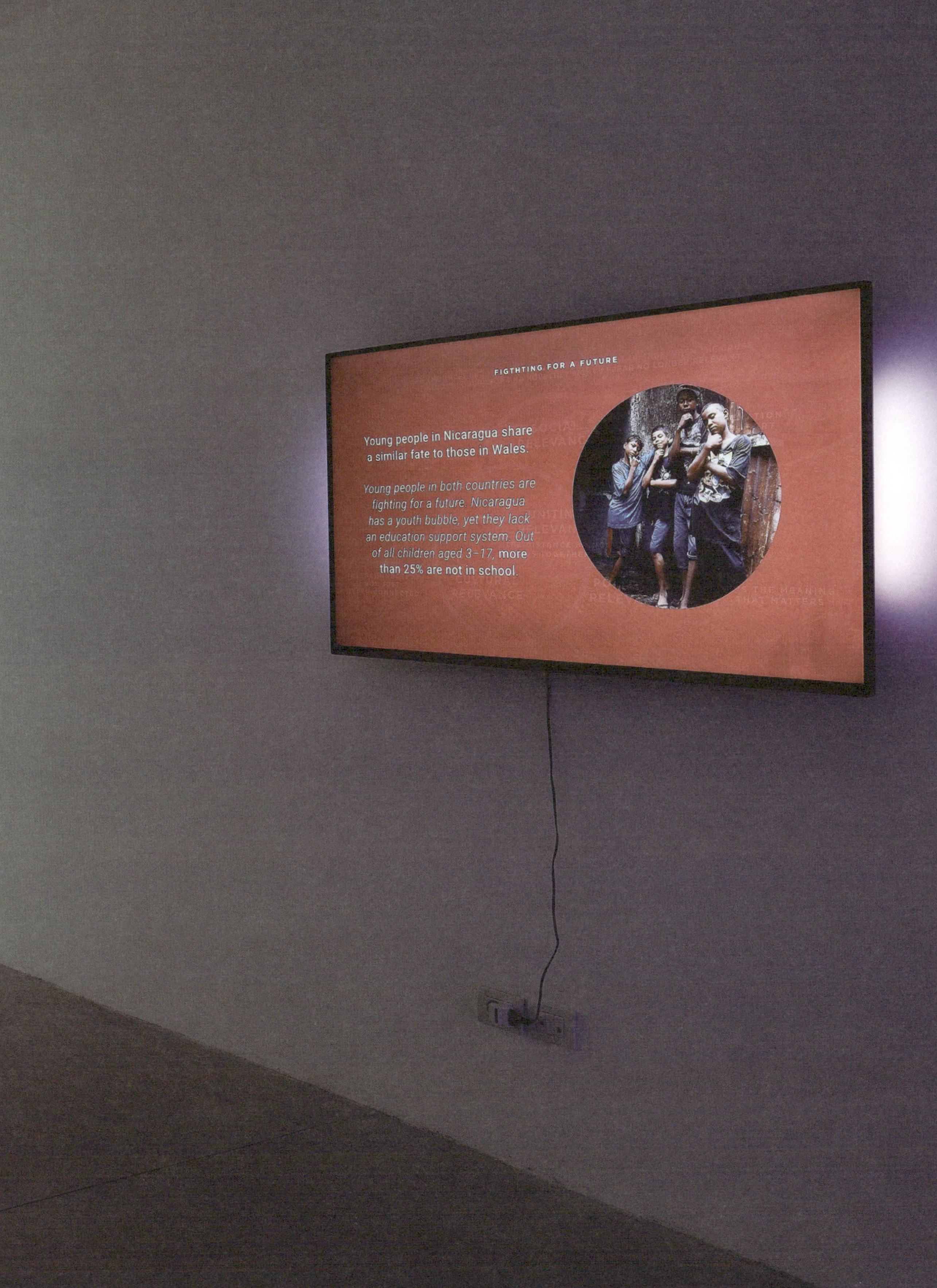
FIGHTING FOR A FUTURE
Young people in Nicaragua share
a similar fate to those in Wales.
Young people in both countries are
fighting for a future. Nicaragua
has a youth bubble, yet they lack
an education support system. Out
of all children aged 3–17, more
than 25% are not in school.

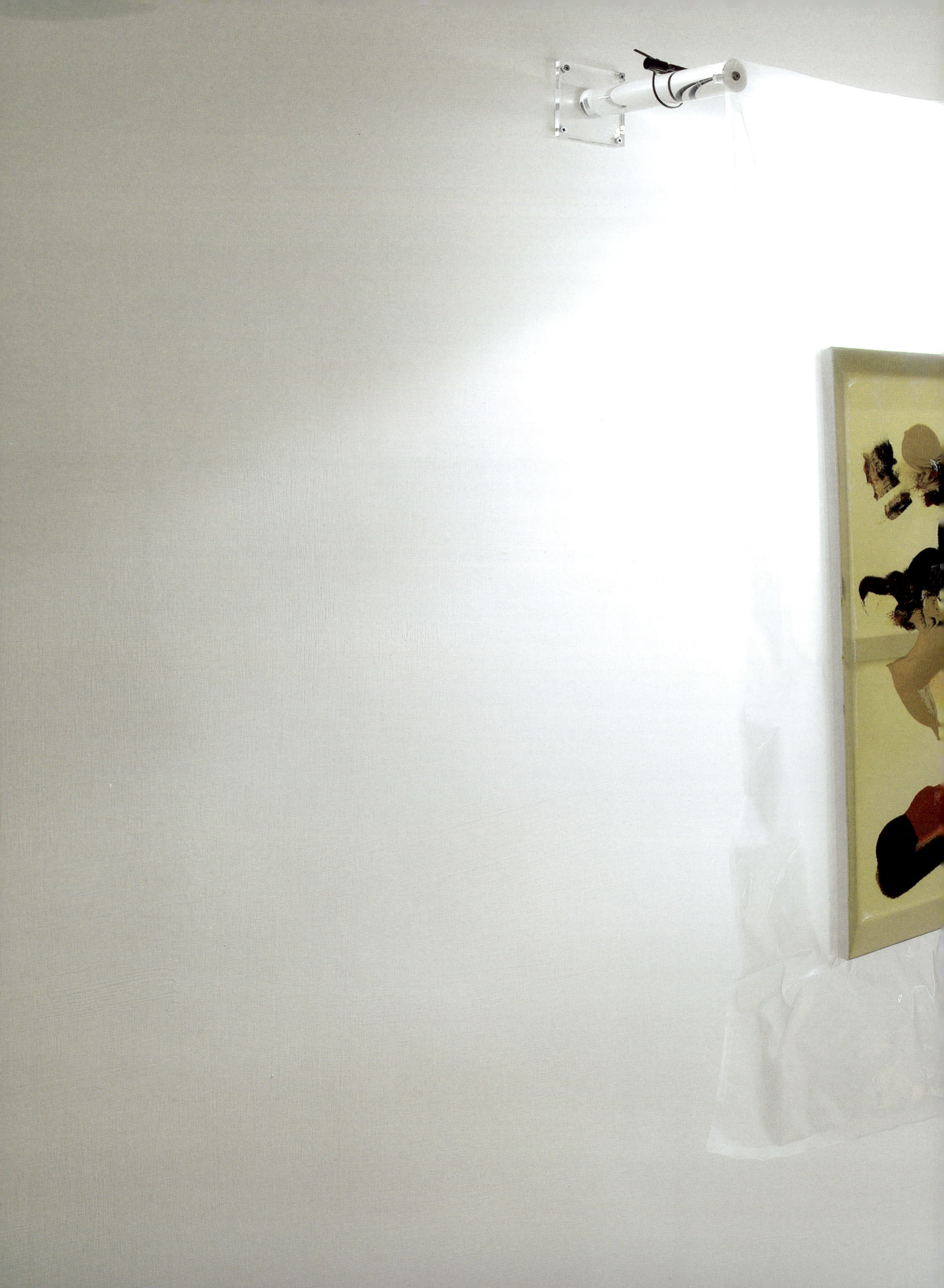

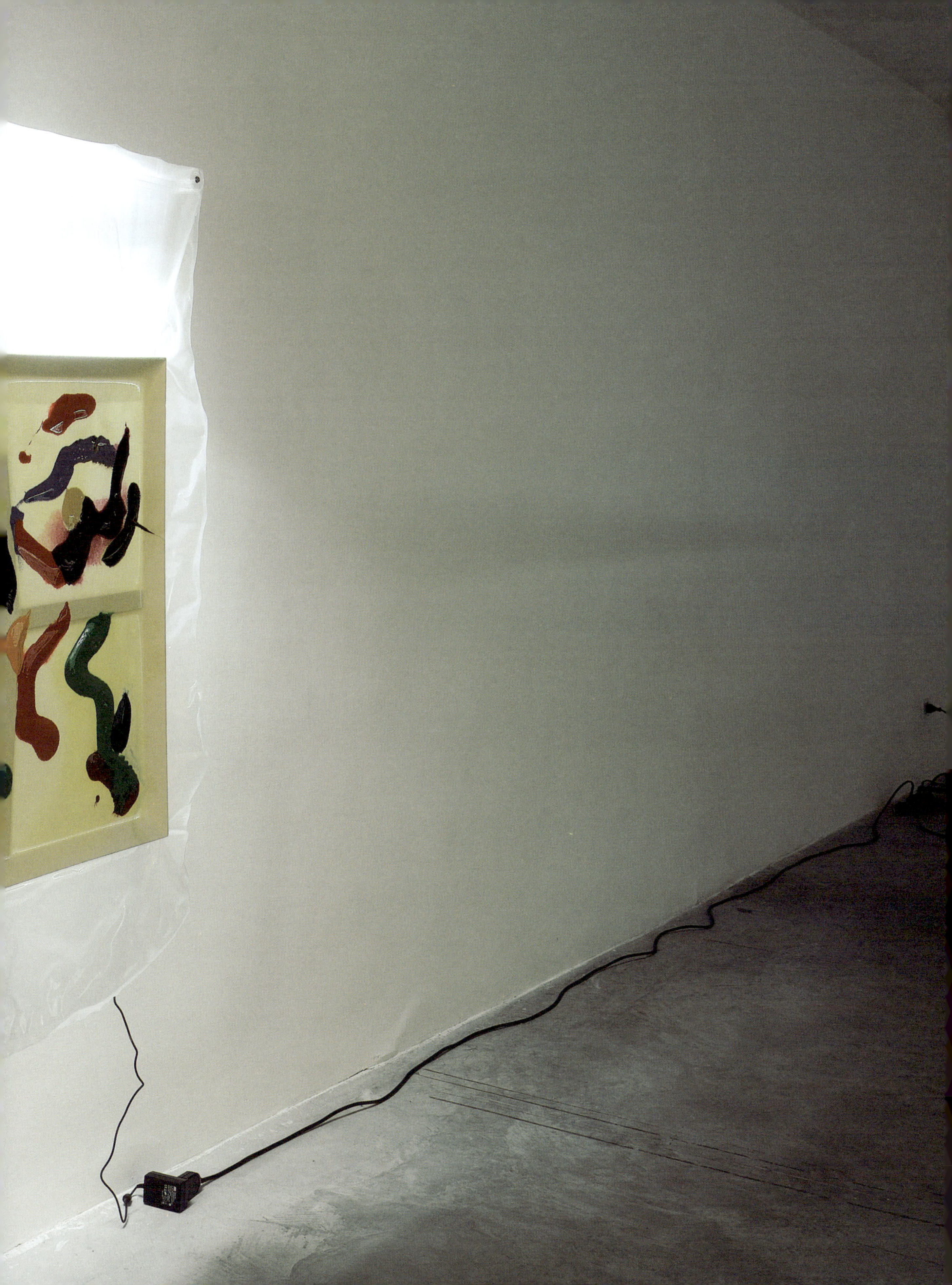

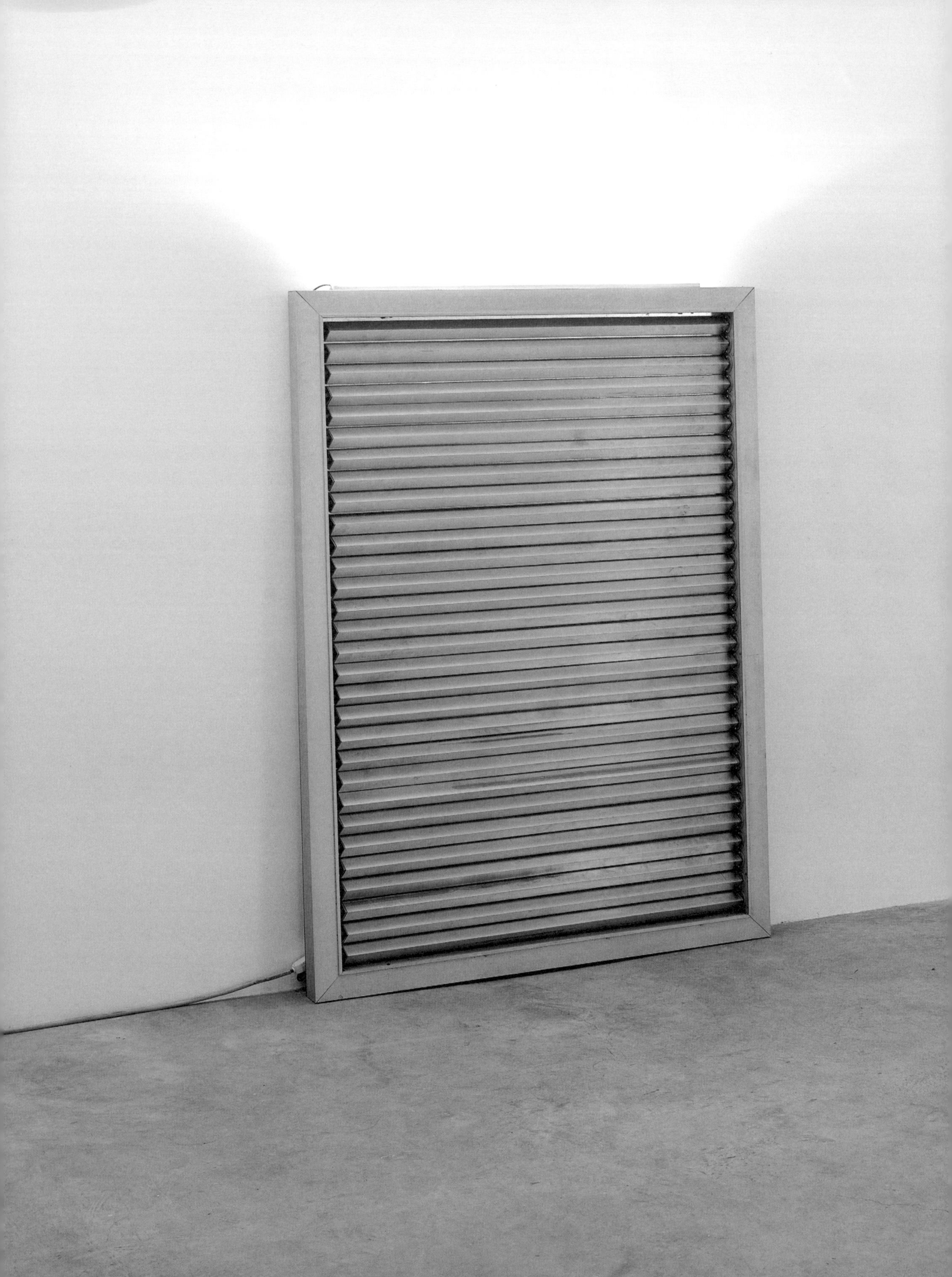

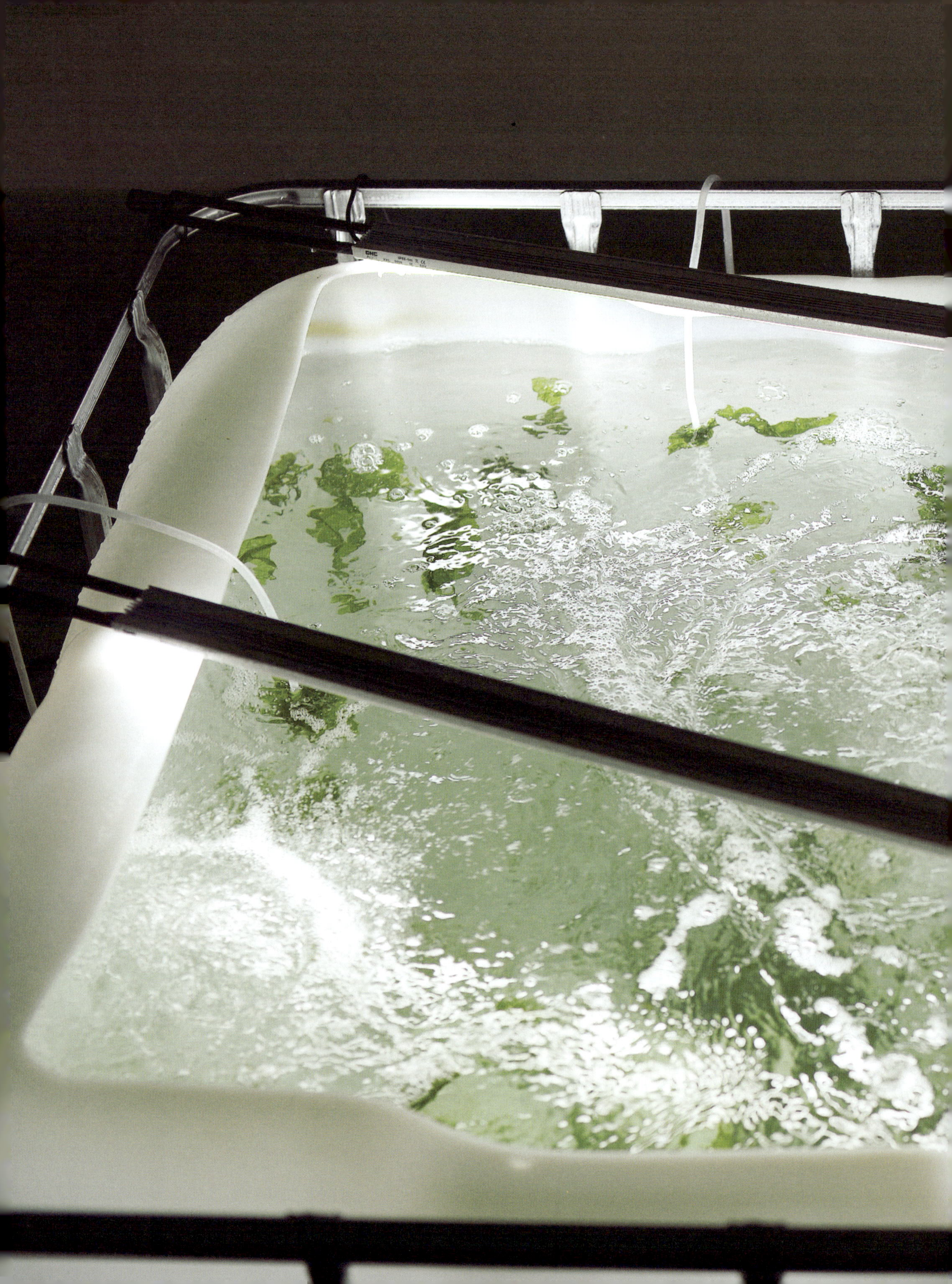

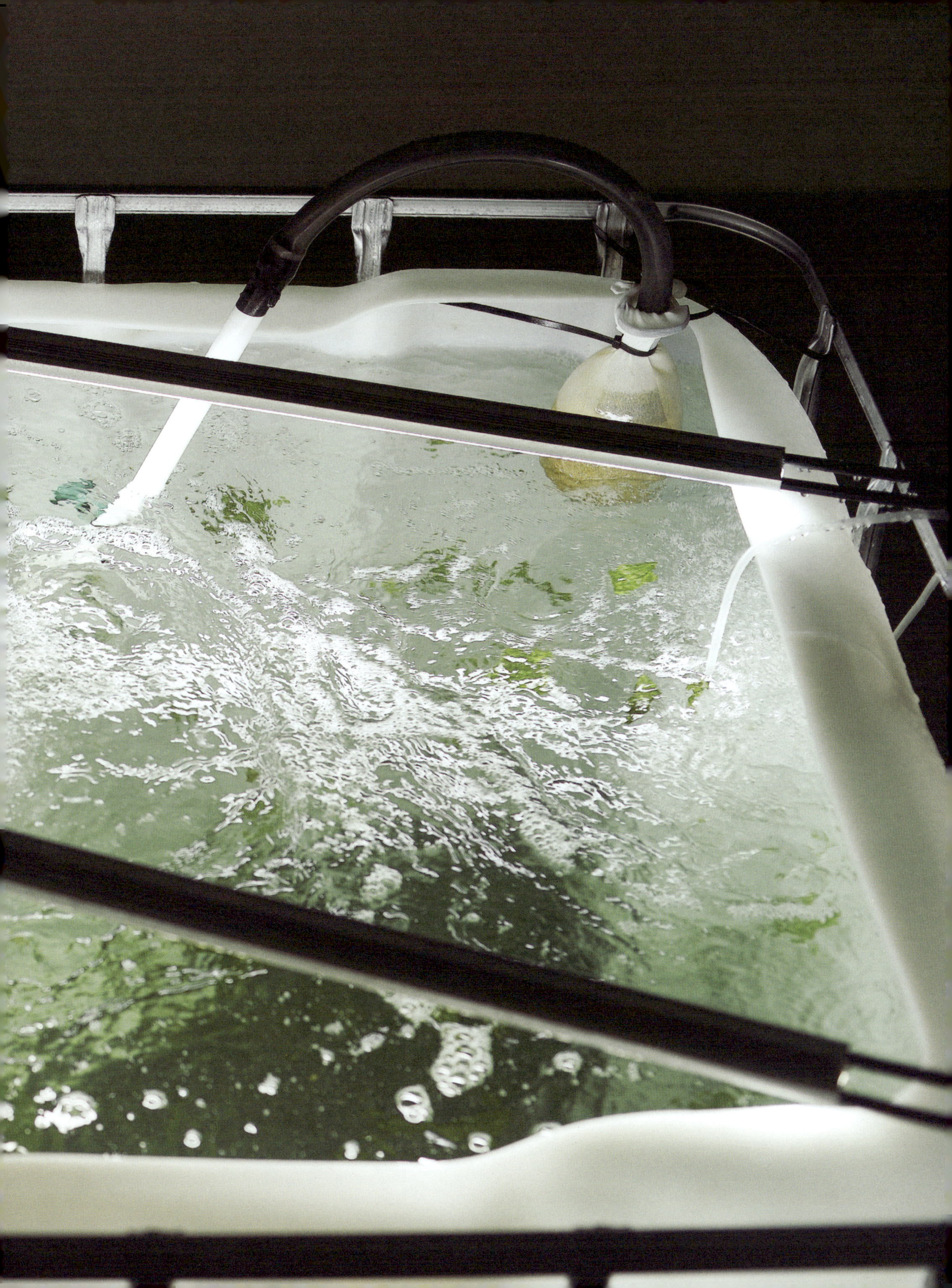

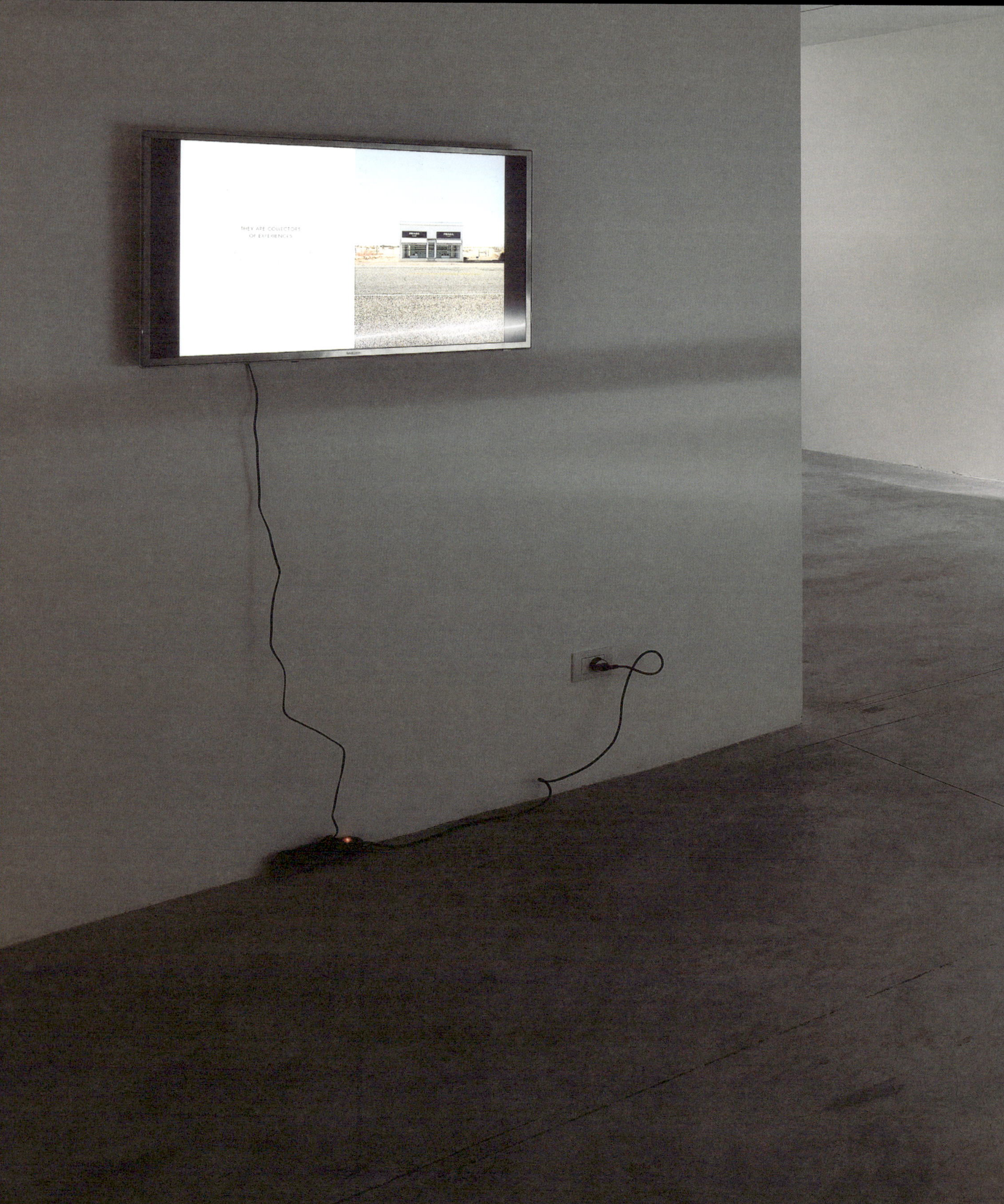
THEY ARE COLLECTORS
OF EXPERIENCES

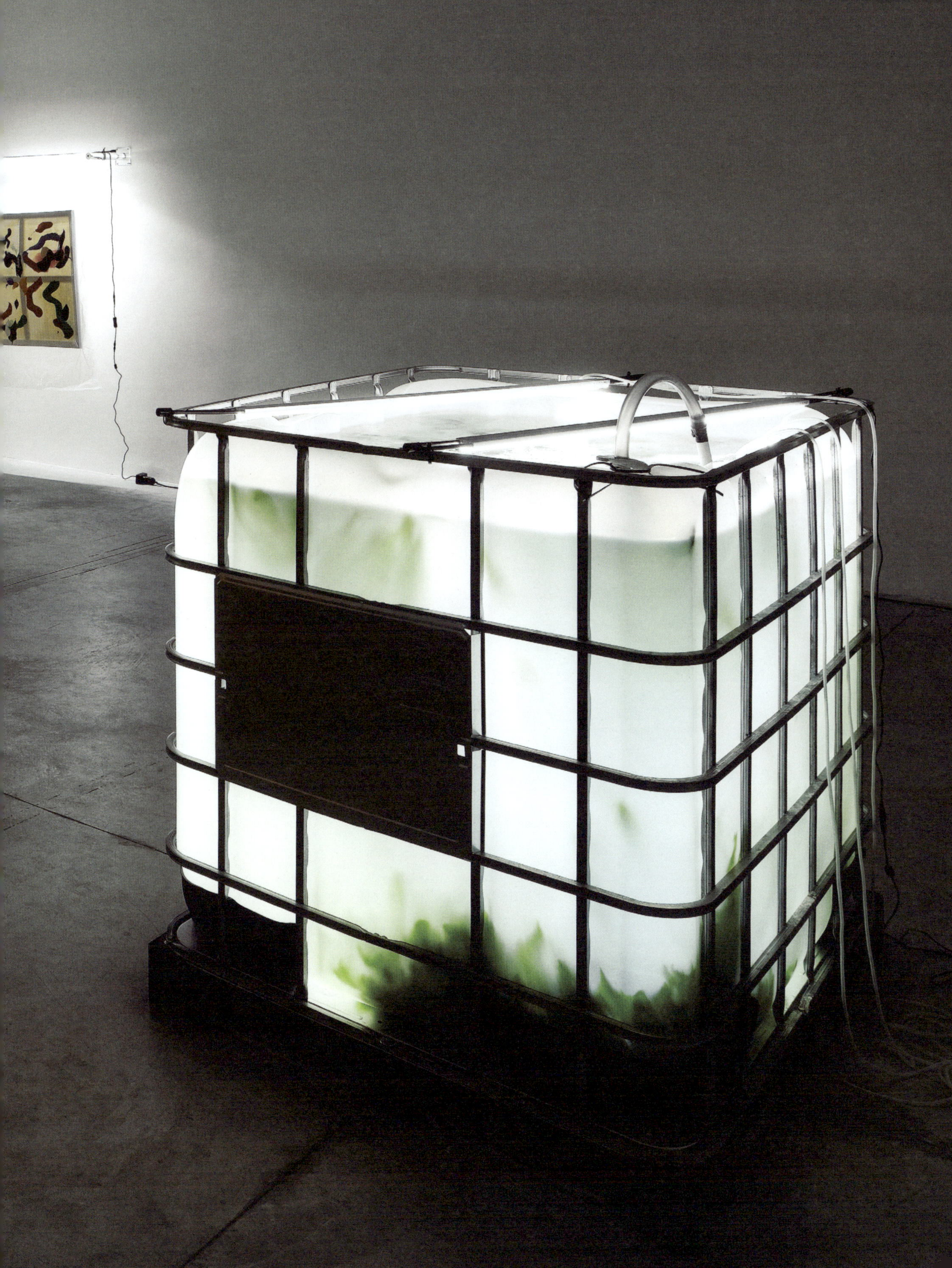

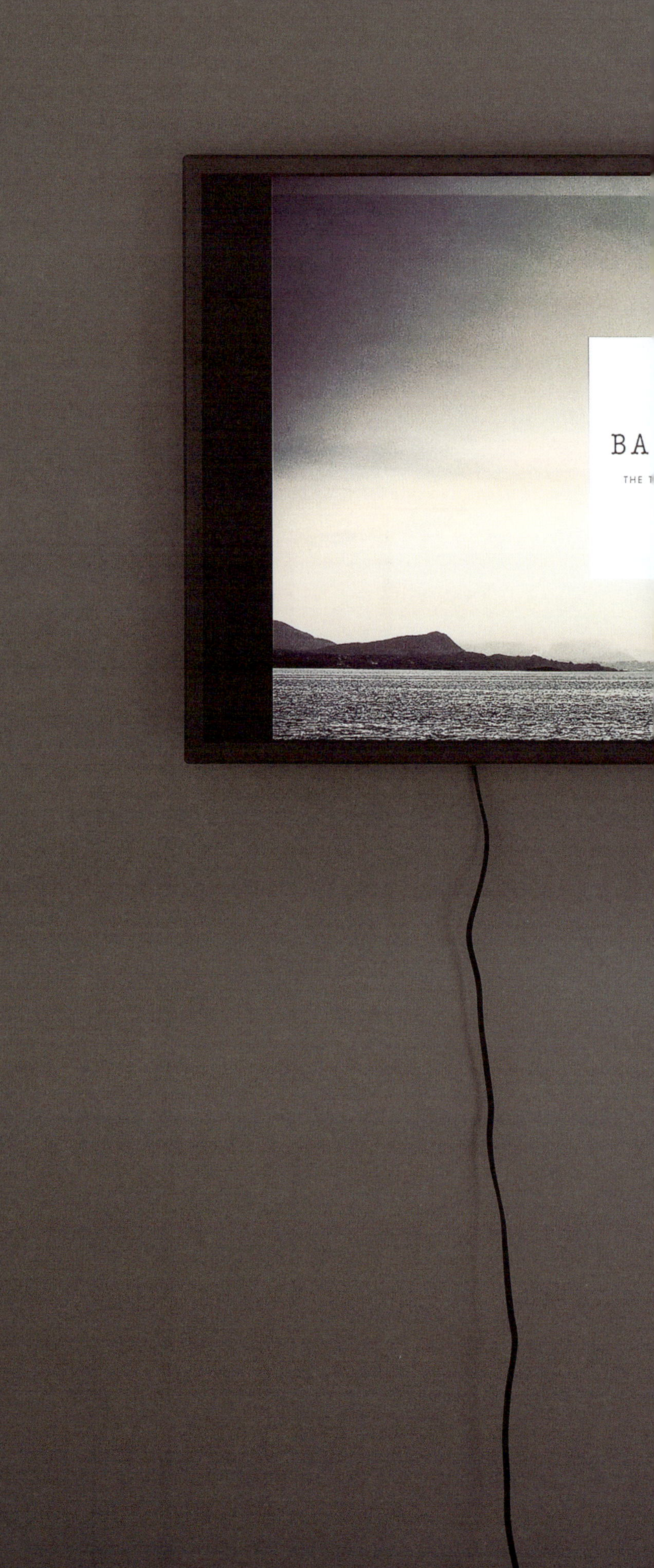

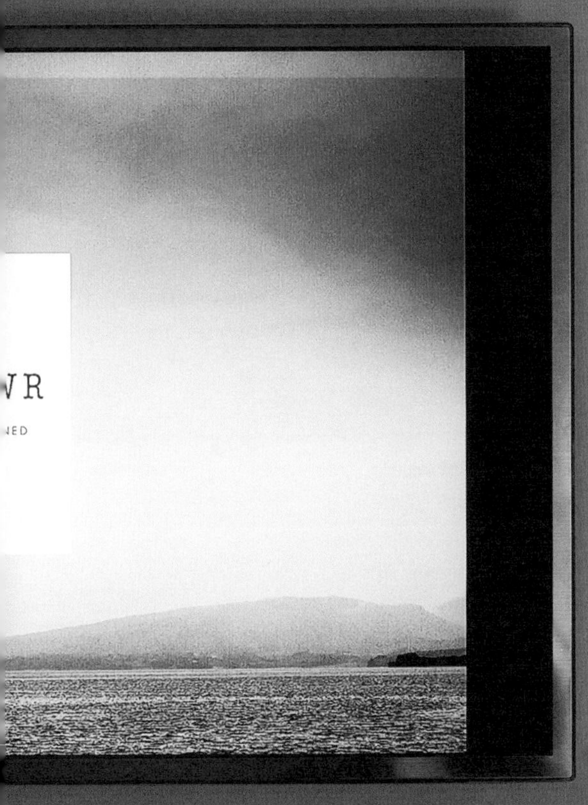
VR
NED

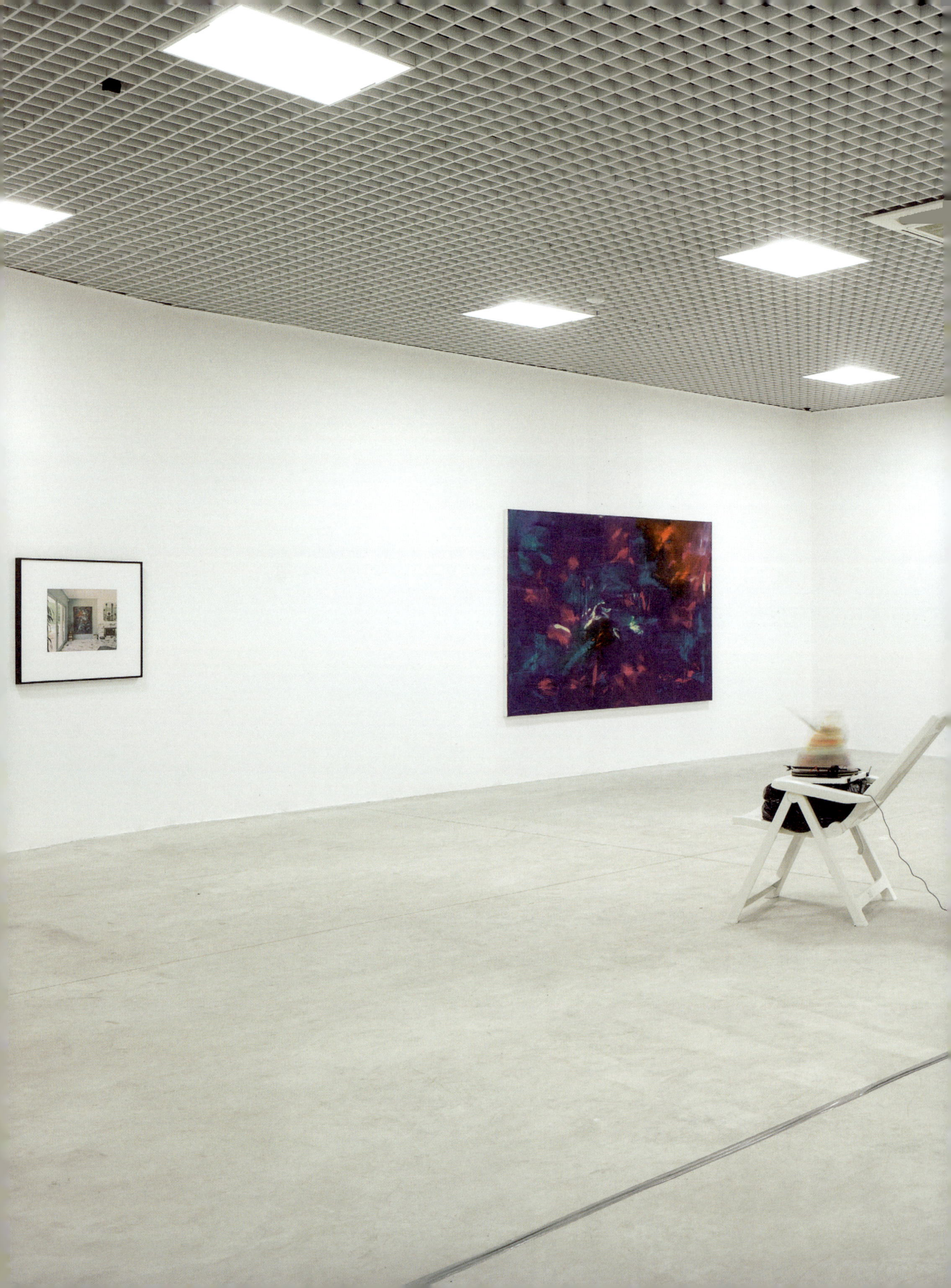

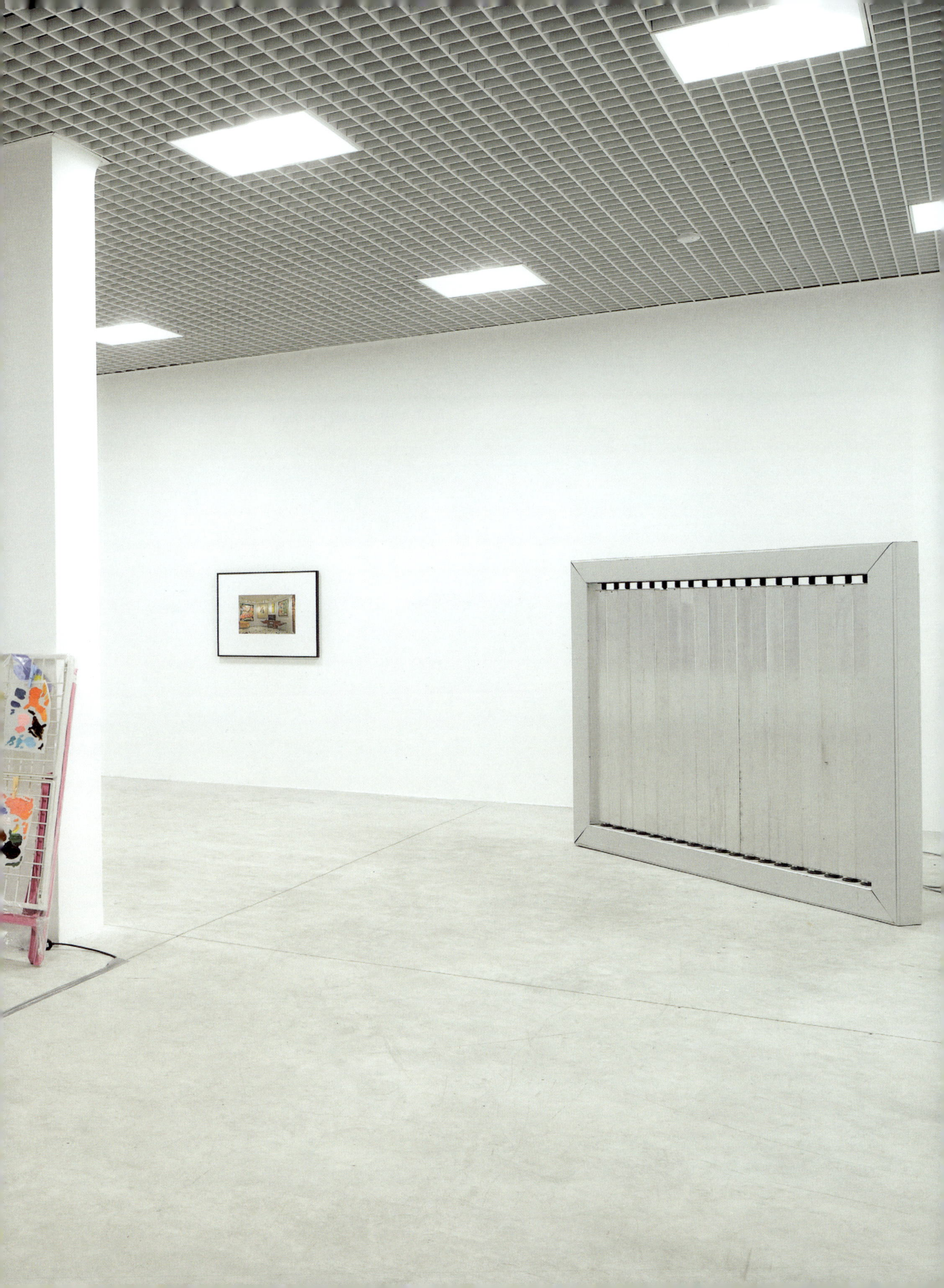

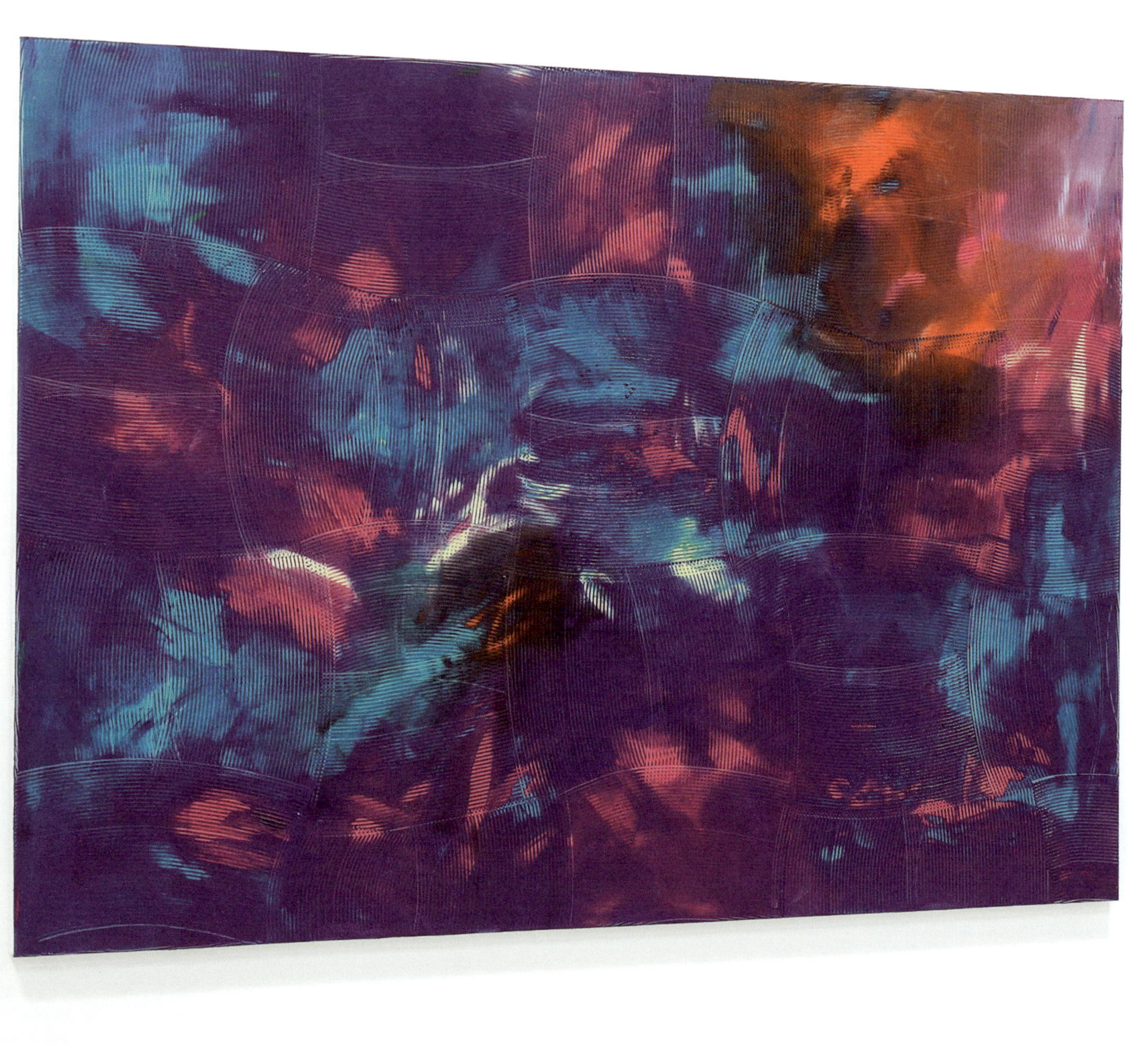

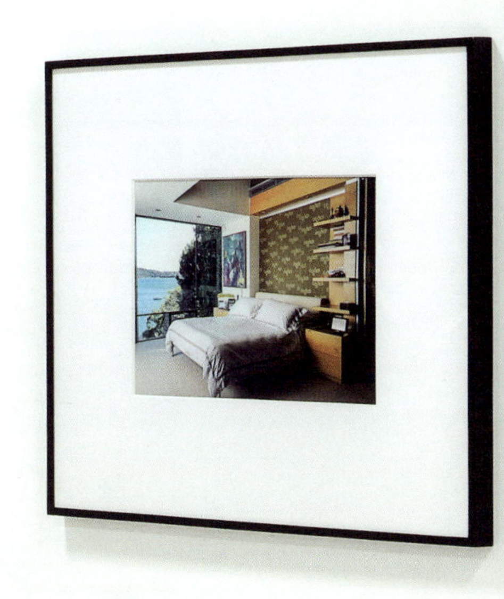

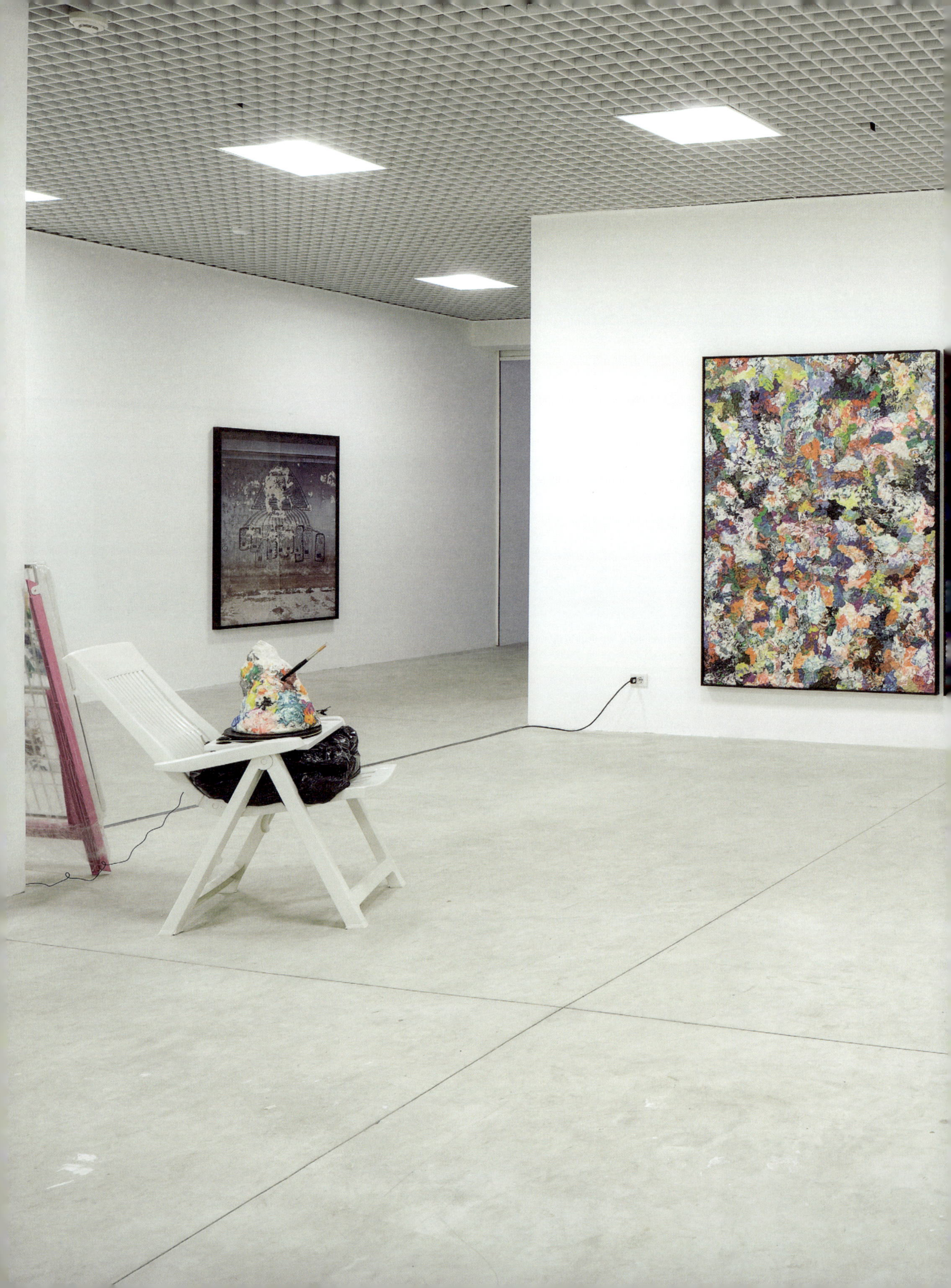

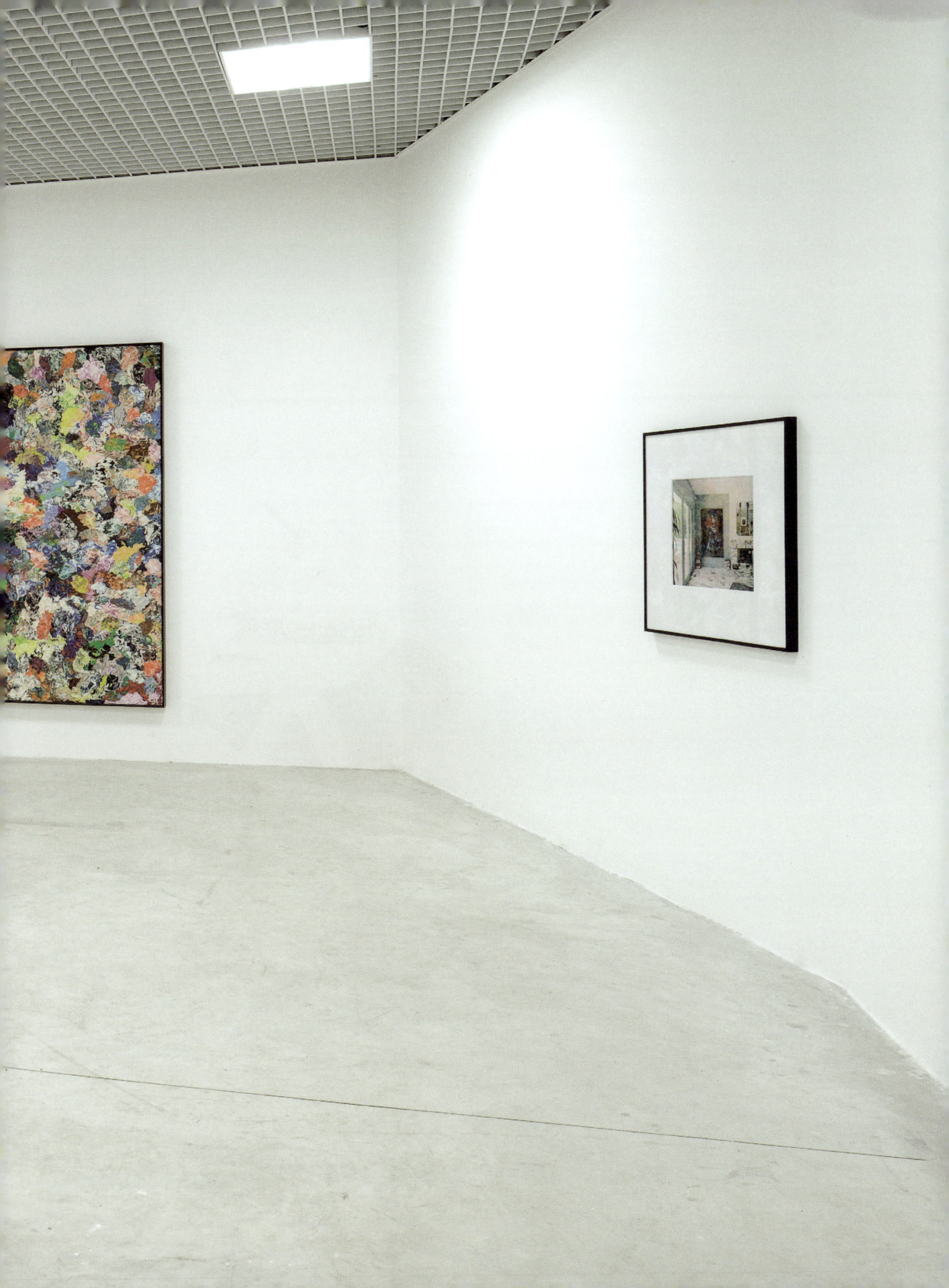

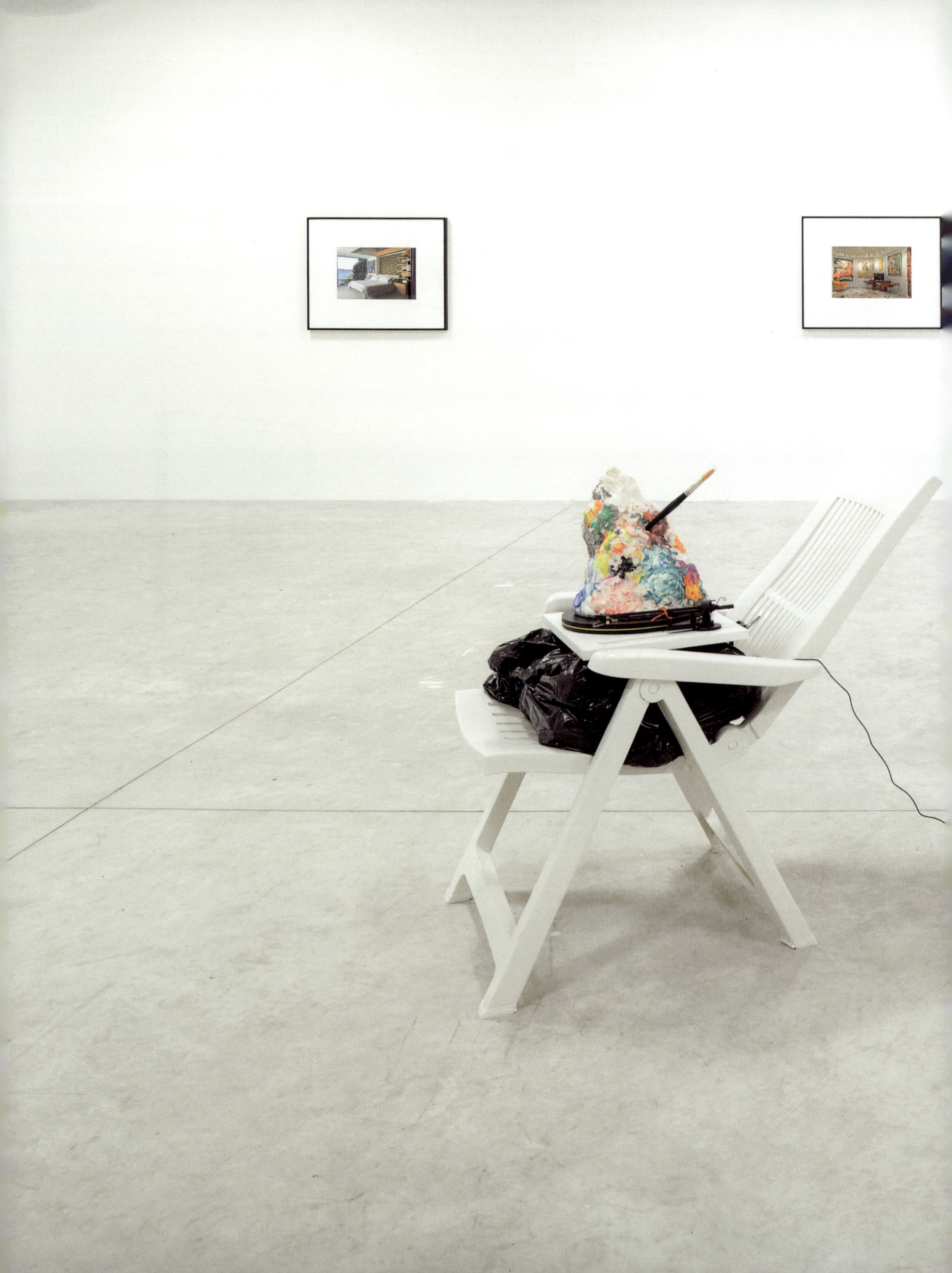

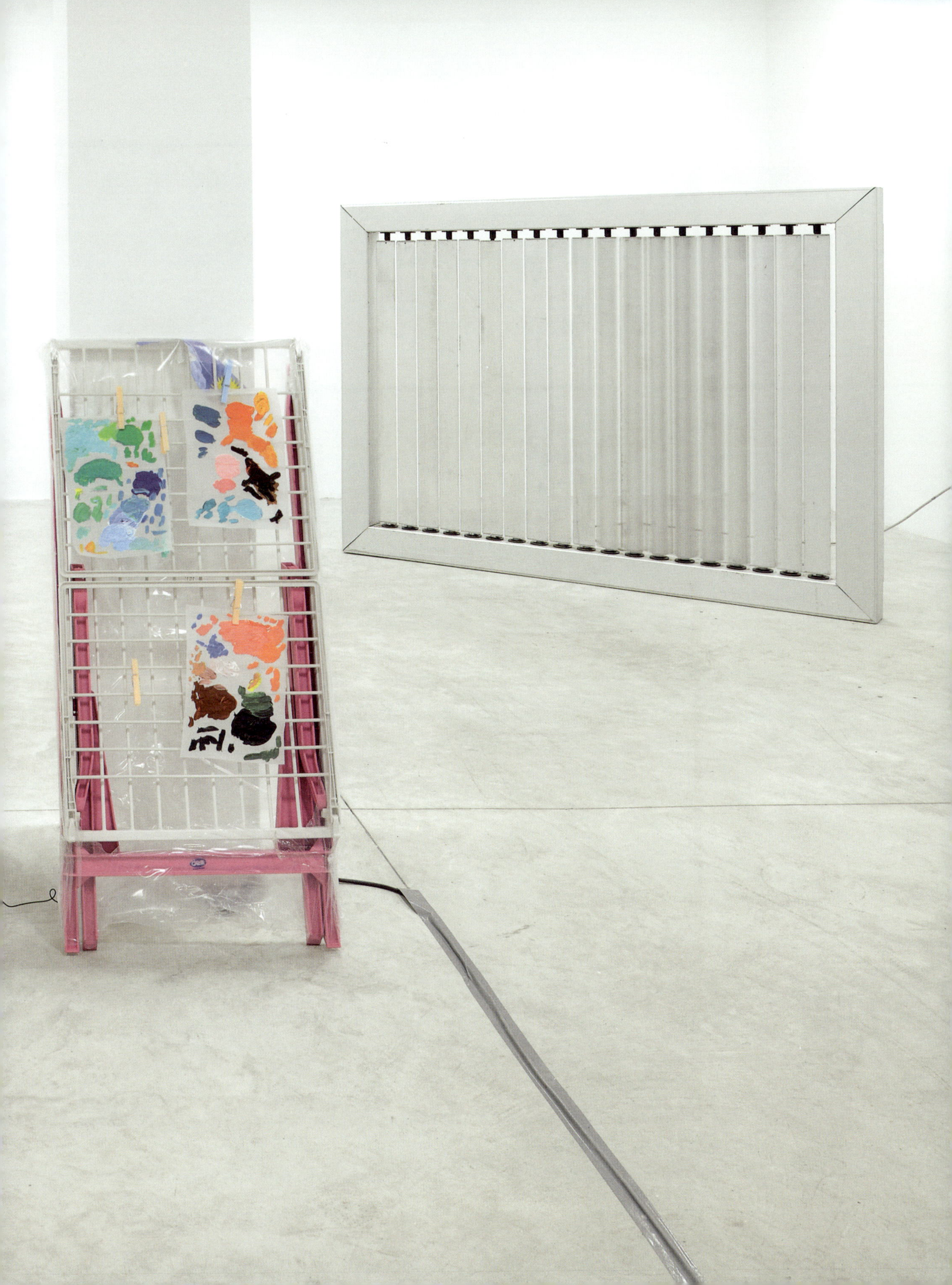

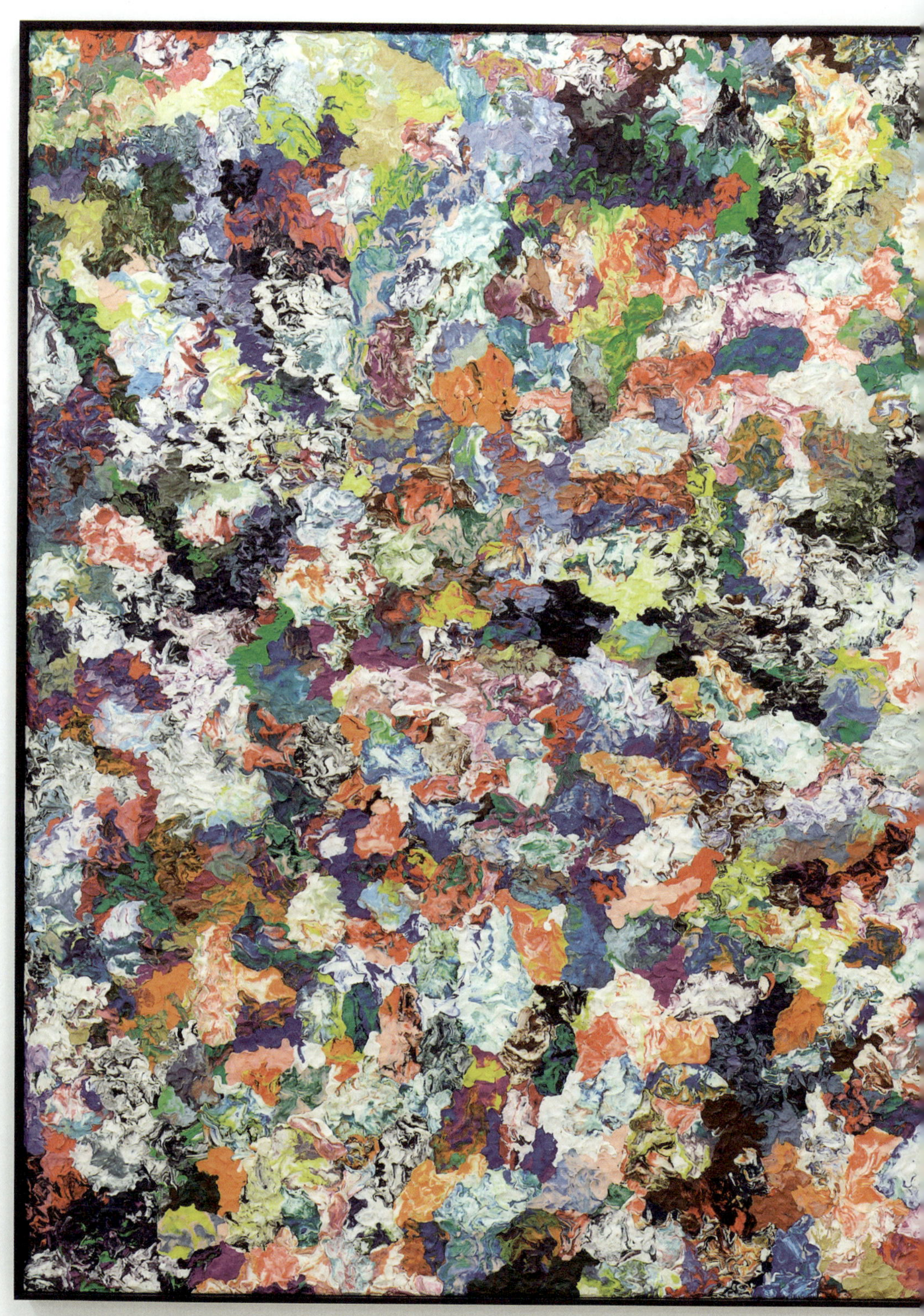

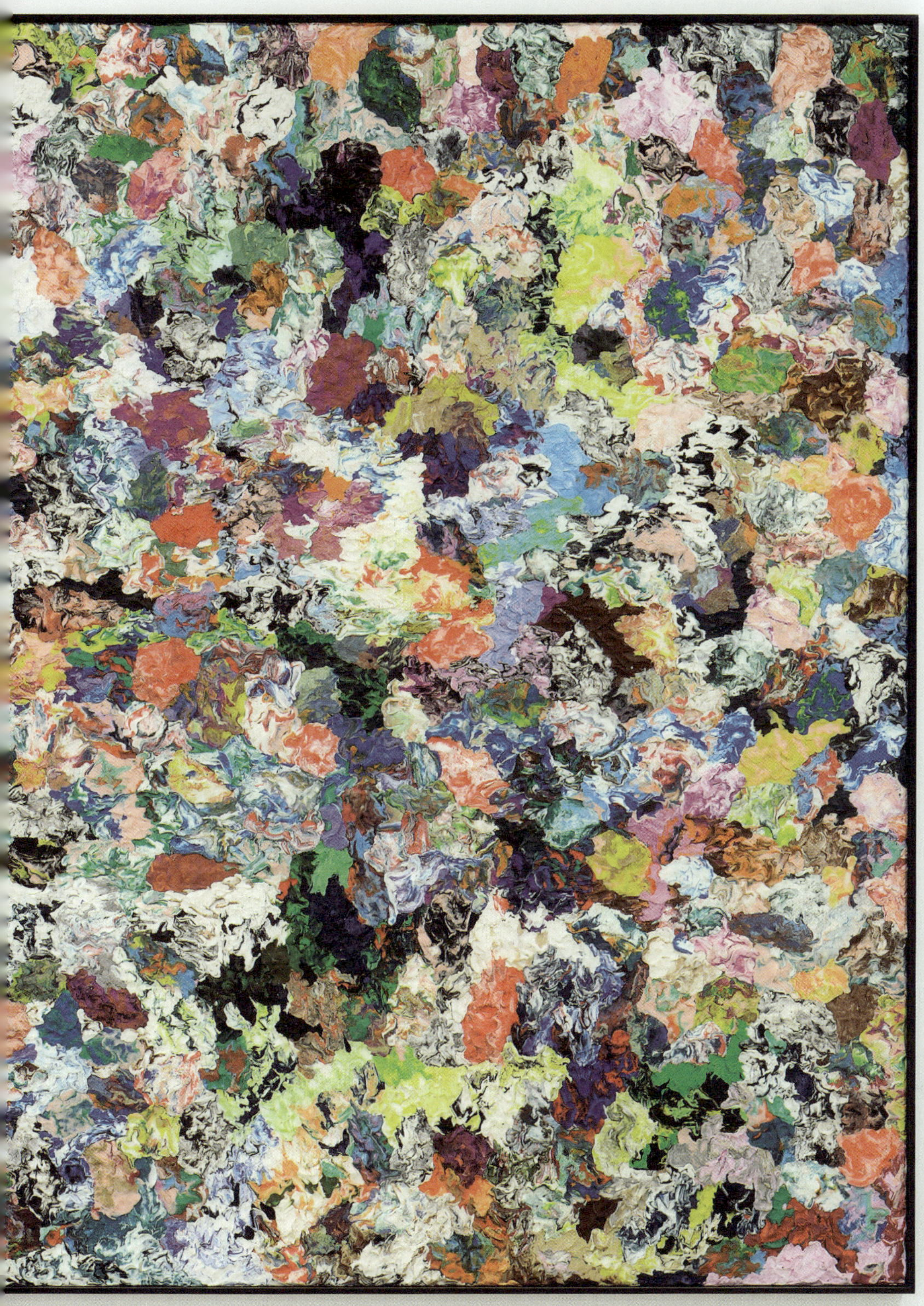

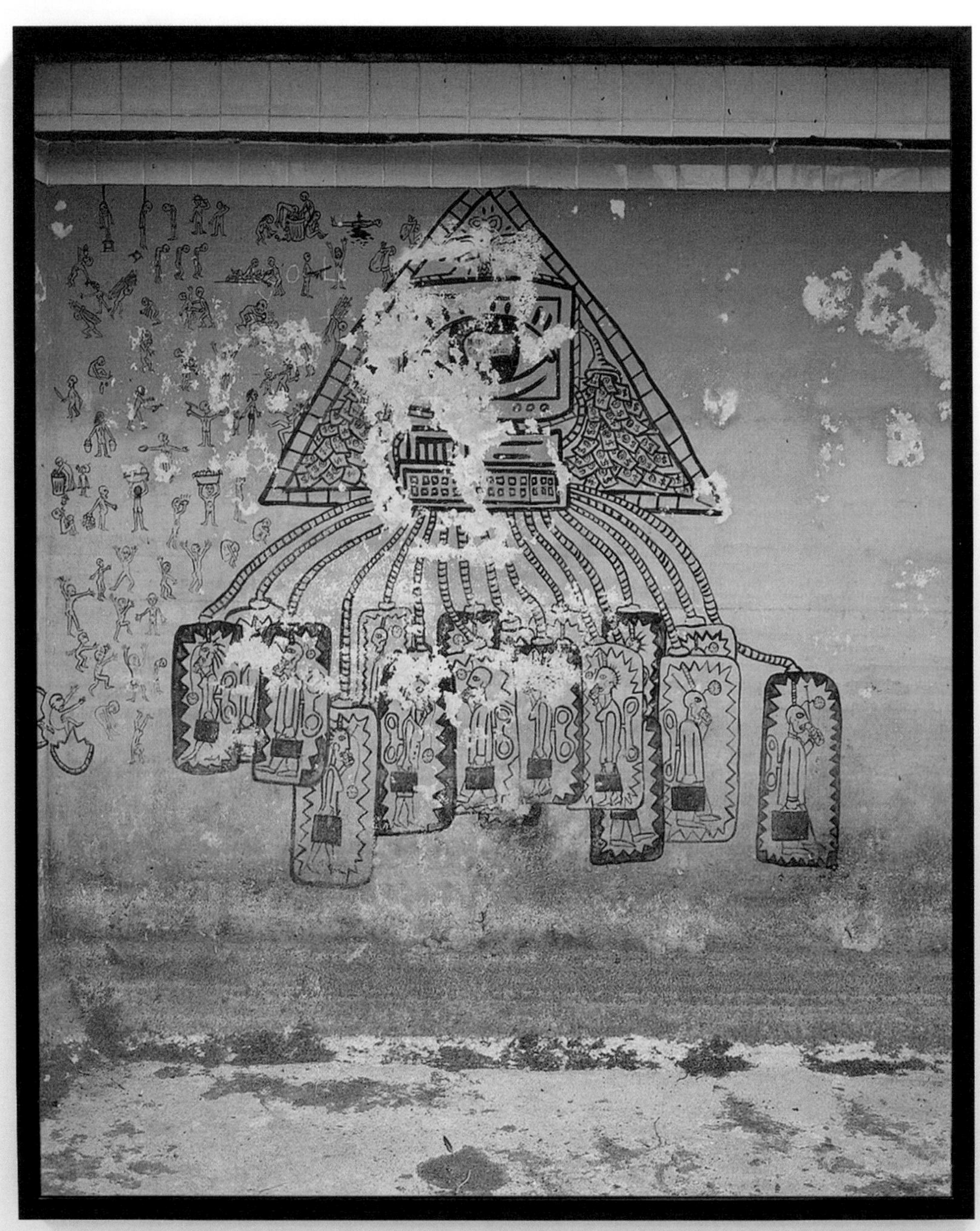

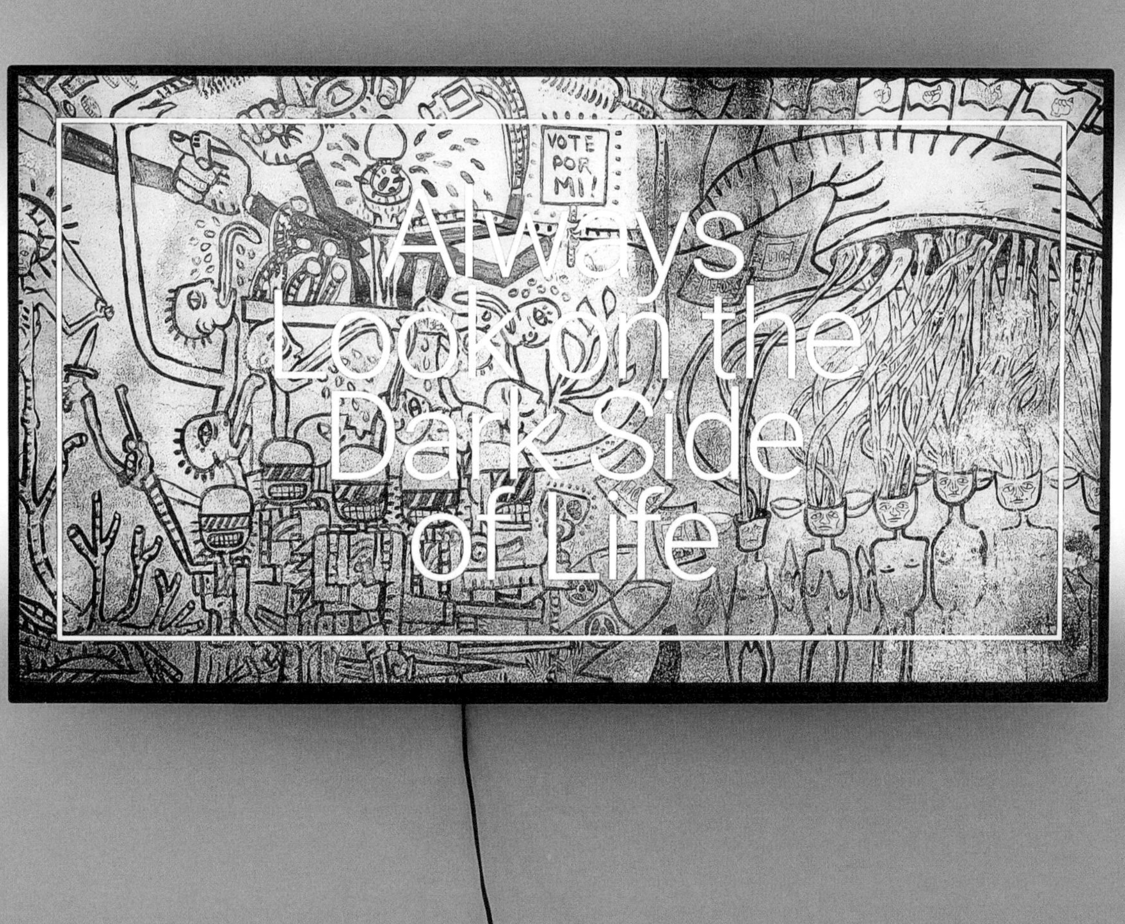

VOTE POR MI!
Always
Look on the
Dark Side
of Life

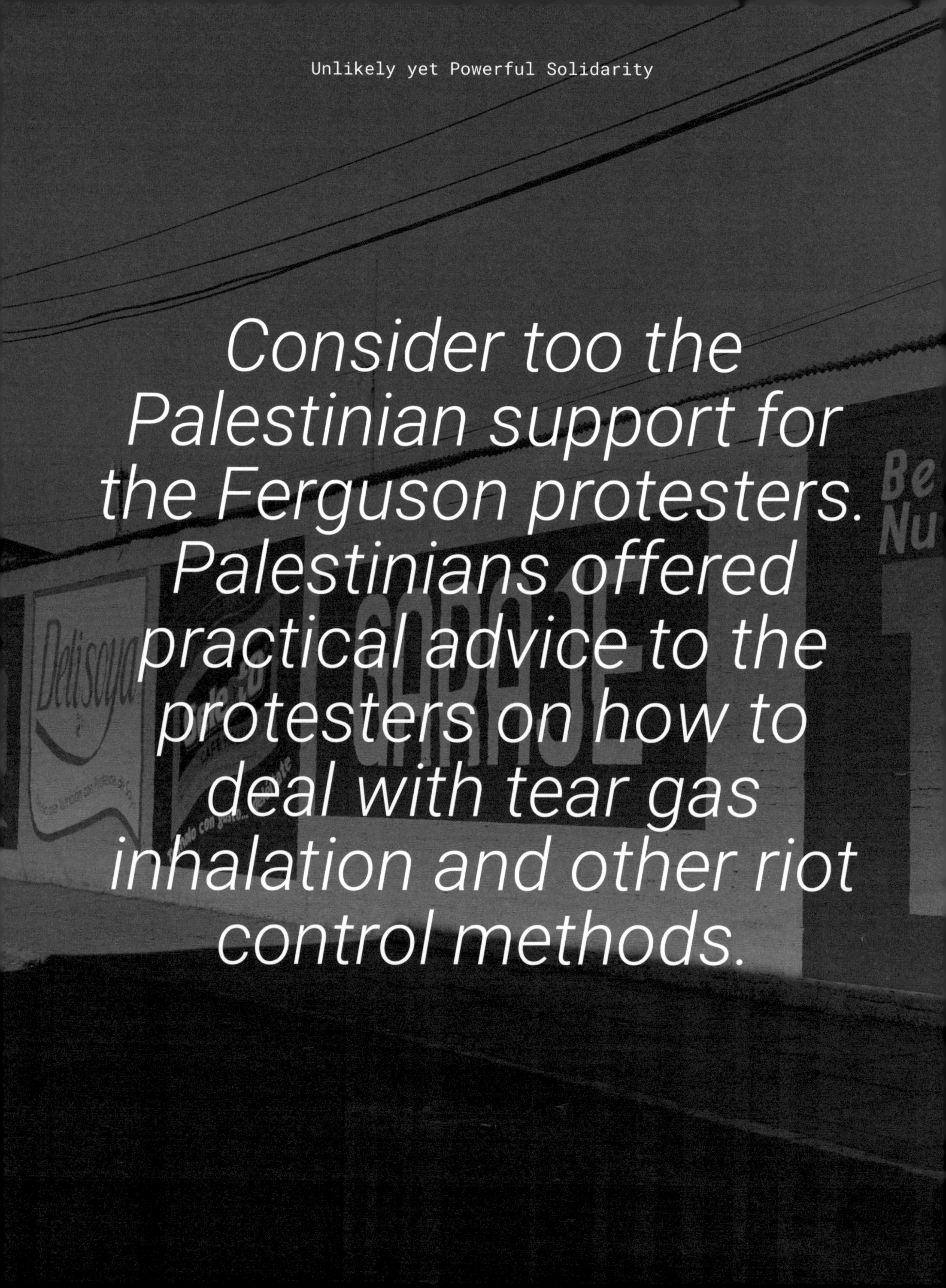

Consider too the Palestinian support for the Ferguson protesters. Palestinians offered practical advice to the protesters on how to deal with tear gas inhalation and other riot control methods.

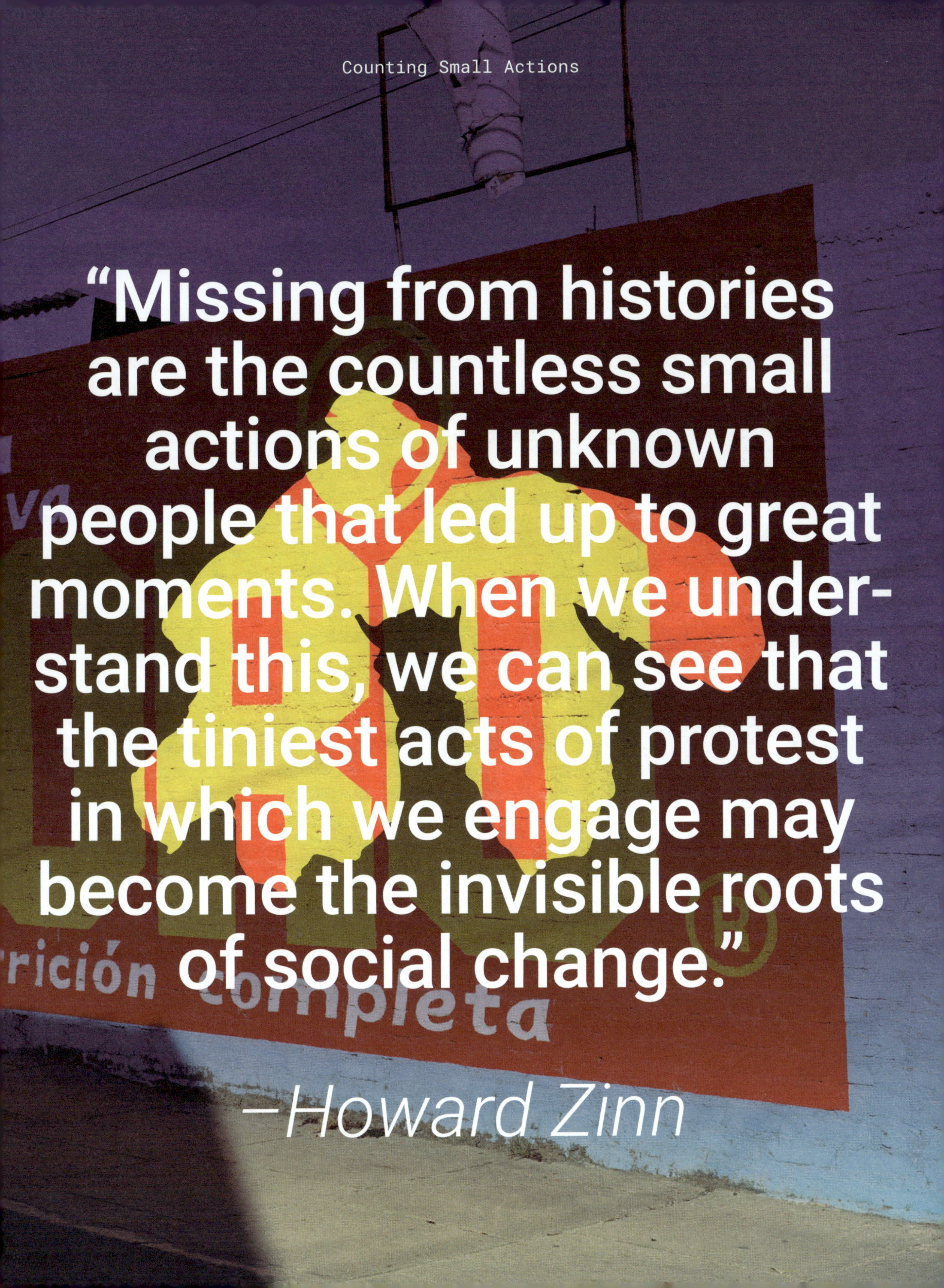

"Missing from histories are the countless small actions of unknown people that led up to great moments. When we understand this, we can see that the tiniest acts of protest in which we engage may become the invisible roots of social change."

–Howard Zinn

How can the Wales NSC be a force for positive social change when the cause they've always fought for and how they fight appear no longer relevant?

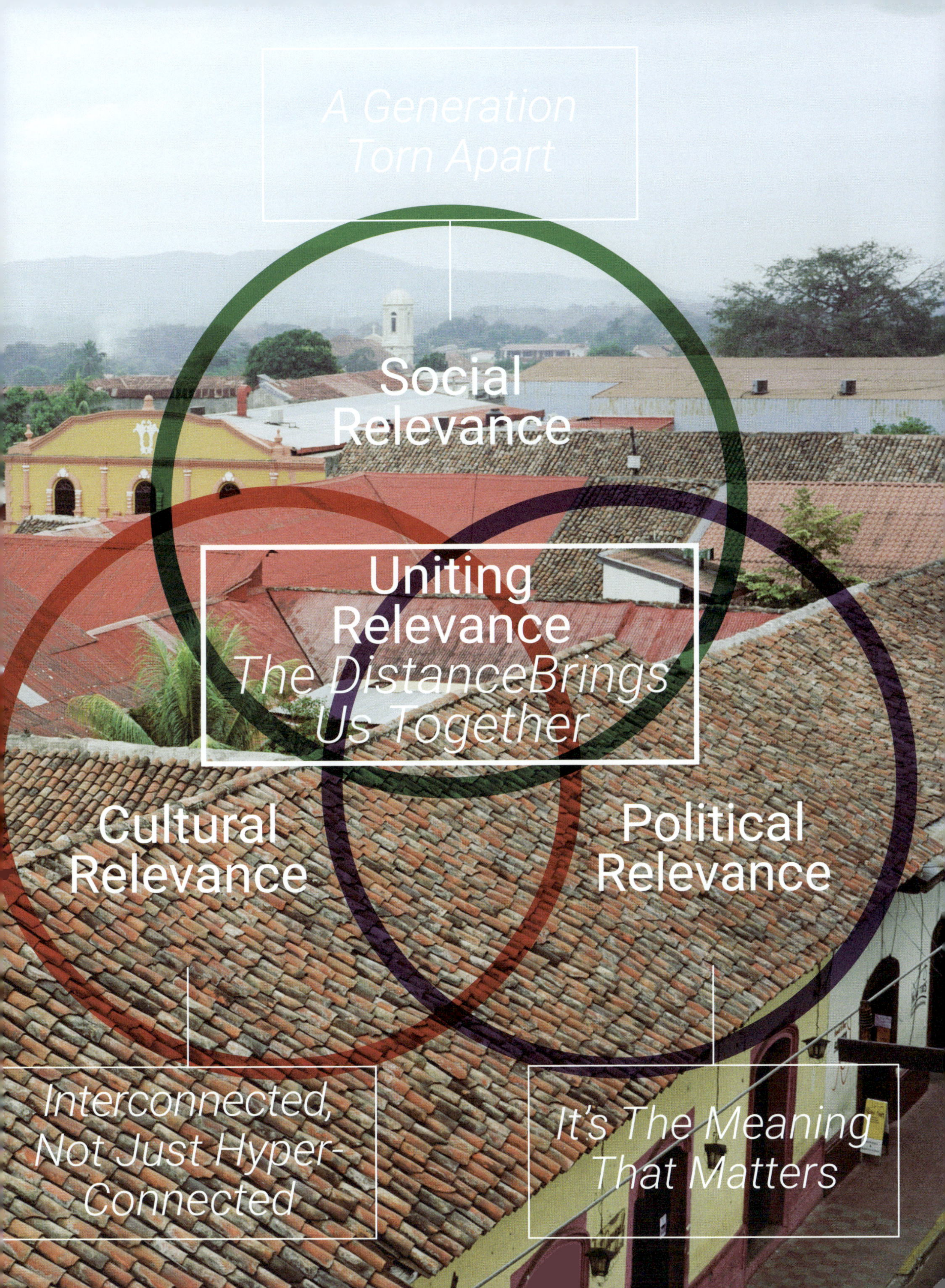

A Generation Torn Apart
Social Relevance
Uniting Relevance
The DistanceBrings Us Together
Cultural Relevance
Political Relevance
Interconnected, Not Just Hyper-Connected
It's The Meaning That Matters

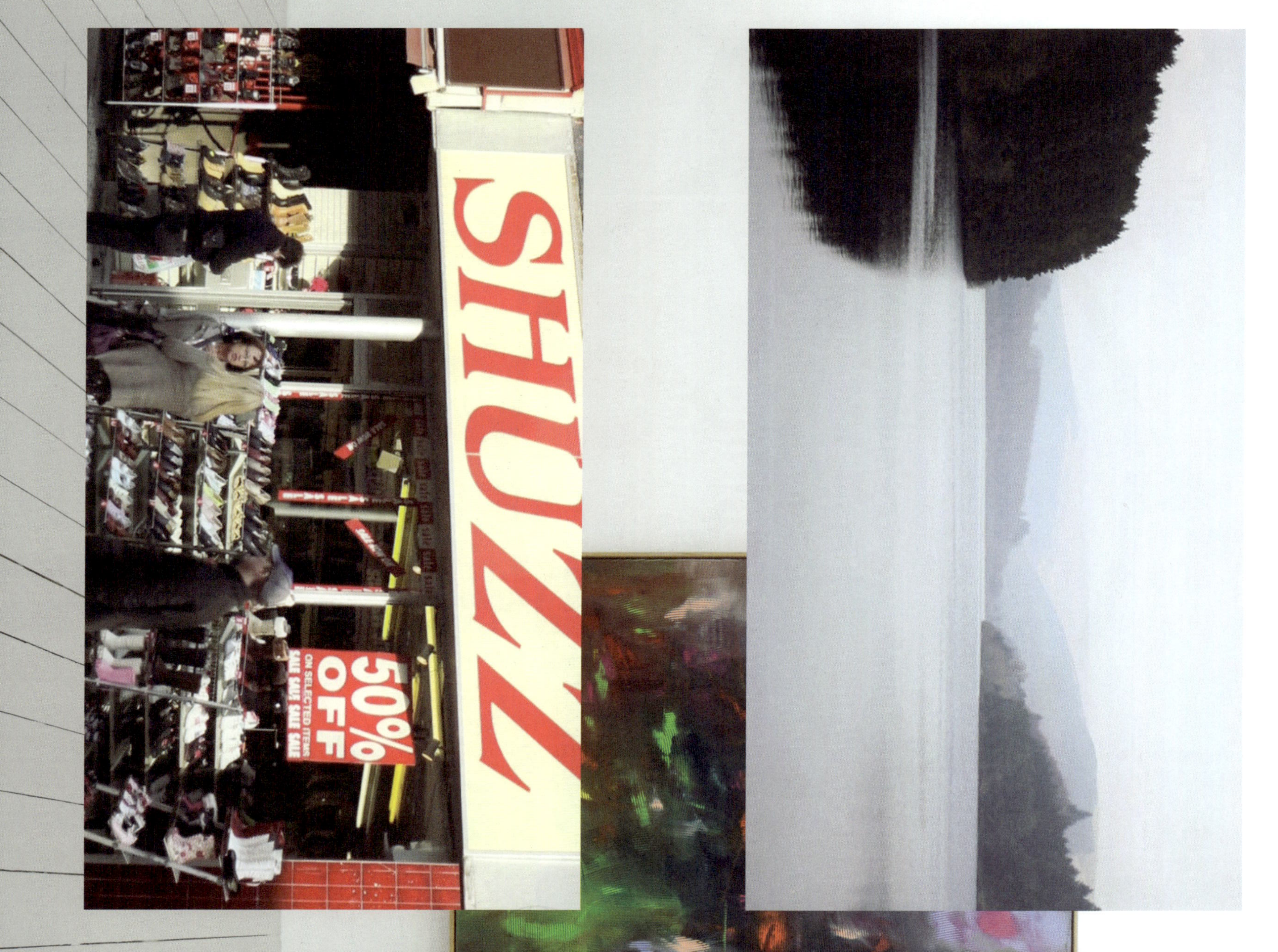

Merthyr Rising (video stills), 2012

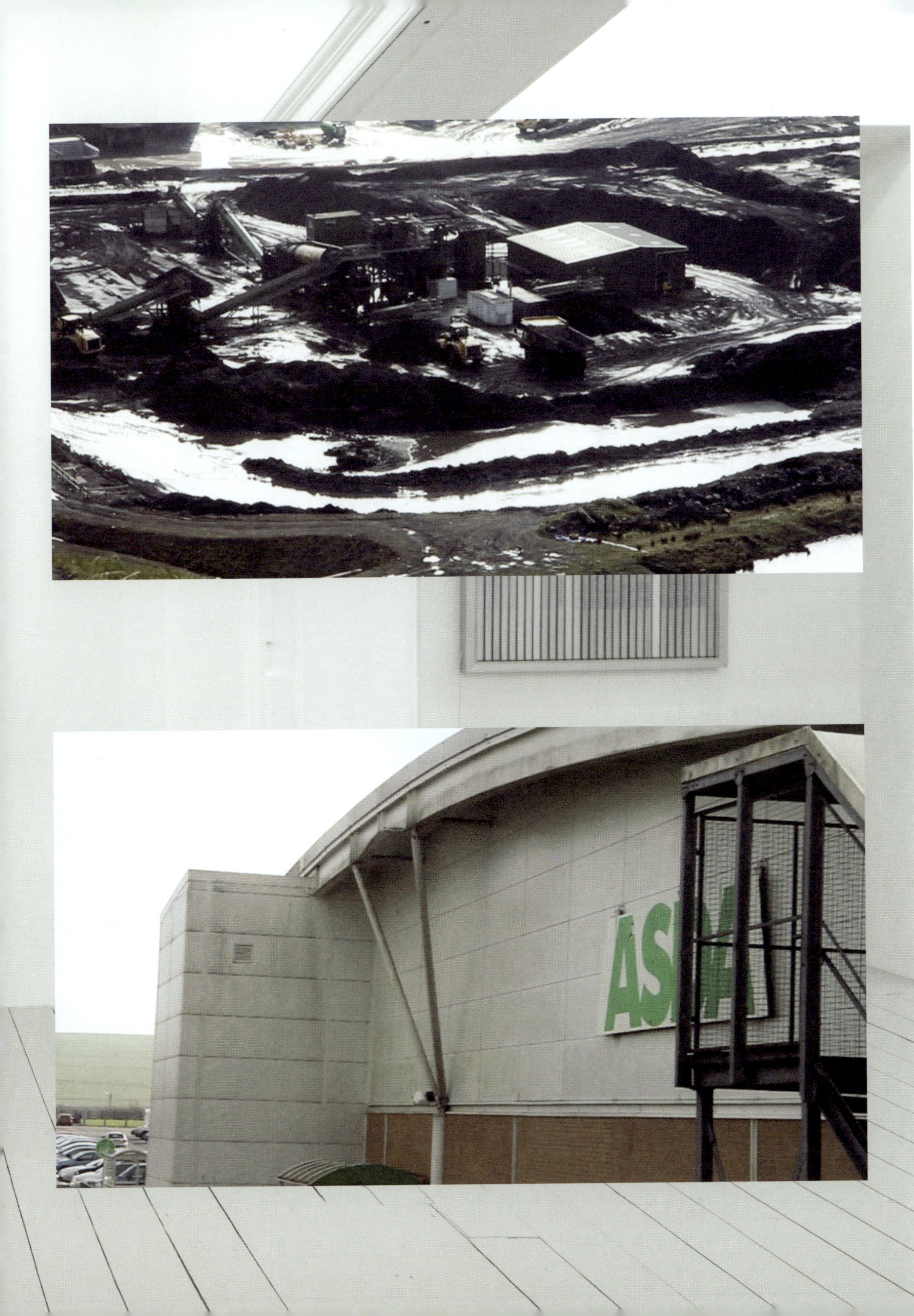

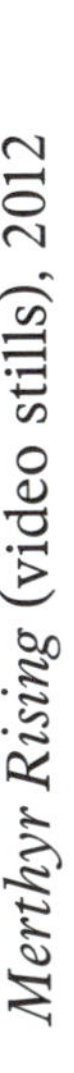

Merthyr Rising (video stills), 2012

Think Local Act Global, 2015, MOT International, Brussels

Artex, 2015

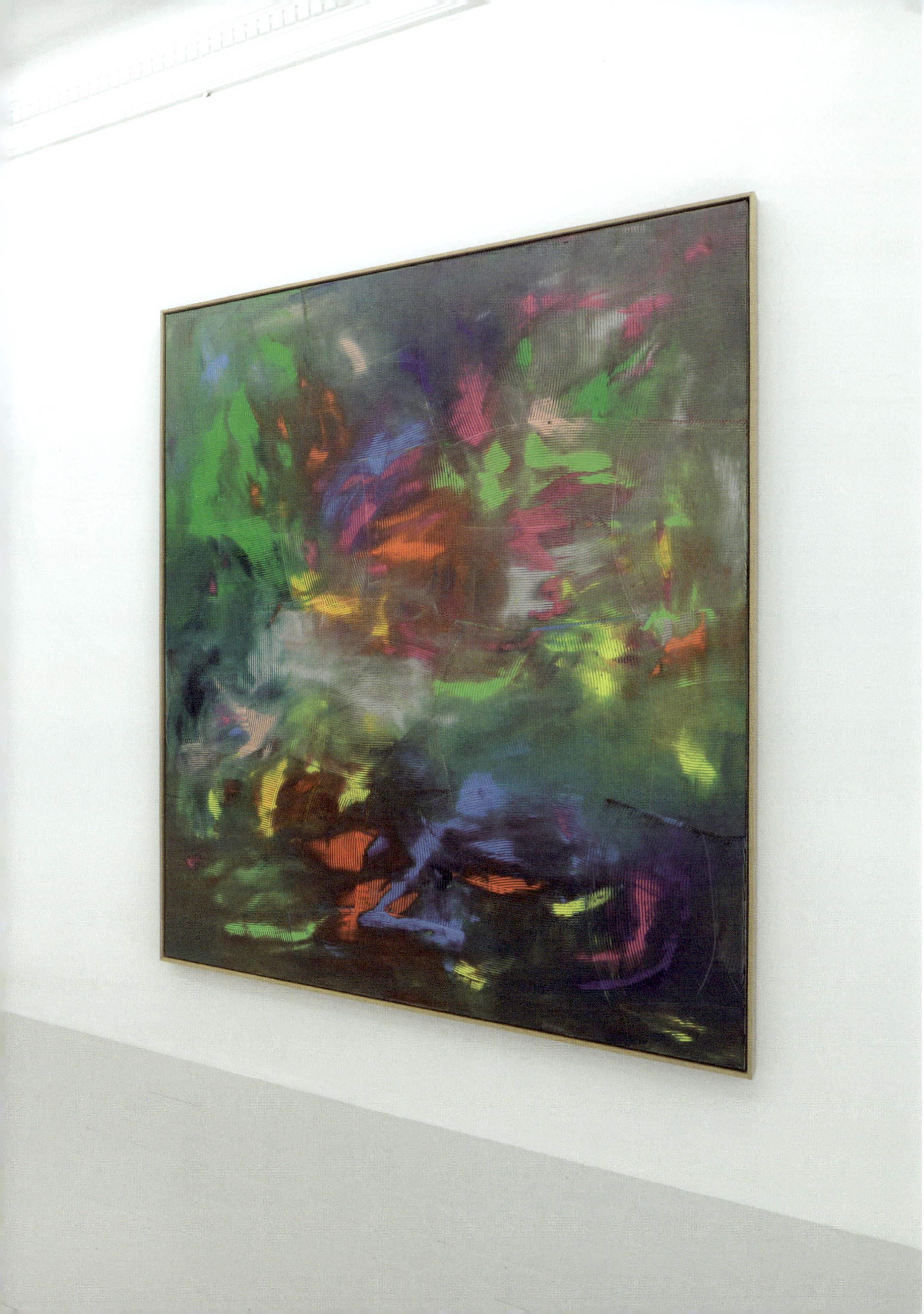

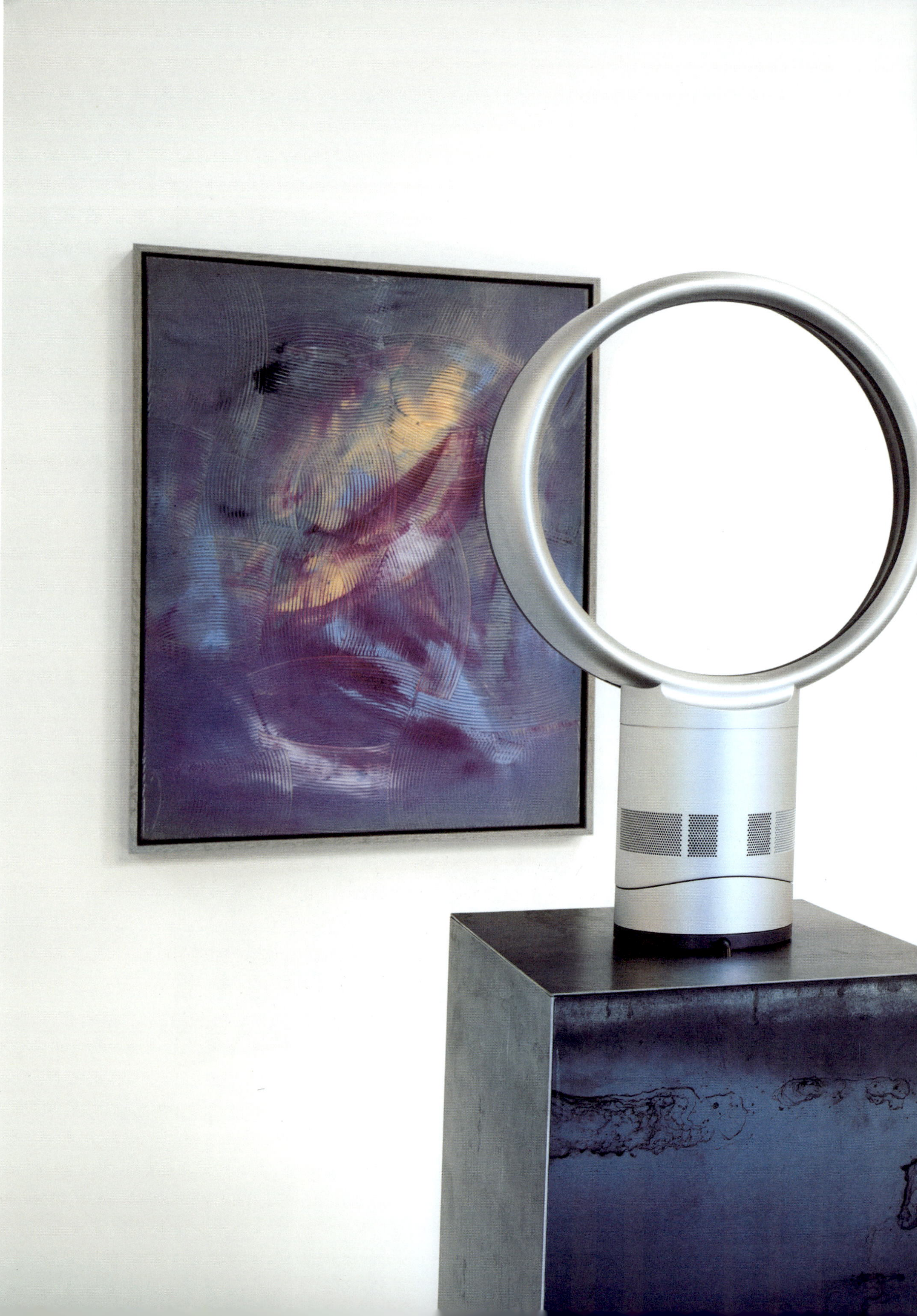

In The Ghetto It Gets Cold But We've Got Something To Warm Our Soles, 2012, Albert Baronian, Brussels

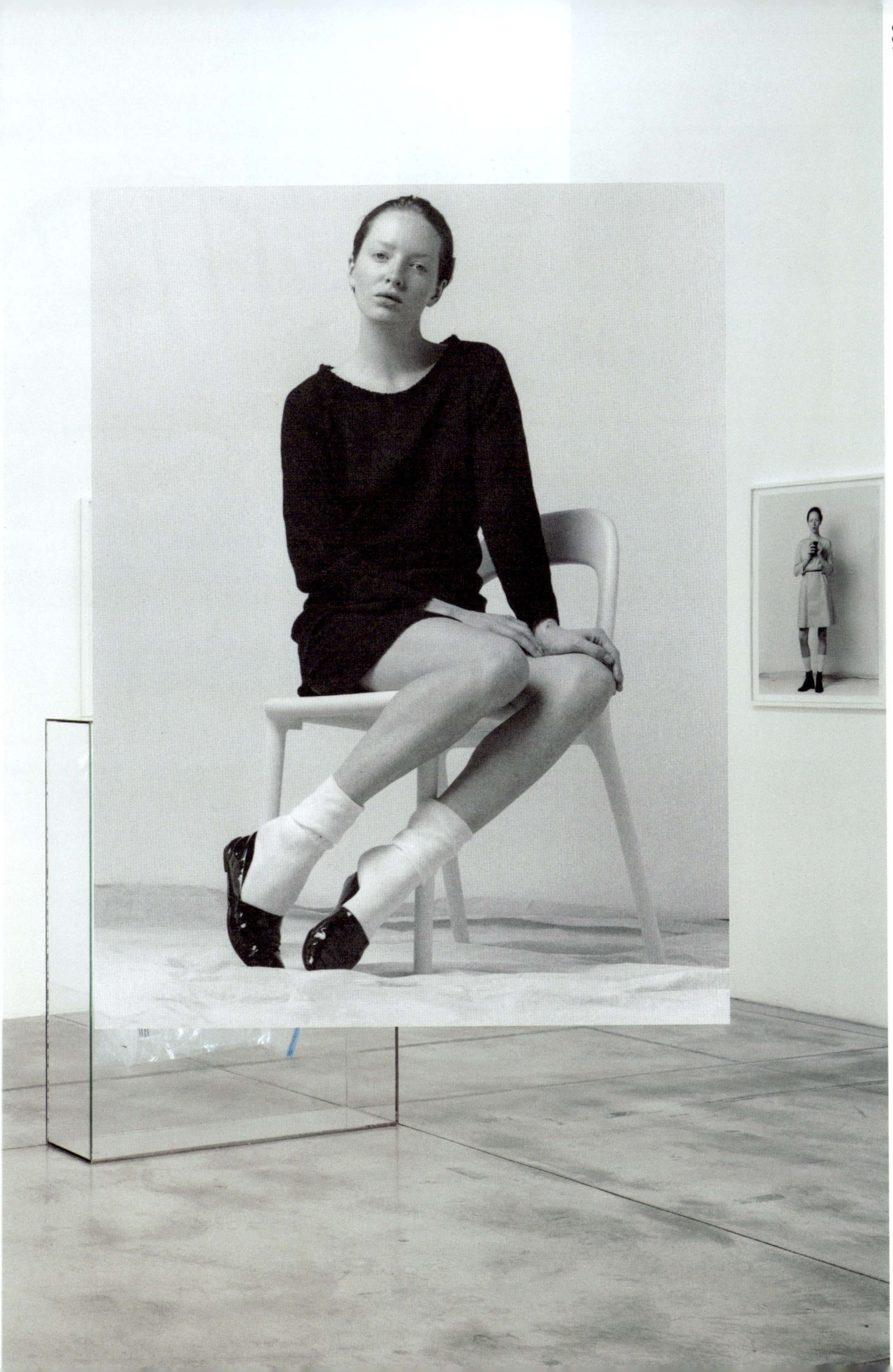

In The Ghetto It Gets Cold But We've Got Something To Warm Our Soles, 2012

Green Room, 2011, Museum der Weltkulturen, Frankfurt

Civic Pride (video stills), 2013

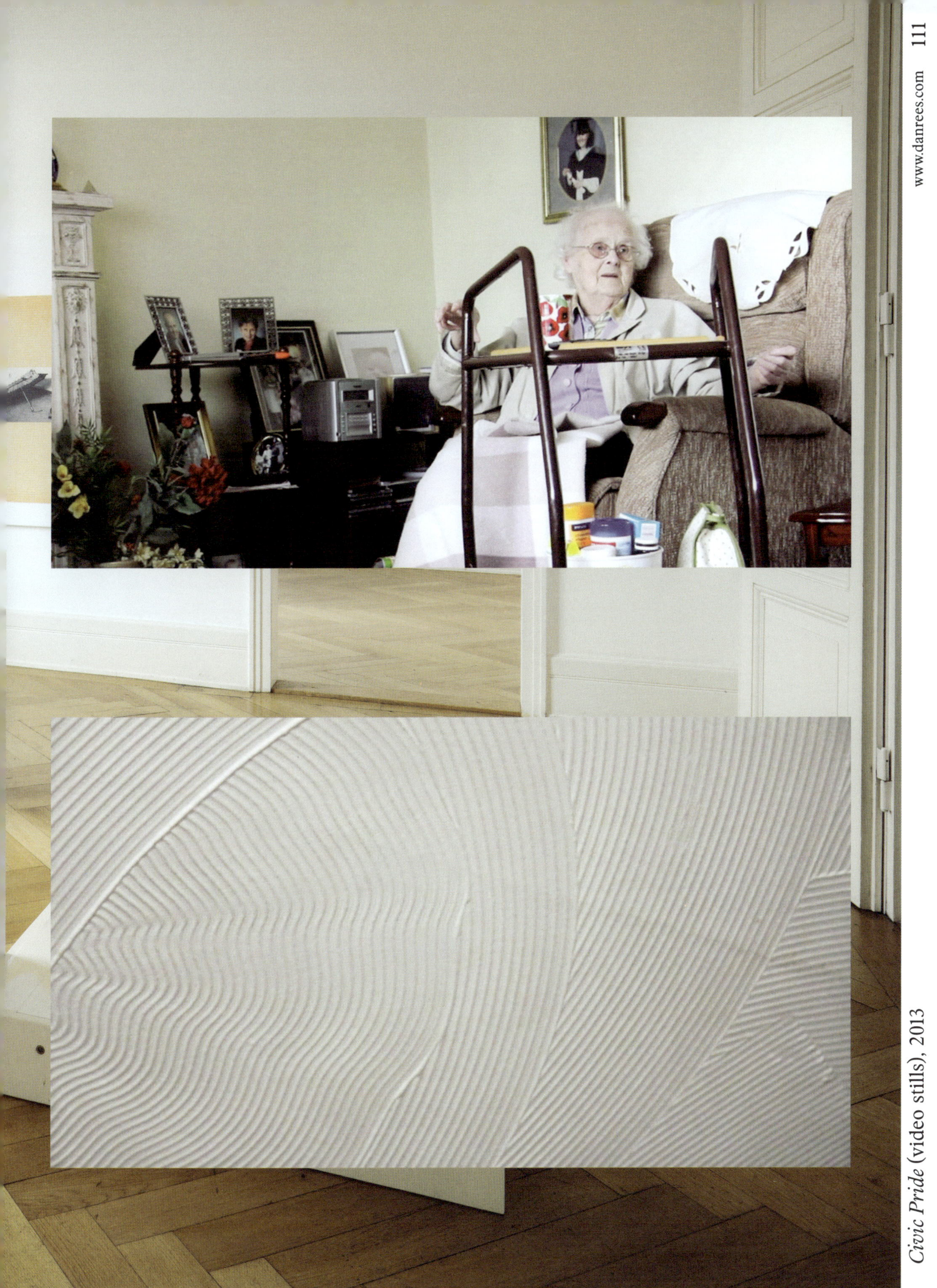

Civic Pride (video stills), 2013

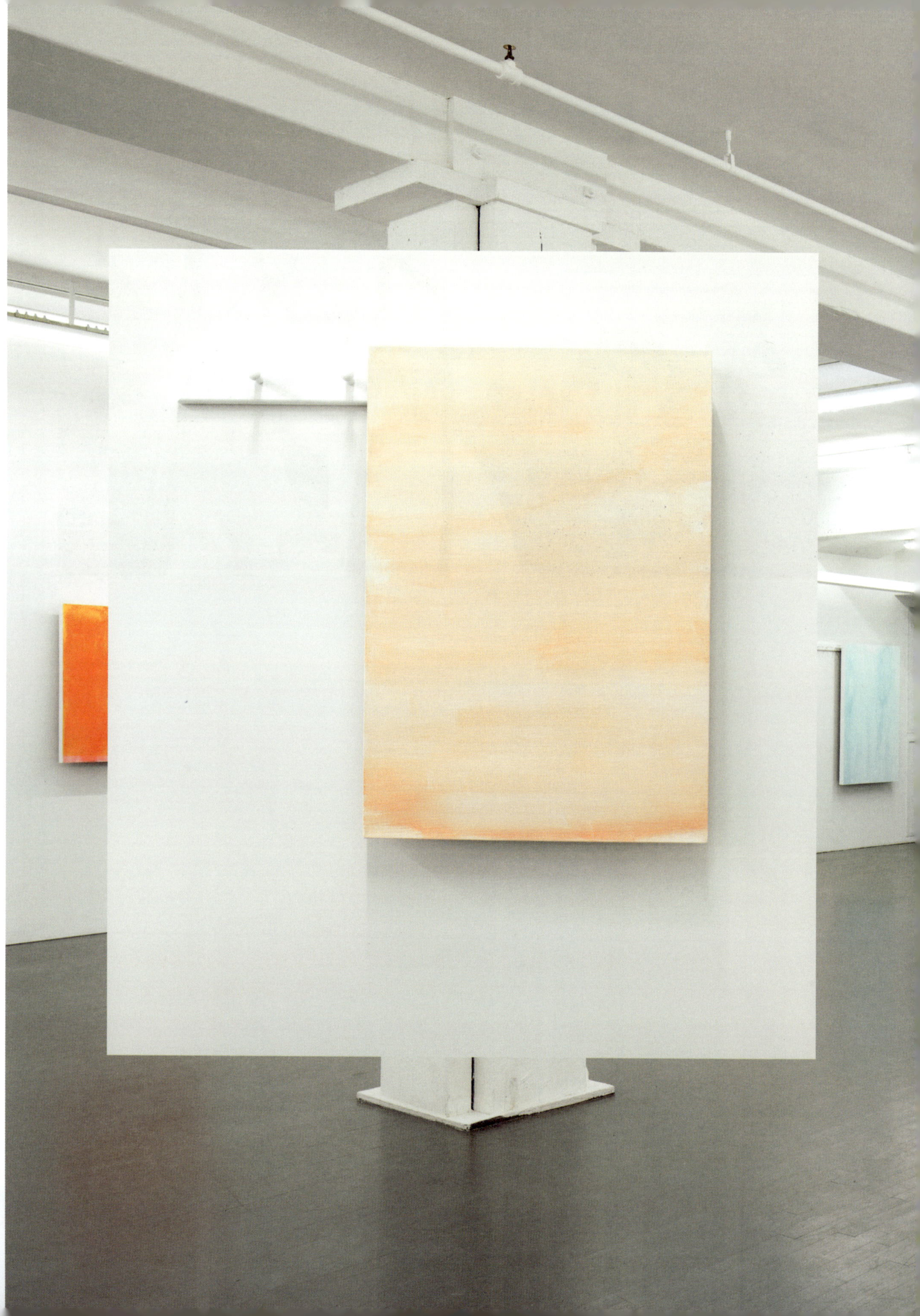

Shakin' Peg Rails (And The Sunsets), 2010, Wallspace, New York

Shaker Peg, 2010

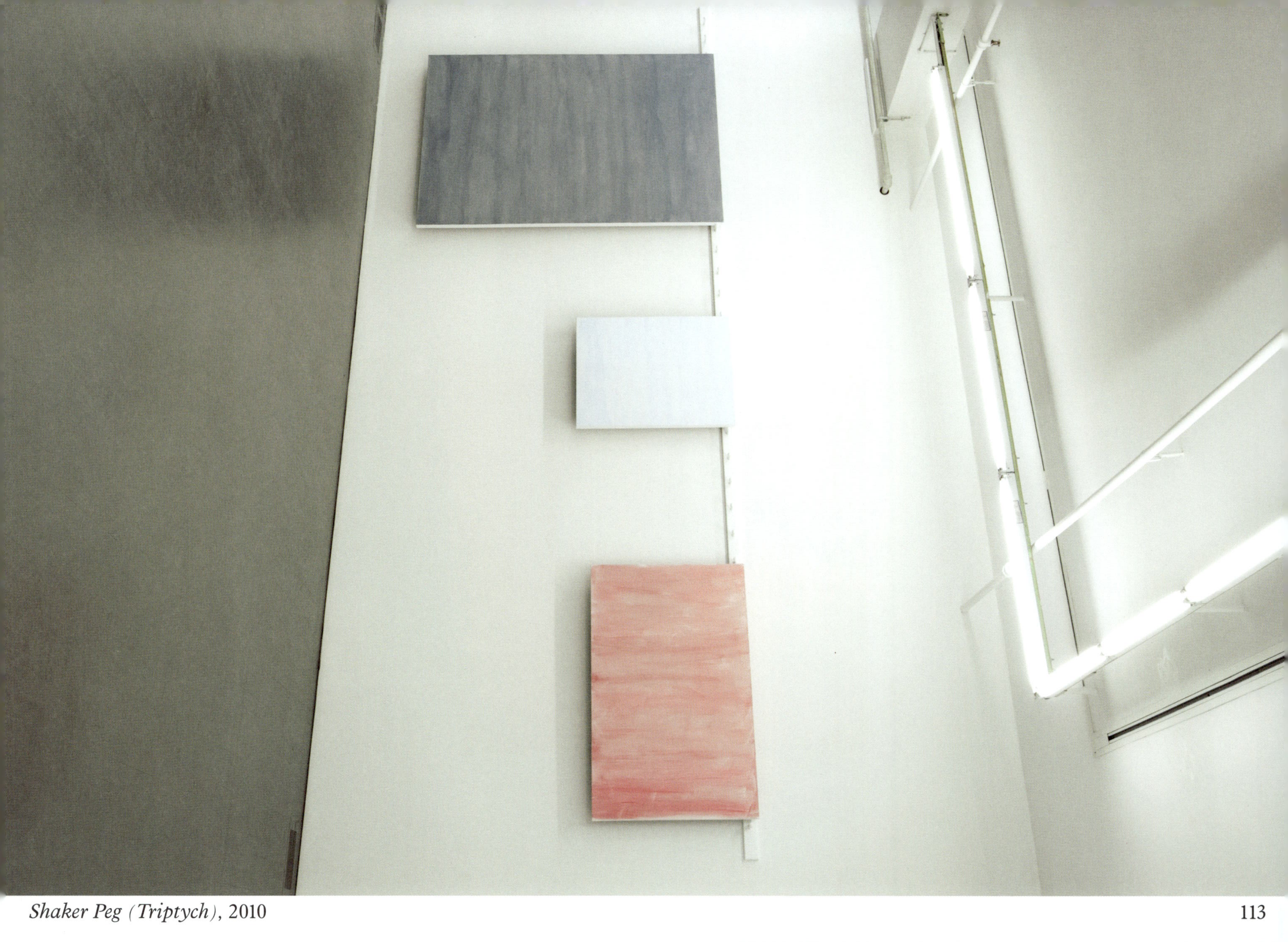

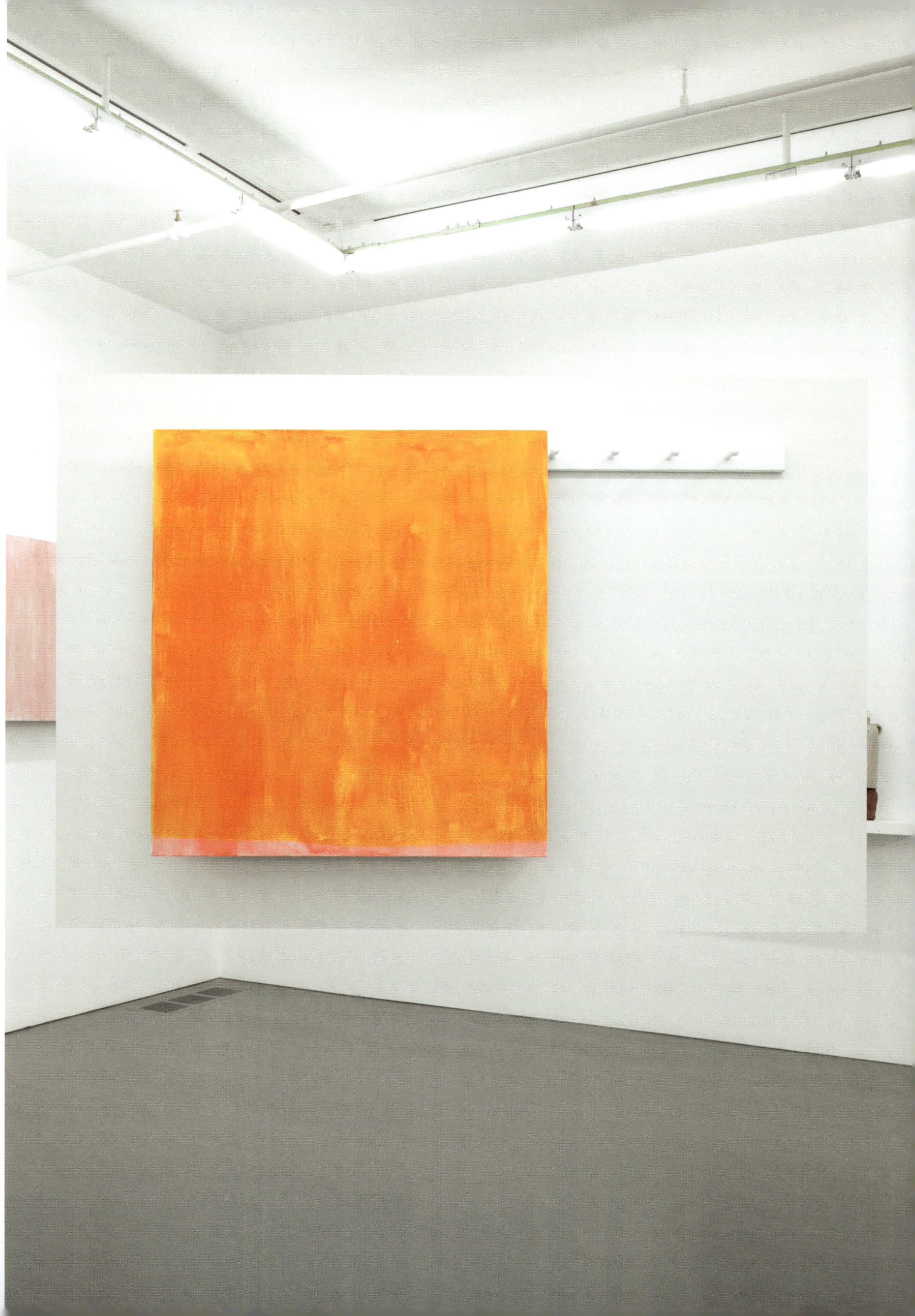

Shaker Peg, 2010

Shakin' Peg Rails (And The Sunsets), 2010, Wallspace, New York

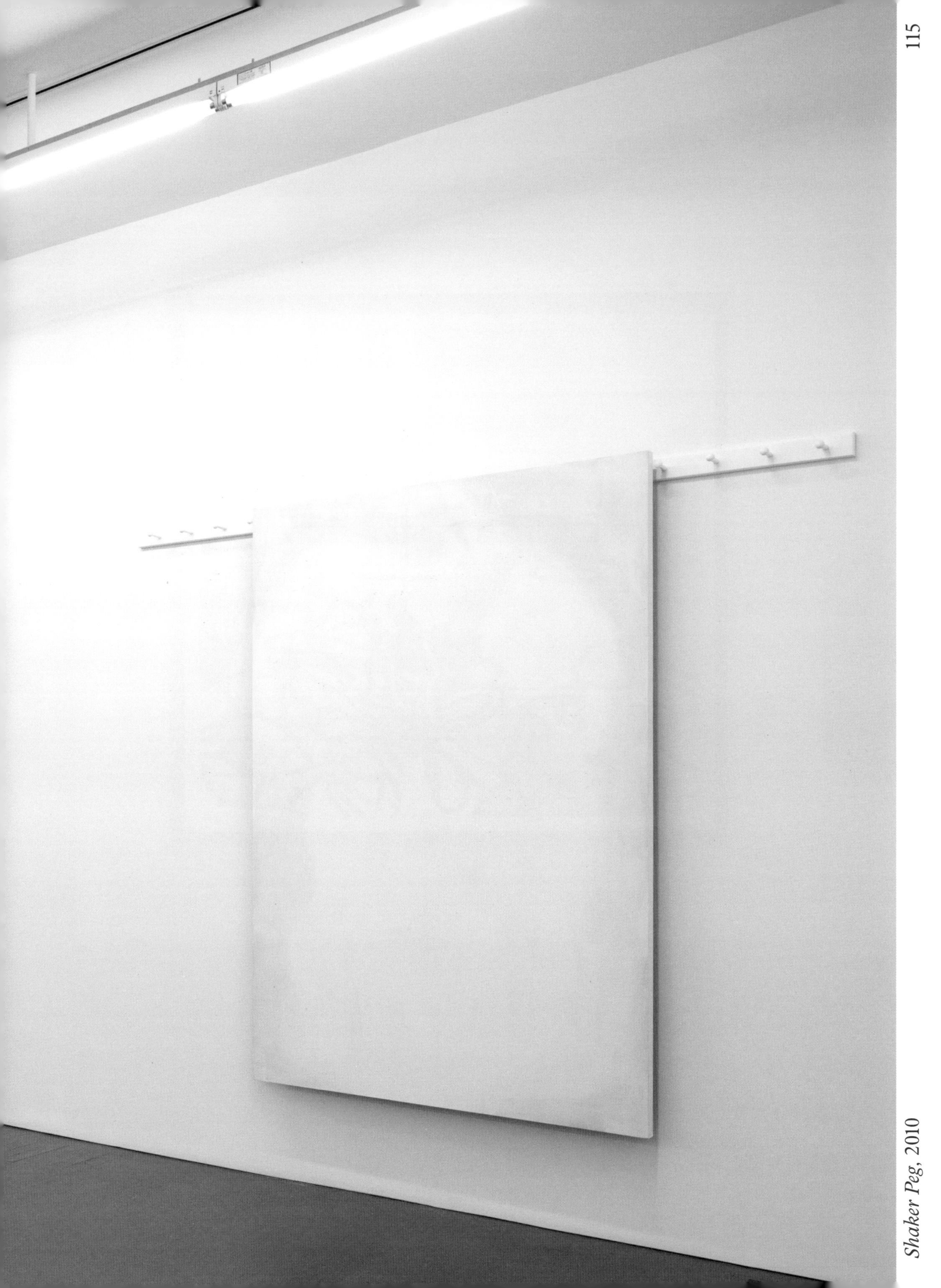

Shaker Peg, 2010

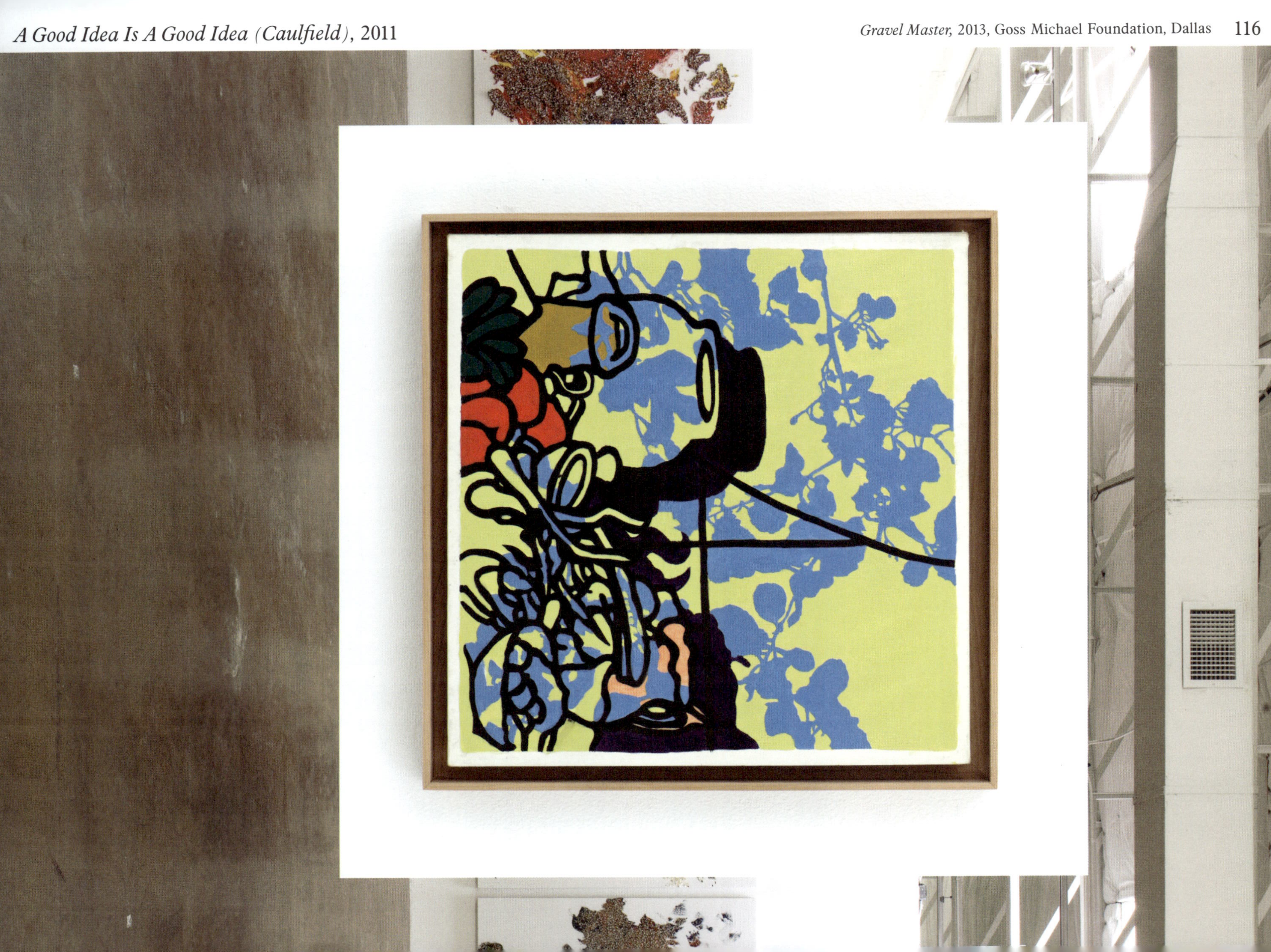

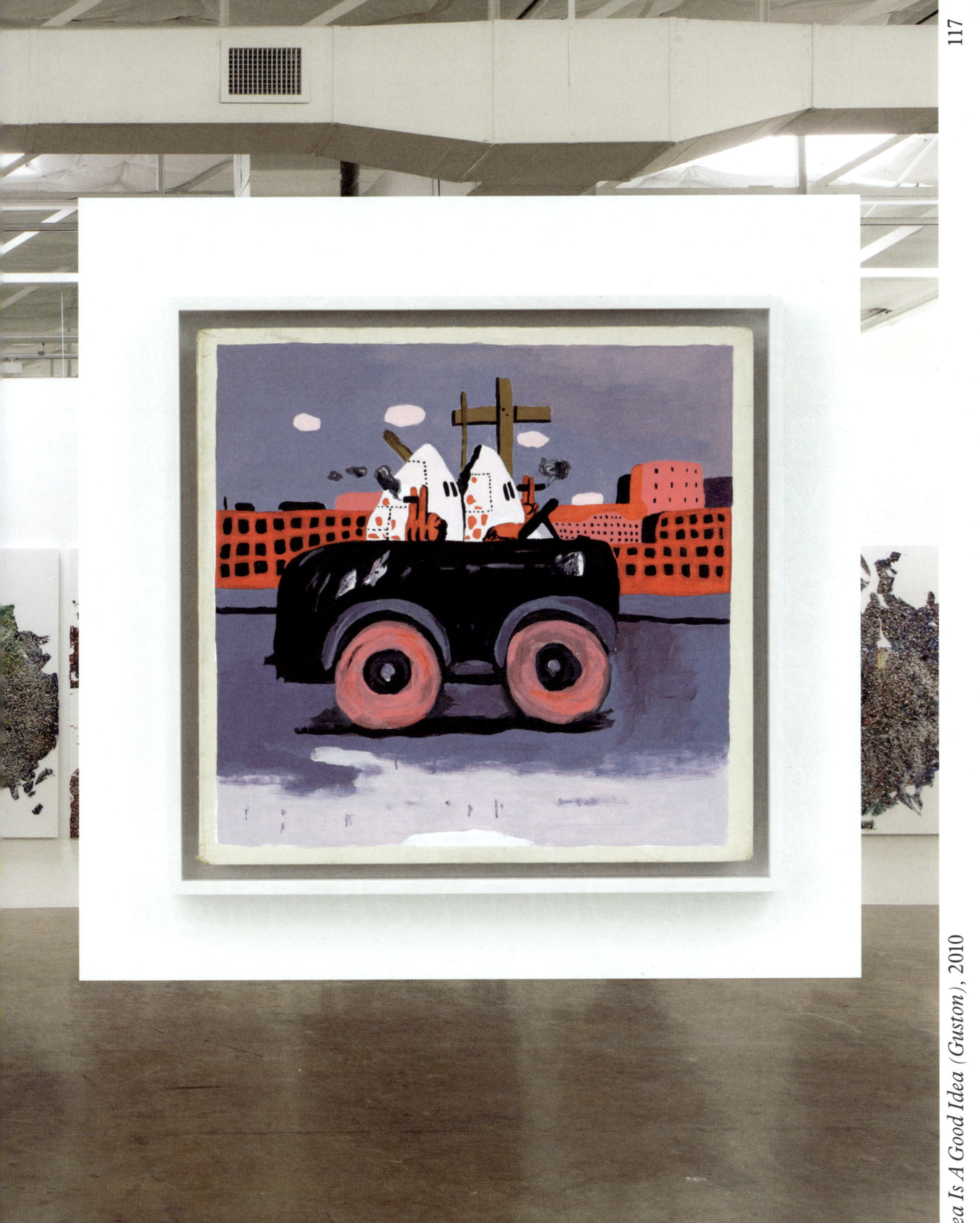

A Good Idea Is A Good Idea (Guston), 2010

Young people in Nicaragua share a similar fate to those in Wales. Young people in both countries are fighting for a future. Nicaragua has a youth bubble, yet they lack an education support system. Out of all children aged 3–17, more than 25% are not in school.

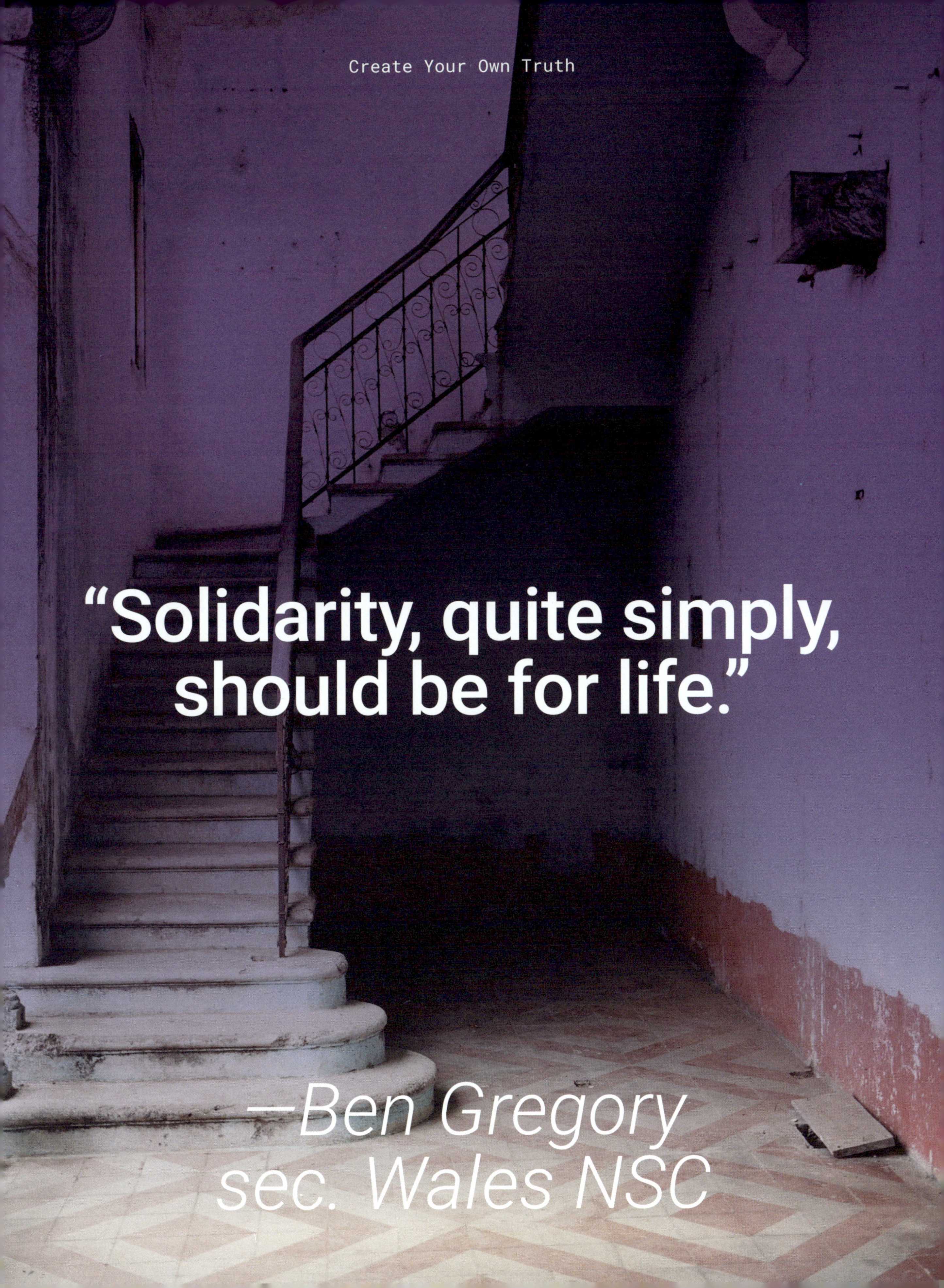

"Solidarity, quite simply, should be for life."

—Ben Gregory
sec. Wales NSC

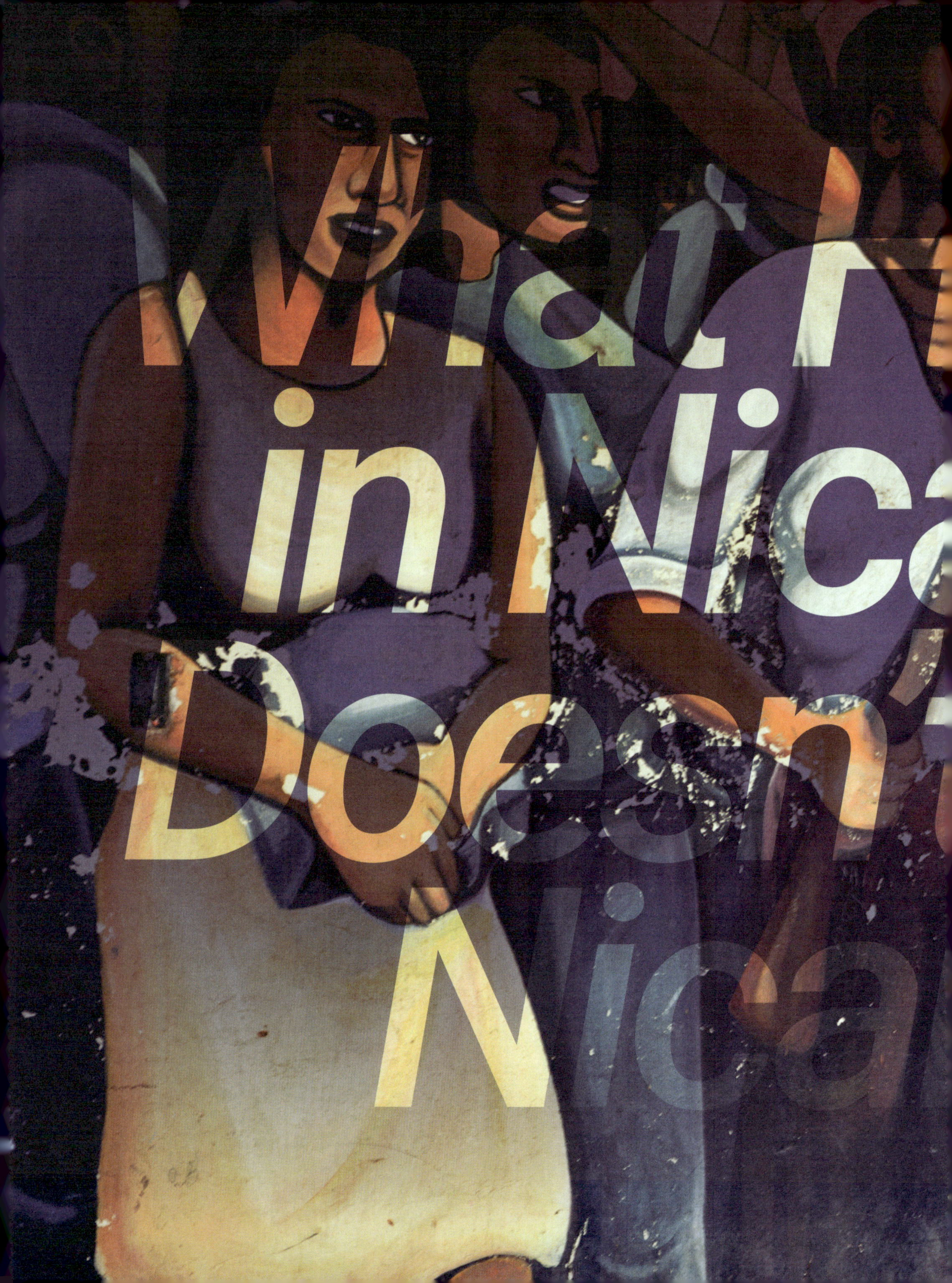
What's
in Nica
Doesn't
Nica

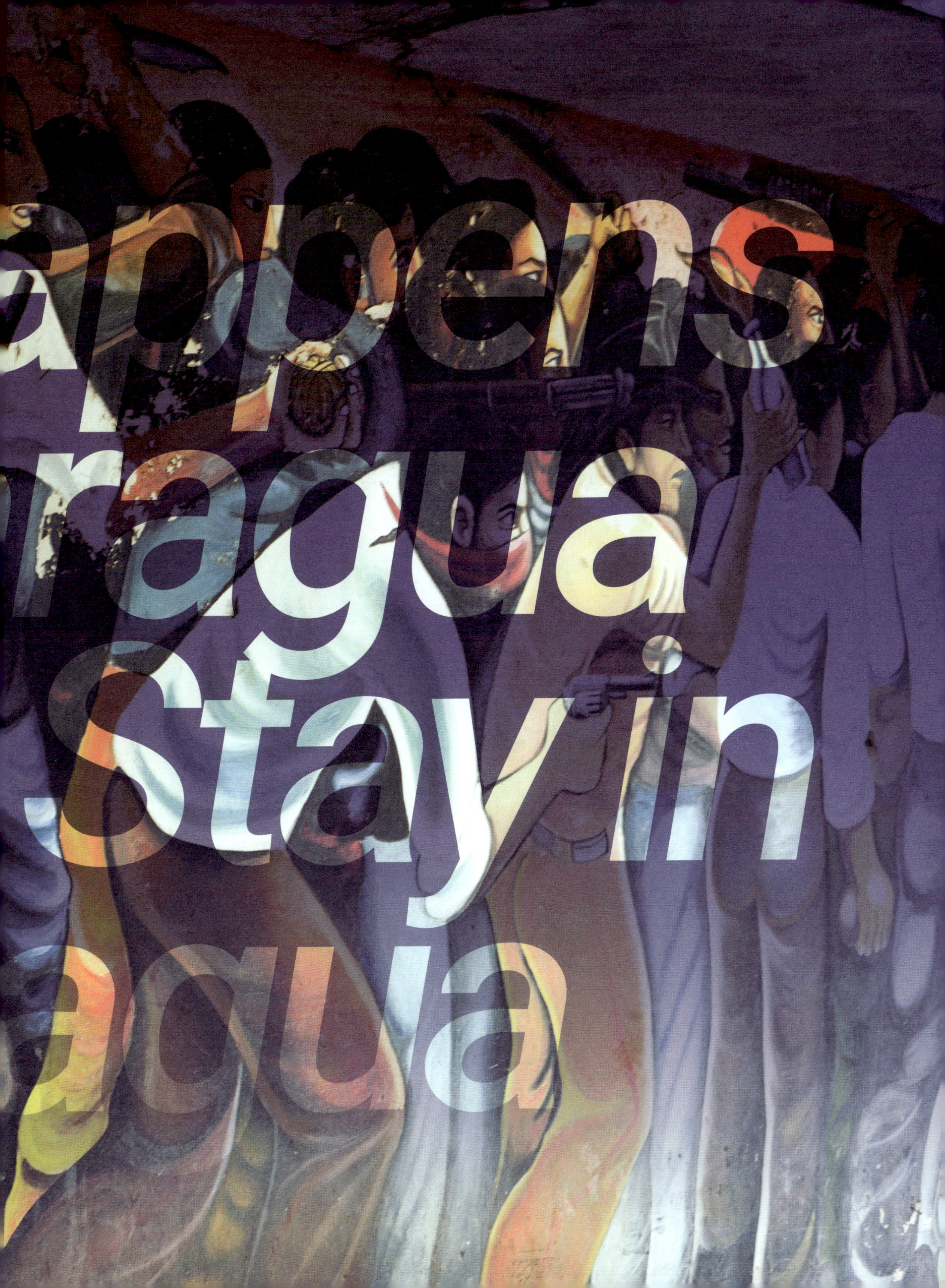
appens
ragua
Stayin
ragua

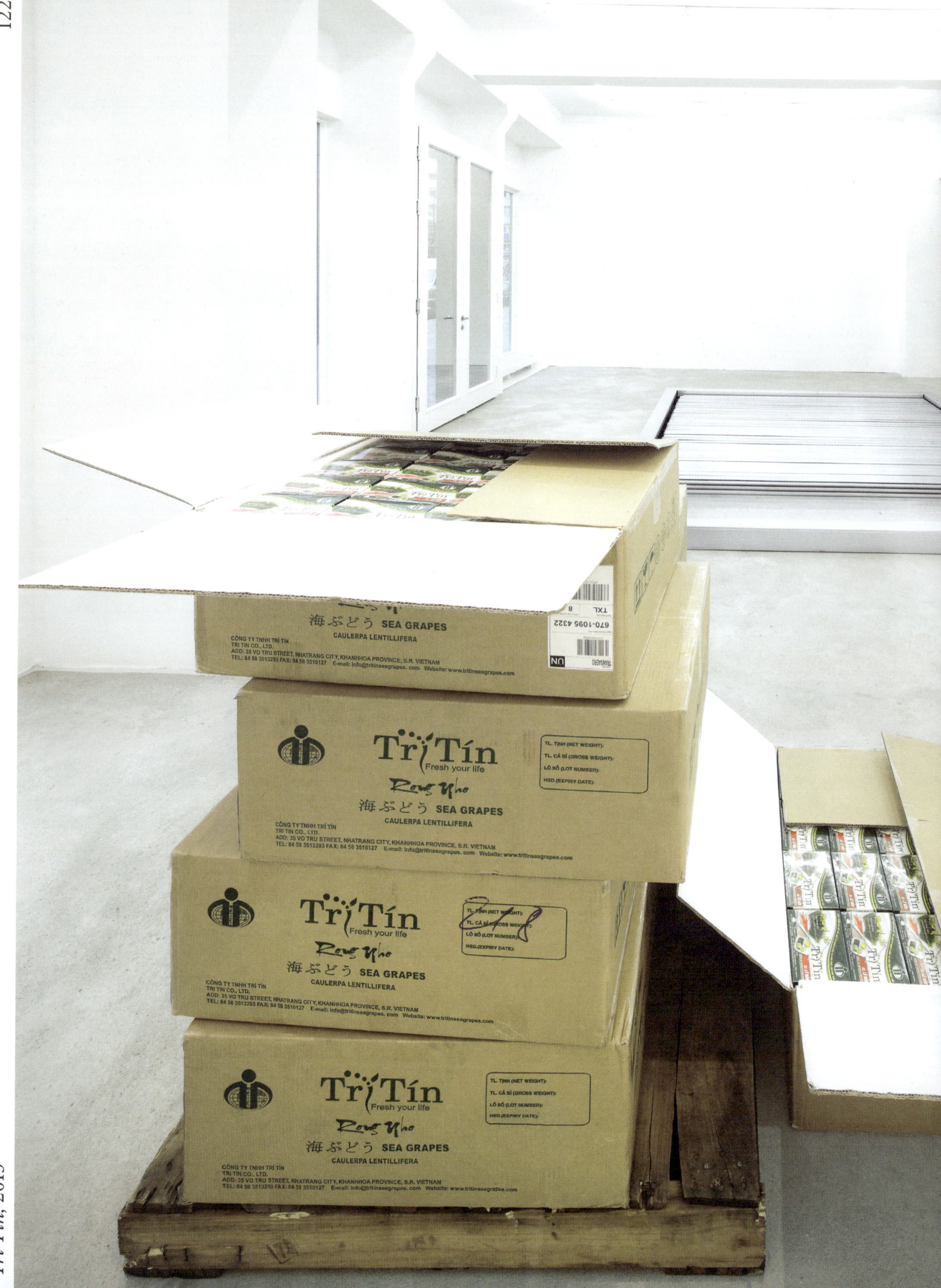
海ぶどう SEA GRAPES
CAULERPA LENTILLIFERA
CÔNG TY TNHH TRÍ TÍN
TRI TIN CO., LTD.
ADD: 35 VO TRU STREET, NHATRANG CITY, KHANHHOA PROVINCE, S.R. VIETNAM
TEL: 84 58 3513293 FAX: 84 58 3510127 E-mail: info@tritinseagrapes.com Website: www.tritinseagrapes.com
670-1095 4322
TXL
UN
TriTín
Fresh your life
Rong Nho
TL. TỊNH (NET WEIGHT):
TL. CẢ BÌ (GROSS WEIGHT):
LÔ SỐ (LOT NUMBER):
HSD.(EXPIRY DATE):

Slate Islands Seaweed Ltd: email: kelpie@slateislandsseaweed.com tel:07736319200

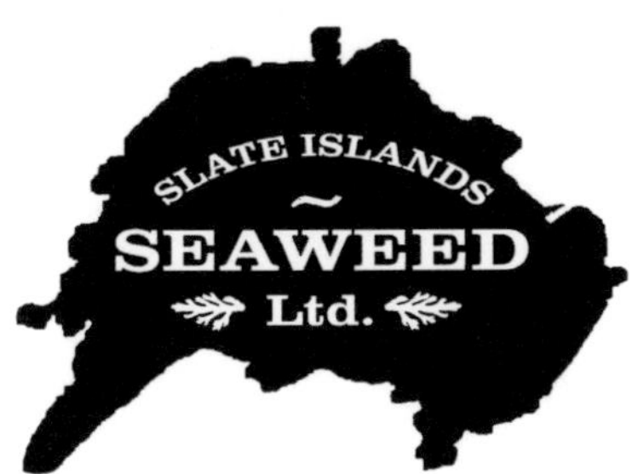

Slate Islands Seaweed Ltd
1B Easdale Island
Oban

1 March 2016

Re: Timetable and quote for Ulva collection and shipping

To: Dan Rees

Dear Dan,

Further to our email conversations about your requirements here is a proposed timetable for collection of sea lettuce (*Ulva lactuca* and *U. linza*). The requirement I have is for 1kg to reach Rome by the 9th of March. I therefore propose collection by courier from Easdale on the afternoon of the 7th. I will look to get an appropriate address for the courier to collect from.
The timetable and quote for the price of the harvested material reflects the difficulty in obtaining the quantity at this time of year and that it is outwith the optimal tidal conditions for harvesting. From the 2nd until the 6th of March, the tidal range is at its minimum (neap tides), generally less than 1m between high water and low water, meaning the water depth is quite high at low water.
In addition the sea lettuce is still quite young and the leaves therefore quite small meaning it will take longer to obtain the required mass, as I will have to most likely snorkel for it. The price is therefore charged per hour of labour rather than per kg to reflect the challenge of harvesting out of season (including working in water) and during non-optimal tides.

There will be no charge for any stock and site assessments undertaken

Proposed timetable:
Wednesday 2nd – Weather dependent assessment of low water depth and Ulva availability (low water 4:38am, 1.87m and 5:52pm, 2.01m)
Thursday 3rd to Saturday 5th – Depending results of tide assessment, should get upto 1hr of harvesting.
Sunday 6th and Monday 7th – Should get 2h harvesting on Sunday and 2h of harvesting Monday.

Cleaning and packing time will total 2h over the 5 days.

Maximum total number of hours work = 9h@ £12/h = **£108**

Slate Islands Seaweed Ltd, 1b Easdale Island, Oban, Argyll, PA34 4TB, Company no. SC519009
kelpie@slateislandsseaweed.com; www.slateislandsseaweed.com;
twitter.com/seaweedonaslate; www.facebook.com/seaweedonaslate

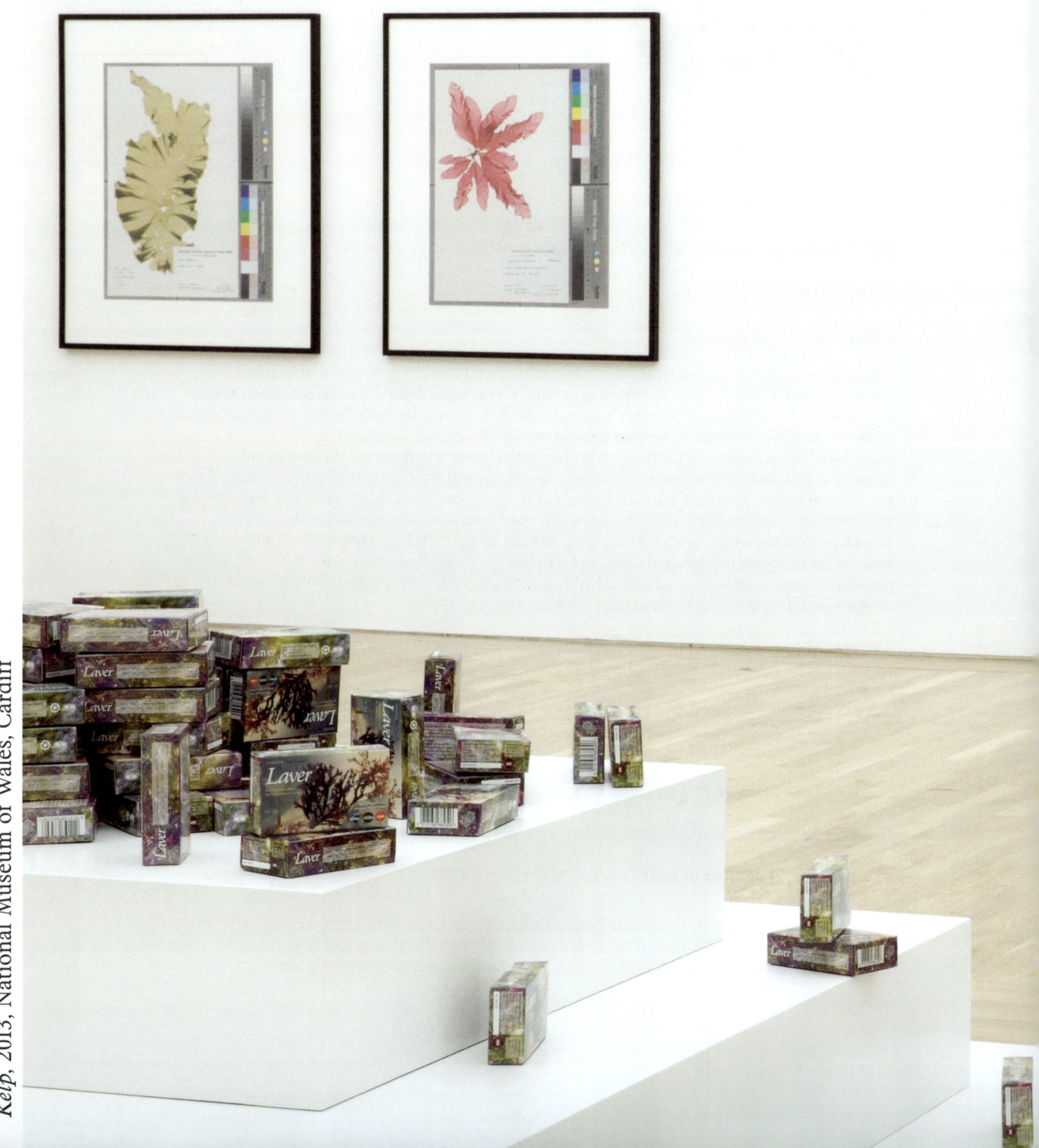

Kelp, 2013, National Museum of Wales, Cardiff

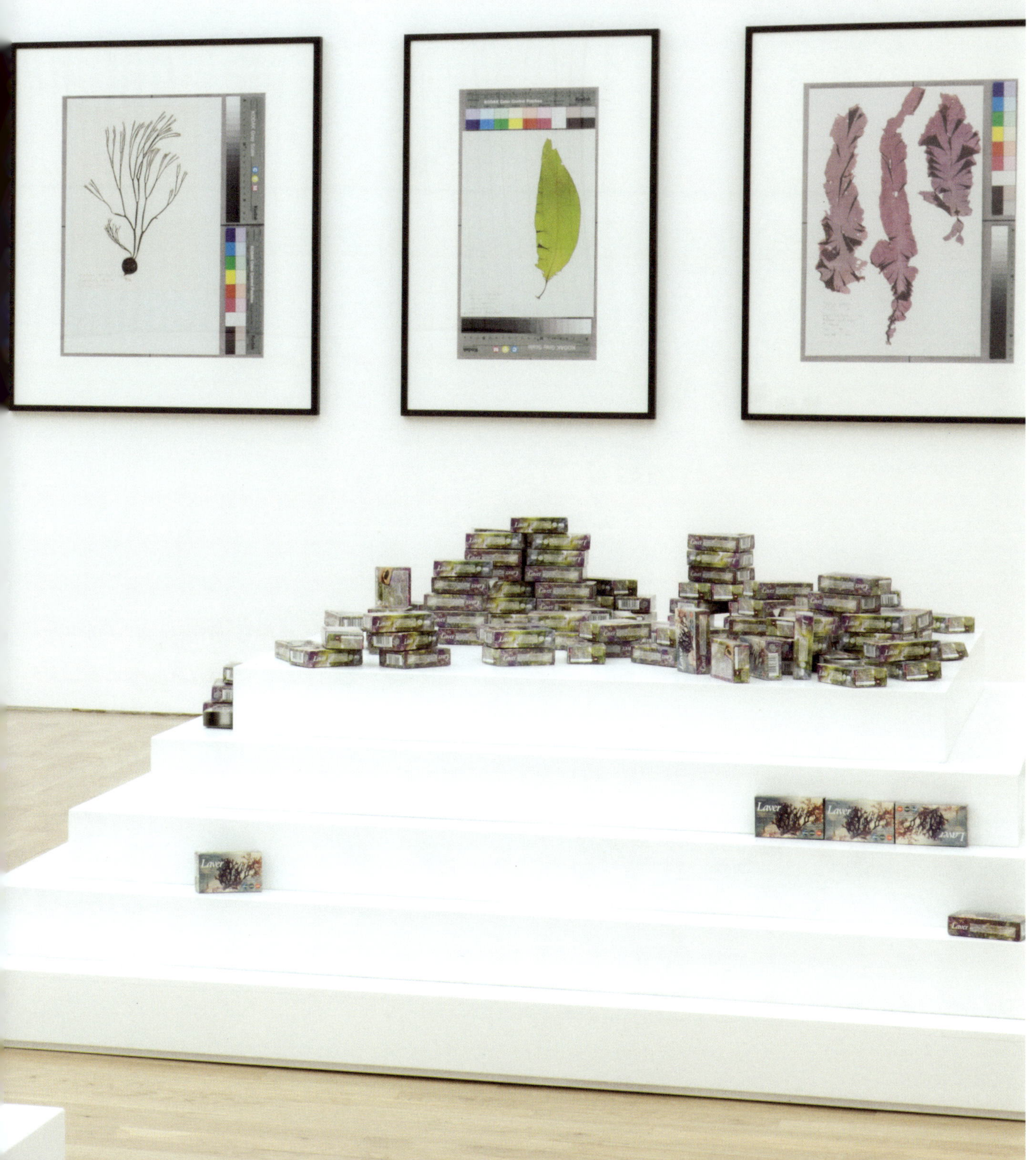

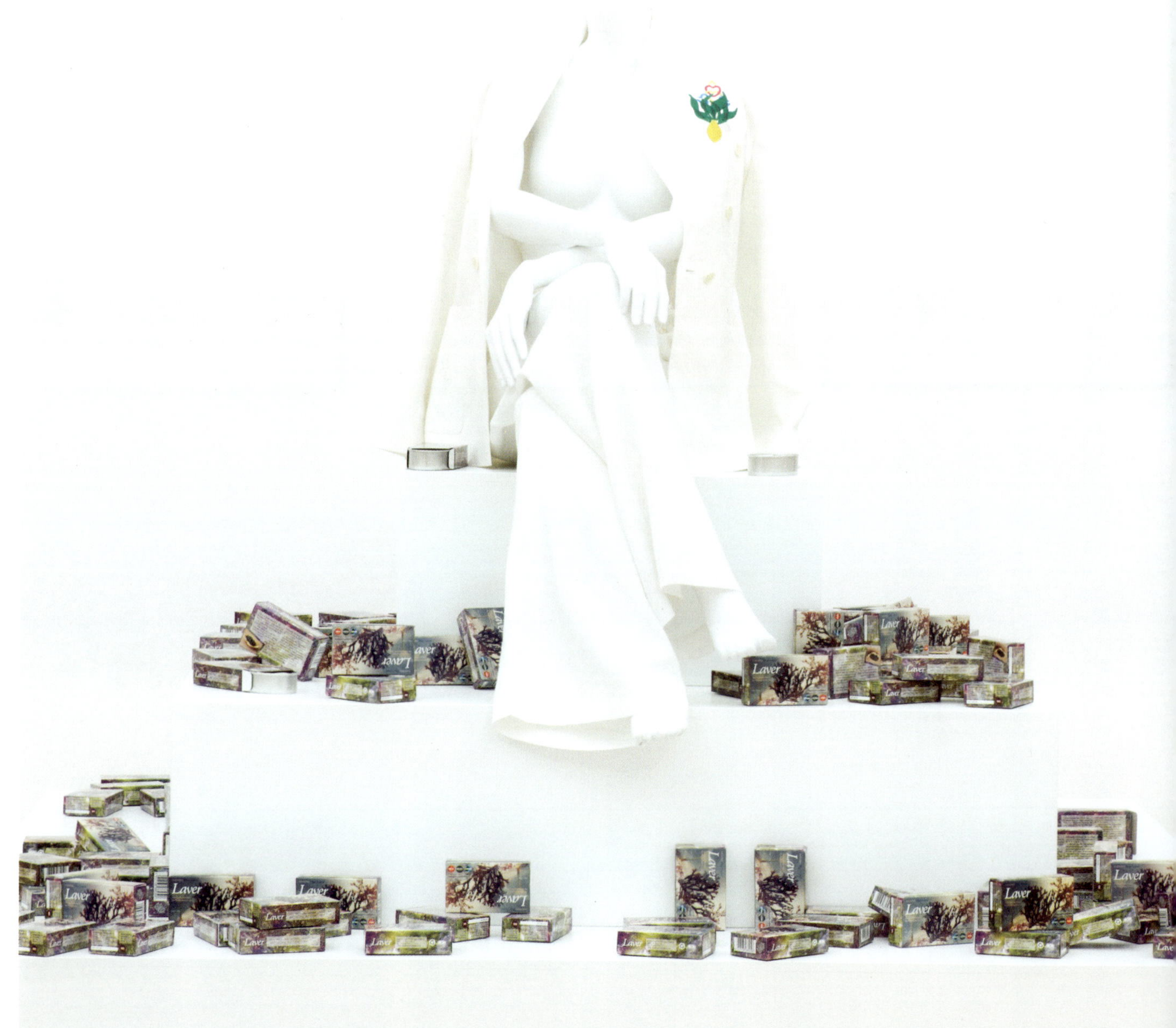

THE OBJECTIVE

Establish Welsh Laverbread as the Next Must Have
luxury item among aspiring affluents.

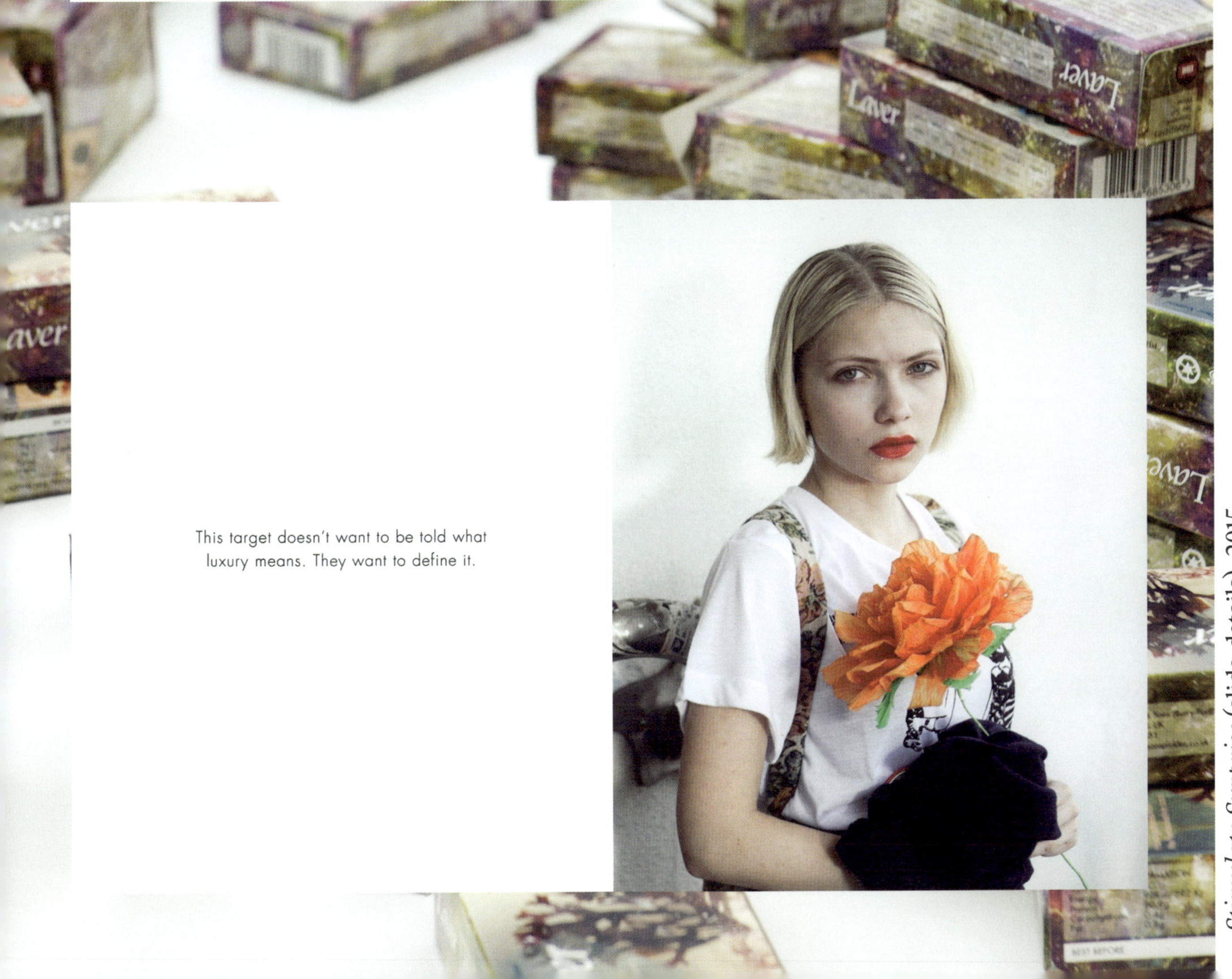

This target doesn't want to be told what
luxury means. They want to define it.

Kelp, 2013, National Museum of Wales, Cardiff   128

THEY ARE COLLECTORS
OF EXPERIENCES

Endless tales of rich, off the beaten path
experiences are true stamps of discernment.

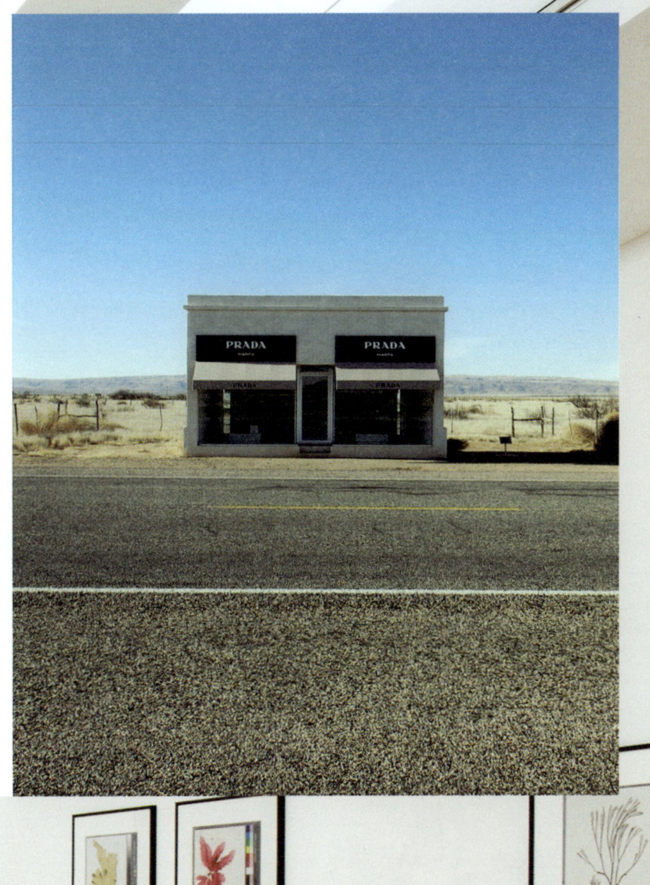

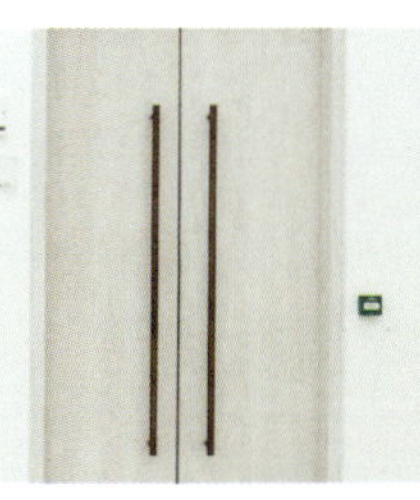
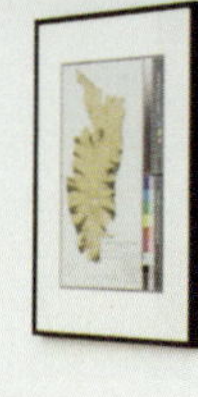
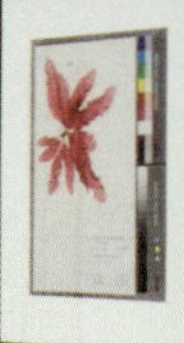

1 ESTABLISH
THE
PROVENANCE

Establish the rich heritage behind
hand gathered Welsh seaweed.

2 EMBODY THE
TENSION

Demonstrate the inherent tension
in found food being used in haute
cuisine.

3 ENRICH THE
EXPERIENCE

Luxury consumption experiences
have rituals, to elevate the
experience we'll need to create
rituals of our own.

4 STIMULATE
SURPRISE

Status stories come from the
unexpected, so we will need to
surprise and delight at every turn.

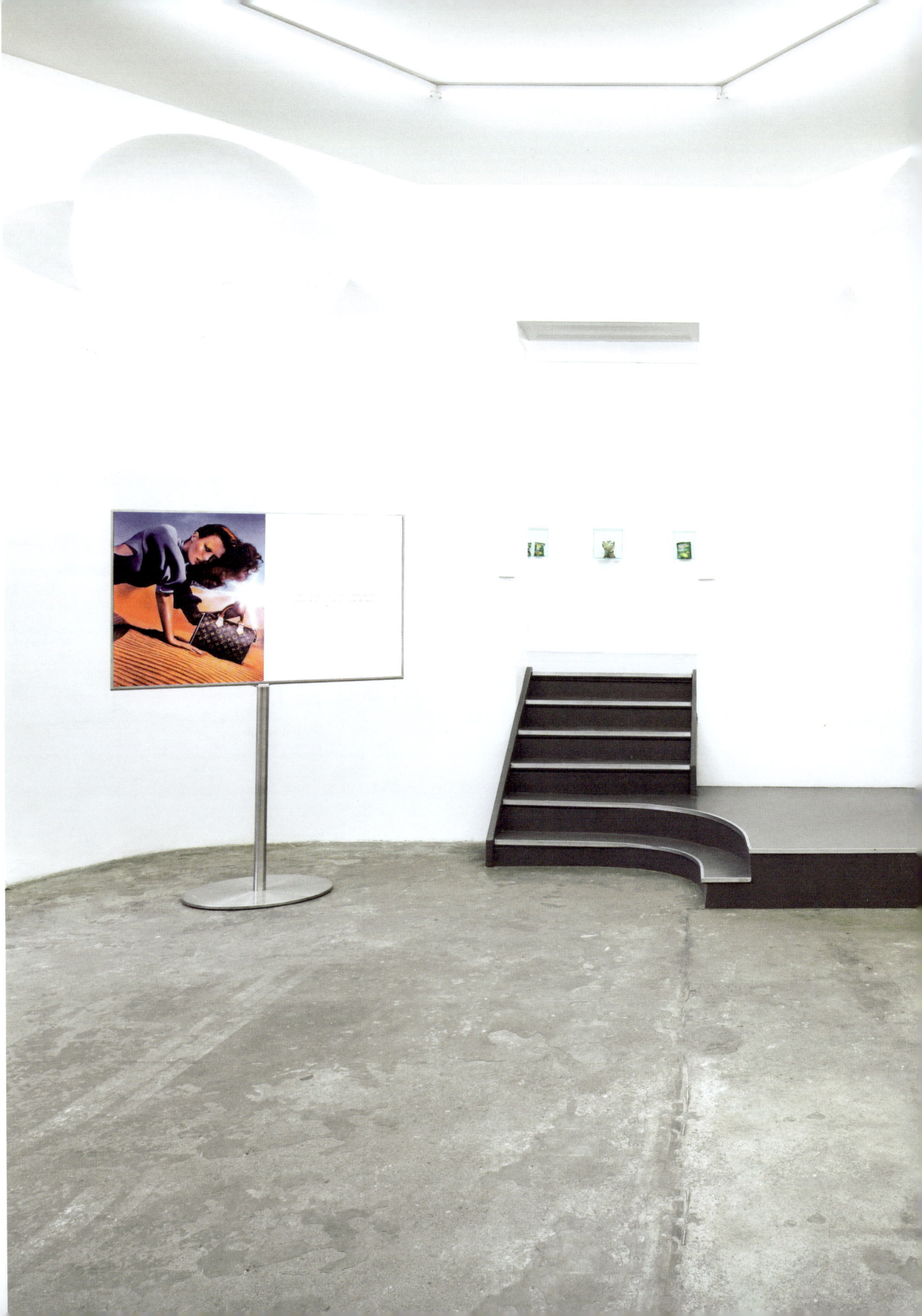

Stimulate Surprise, 2015, Tanya Leighton, Berlin

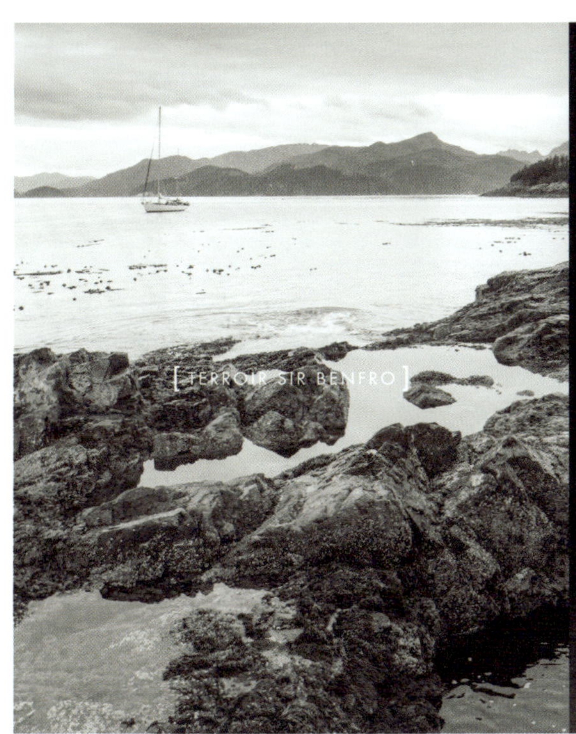
[TERROIR SIR BENFRO]

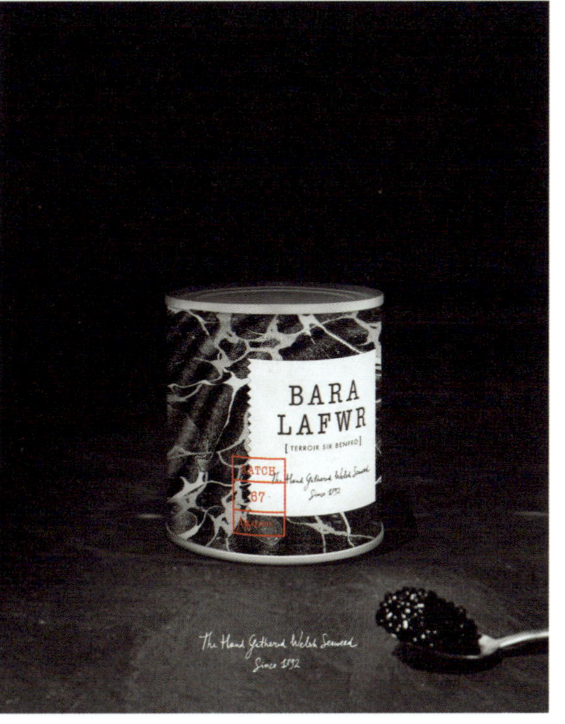
BARA
LAFWR
[TERROIR SIR BENFRO]
BATCH
187
The Hand Gathered Welsh Seaweed
Since 1992

Snacks; Super Crisp, Pringles, 2015

3 ENRICH THE EXPERIENCE

To tap into groups of influential tastemakers we propose working with carefully selected partners such as the Ace Hotel or the Fat Radish to have private tasting sessions featuring seaweed dishes and seaweed based cocktails.

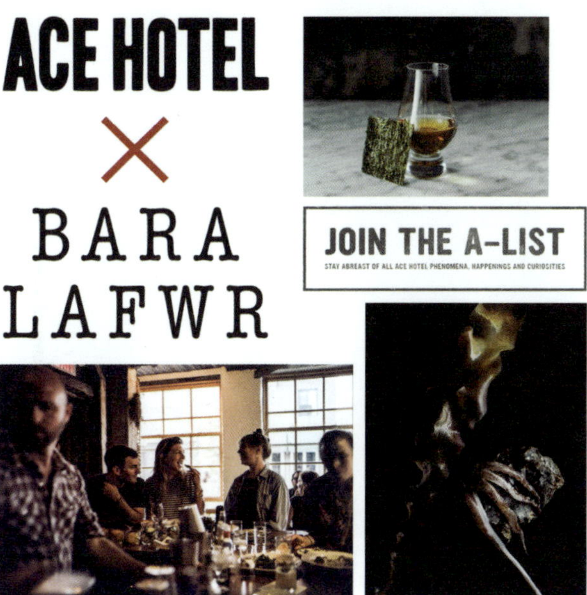

Pop-up experience

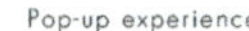

4 STIMULATE SURPRISE

To further extend the brand we can take it into luxury perfumery with a limited edition run of scents.

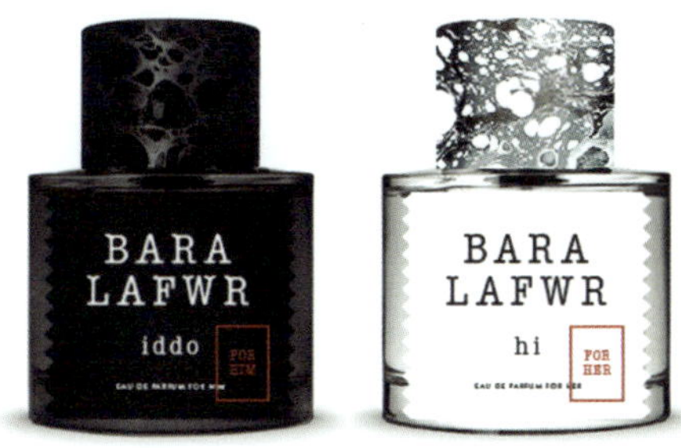

Products

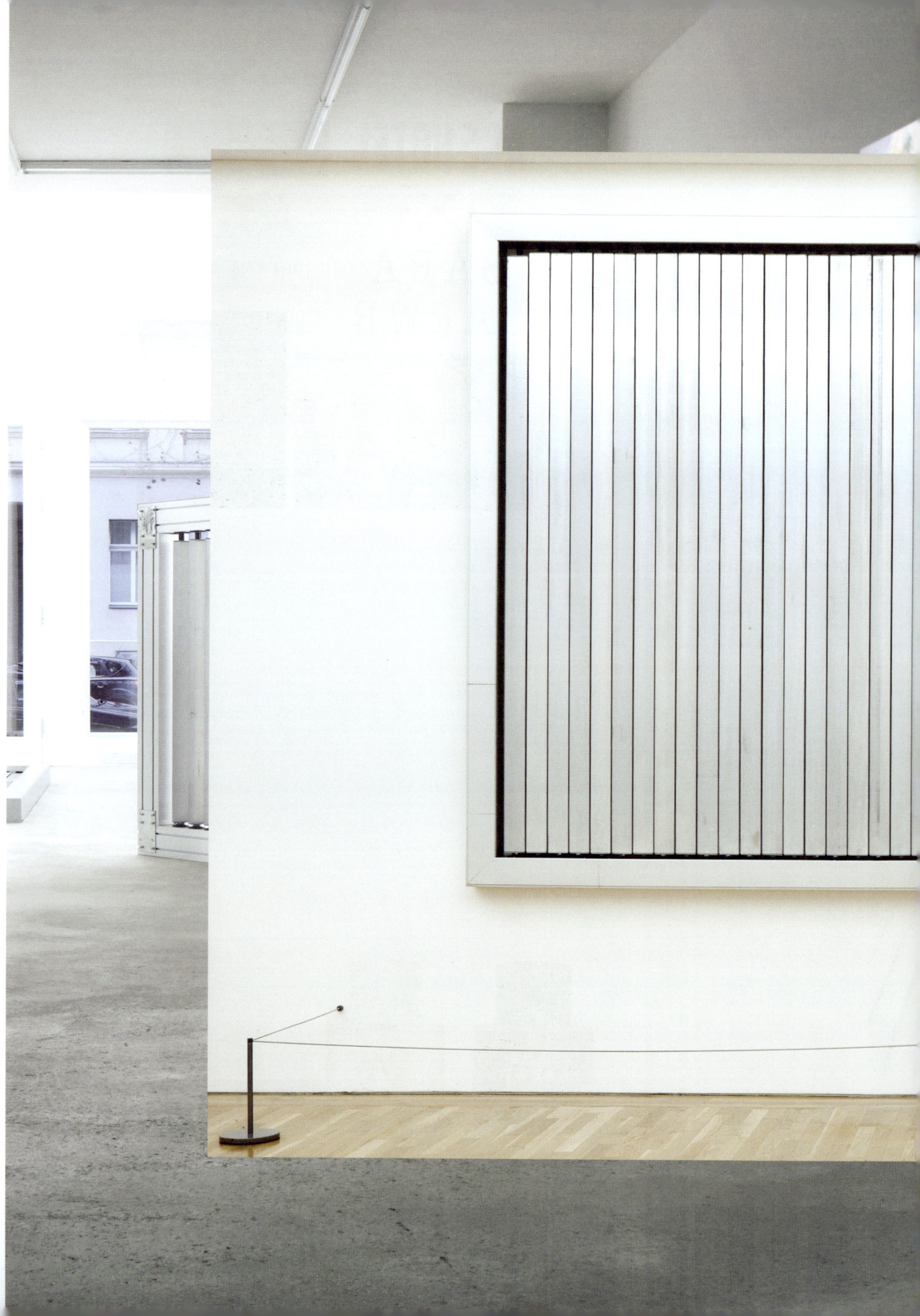

Stimulate Surprise, 2015, Tanya Leighton, Berlin 134

Trivision Billboard, 2013

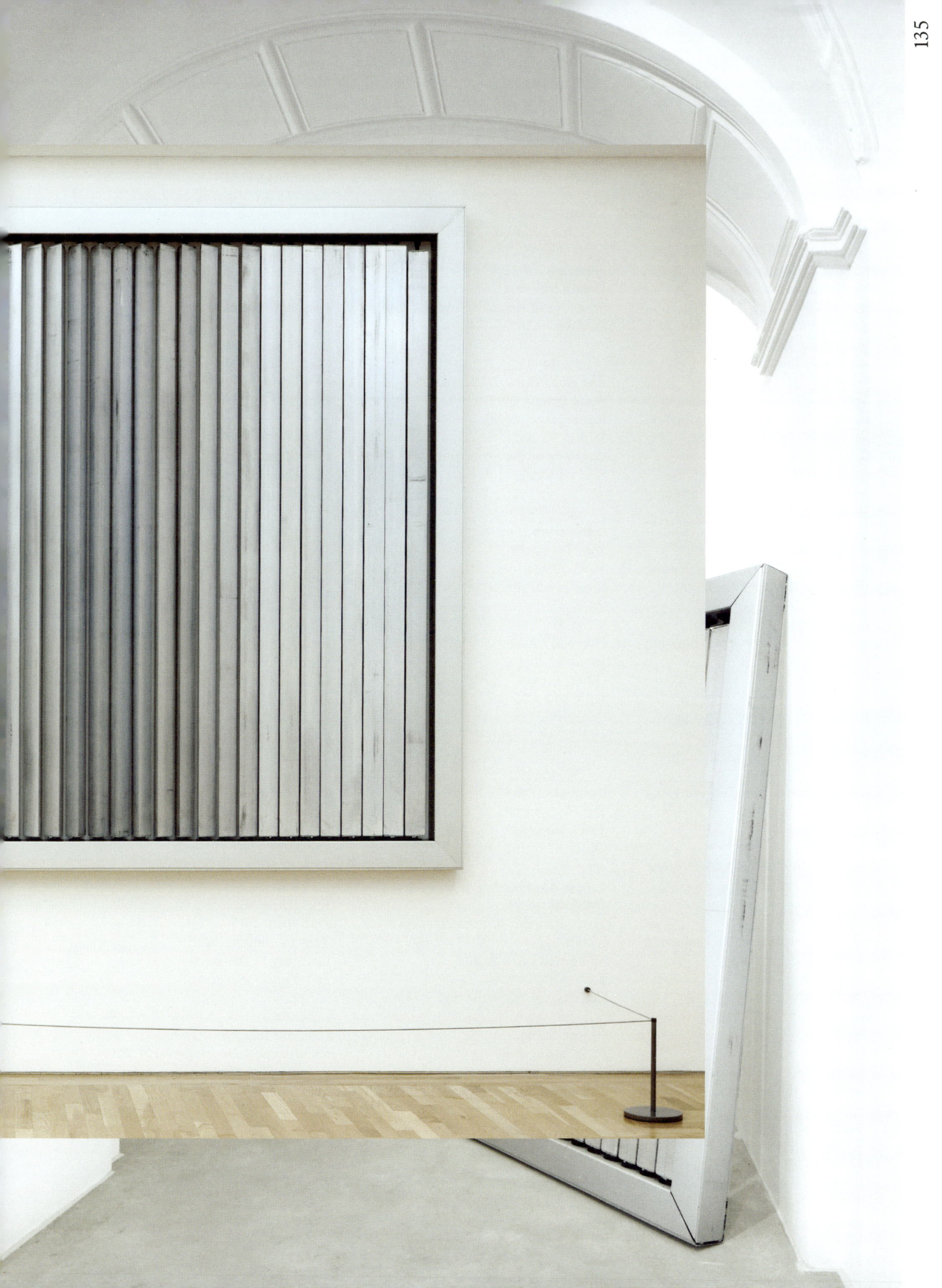

pp. 4–5
A Misunderstood Weed (detail), 2016
IBC tank, salt water, seaweed, plastic,
LED lights, pump, filter
100 × 120 × 117 cm
Road Back To Relevance, 2016
Nomas Foundation, Rome
Courtesy of the artist

pp. 6–7
A Misunderstood Weed (detail), 2016
IBC tank, salt water, seaweed, plastic,
LED lights, pump, filter
100 × 120 × 117 cm
Road Back To Relevance, 2016
Nomas Foundation, Rome
Courtesy of the artist

pp. 16–17
Intended Circulation, 2013–ongoing
Courtesy of the artist

pp. 18–19
Intended Circulation, 2013–ongoing
Courtesy of the artist

pp. 20–21
Intended Circulation, 2013–ongoing
Courtesy of the artist

pp. 22–23
Intended Circulation, 2013–ongoing
Courtesy of the artist

pp. 24–25
Intended Circulation, 2013–ongoing
Courtesy of the artist

pp. 26–27
Intended Circulation, 2013–ongoing
Courtesy of the artist

p. 28
Intended Circulation, 2013–ongoing
Courtesy of the artist

p. 32
Intended Circulation, 2013–ongoing
Courtesy of the artist

pp. 38–39
*Something To Fill That
Empty Feeling*, 2007
16 mm film installation,
T293, Naples
Courtesy of the artist and T293

pp. 40–41
*Something To Fill That
Empty Feeling*, 2007
16 mm film installation
T293, Naples
Courtesy of the artist and T293

p. 40
Overlaid images
The Postman's Decision Is Final,
2006–ongoing
Postcards, glue, shelf
Dims variable
Courtesy of the artist

pp. 42–43
The Road Back To Relevance
(slide detail), 2015
Presentation deck
13 min 53 sec
Courtesy of the artist and MOT
International

pp. 44–45
The Road Back To Relevance
(slide detail), 2015
Presentation deck
13 min 53 sec
Courtesy of the artist and MOT
International

pp. 46–47
Installation shot
Top Heavy, 2013
T293, Rome
Courtesy of the artist and T293

p. 47
Overlaid image
Vacuum, 2012
Oil on canvas, plastic, glass
110 × 140 × 25 cm
Courtesy of the artist
and Tanya Leighton

pp. 48–49
Installation shot
Top Heavy, 2013
T293, Rome
Courtesy of the artist and T293

pp. 48–49
Overlaid image
Space Invader (Chartist Mural)
(detail), 2013
40 framed inket prints
210 × 330 cm
Courtesy of the artist and T293

pp. 50–51
Installation shot
*They Don't Make Them Like This
Anymore*, 2009
T293, Naples
Courtesy of the artist and T293

p. 51
Overlaid image
*Black And White Things In Black
And White (Panda) (Guinness)*,

2006
Black and white photograph
13 x 19 cm (each)
Courtesy of the artist and T293

pp. 52–53
Installation shot
*They Don't Make Them Like
This Anymore*, 2009
T293, Naples
Courtesy of the artist and T293

p. 52
Overlaid images
*Black And White Things In Black
And White (Zebra)*, 2006
Black and white photograph
19 × 13 cm
Courtesy of the artist and T293

p. 53
Overlaid images
*Black And White Things In Black
And White (Rush)*, 2006
Black and white photograph
19 × 13 cm
Courtesy of the artist and T293

pp. 54–55
The Road Back To Relevance
(slide detail), 2015
Presentation deck
13 min 53 sec
Courtesy of the artist
and MOT International

pp. 56–57
The Road Back To Relevance
(slide detail), 2015
Presentation deck
13 min 53 sec
Courtesy of the artist
and MOT International

p. 58
Installation Shot
Dan Rees, 2013
Tanya Leighton, Berlin
Courtesy of the artist
and Tanya Leighton

p. 58
Overlaid image
Swansea Self Development 3, 2011
Framed photograph
63 × 53 cm
Courtesy of the artist

p. 59
*Opposite The Church, Workers
In A Wheelbarrow*, 2013
C-print on archival paper
127 × 159 cm

Dan Rees, 2013
Tanya Leighton, Berlin
Courtesy of the artist
and Tanya Leighton

p. 60
Boys Sharing Flip-Flops, 2013
C-print on archival paper
159 × 127 cm
Dan Rees, 2013
Tanya Leighton, Berlin
Courtesy of the artist
and Tanya Leighton

p. 61
Hotel Swimming Pool, 2013
Esteli Bus Stop, 2013
C-print on archival paper
159 × 127 cm, 127 × 159 cm
Dan Rees, 2013
Tanya Leighton, Berlin
Courtesy of the artist
and Tanya Leighton

p. 62
Hotel Swimming Pool, 2013
C-print on archival paper
159 × 127 cm
Dan Rees, 2013
Tanya Leighton, Berlin
Courtesy of the artist
and Tanya Leighton

p. 63
Heroes And Martyrs, 2013
C-print on archival paper
127 × 159 cm
Dan Rees, 2013
Tanya Leighton, Berlin
Courtesy of the artist
and Tanya Leighton

p. 67
Disused Pool Graffiti, 2013
C-print on archival paper
159 × 127 cm
Dan Rees, 2013
Tanya Leighton, Berlin
Courtesy of the artist
and Tanya Leighton

p. 67
Overlaid image
Archive image
Lesbians & Gays Support
The Miners, 1985
Working Class Movement
Library

p. 71
Installation Shot
Dan Rees, 2013
Tanya Leighton, Berlin

Courtesy of the artist
and Tanya Leighton

p. 71
Overlaid image
Archive image
Neath and the Spanish Civil War
1936–39
South Wales Miner's Library

pp. 72–73
The Road Back To Relevance
(slide detail), 2015
Presentation deck
13 min 53 sec
Courtesy of the artist
and MOT International

pp. 74–75
The Road Back To Relevance
(slide detail), 2015
Presentation deck video
13 min 53 sec
Courtesy of the artist
and MOT International

pp. 76–77
Installation shot
Road Back To Relevance, 2016
Nomas Foundation, Rome
Courtesy of the artist

pp. 78–79
Vacuum, 2016
Oil on canvas, plastic, Perspex,
LED light
130 × 110 × 30 cm
Road Back To Relevance, 2016
Nomas Foundation, Rome
Courtesy of the artist and T293

pp. 80–81
China Trivision 1, 2015
Aluminium trivision billboard
145 × 100 × 5 cm
Road Back To Relevance, 2016
Nomas Foundation, Rome
Courtesy of the artist

pp. 82–83
A Misunderstood Weed (detail), 2016
IBC tank, salt water, seaweed, plastic,
LED lights, pump, filter
100 × 120 × 117 cm
Road Back To Relevance, 2016
Nomas Foundation, Rome
Courtesy of the artist

pp. 84–85
Installation shot
Road Back To Relevance, 2016
Nomas Foundation, Rome
Courtesy of the artist

pp. 86–87
Stimulate Surprise, 2015
Presentation Deck
7 mins 4 sec
Road Back To Relevance, 2016
Nomas Foundation, Rome
Courtesy of the artist
and Tanya Leighton

pp. 88–89
Installation shot
Road Back To Relevance, 2016
Nomas Foundation, Rome
Courtesy of the artist

pp. 90–91
Artex, 2016
Oil on canvas
160 × 210 cm
Intended Circulation, 2013–ongoing
Digital photograph
64 × 79 cm
Road Back To Relevance, 2016
Nomas Foundation, Rome
Courtesy of the artist and T293

pp. 92–93
Installation shot
Road Back To Relevance, 2016
Nomas Foundation, Rome
Courtesy of the artist

pp. 94–95
Installation shot
Road Back To Relevance, 2016
Nomas Foundation, Rome
Courtesy of the artist

pp. 96–97
Untitled (Diptych), 2014
Plasticine on wood
200 × 150 cm (each)
Road Back To Relevance, 2016
Nomas Foundation, Rome
Courtesy of the artist and T293

p. 98
Disused Pool Graffiti, 2013
C-print on archival paper
159 × 127 cm
Road Back To Relevance, 2016
Nomas Foundation, Rome
Courtesy of the artist
and Tanya Leighton

p. 99
The Road Back To Relevance, 2015
Presentation deck
13 min 53 sec
Road Back To Relevance, 2016
Nomas Foundation, Rome
Courtesy of the artist
and MOT International

List of Works

printed cardboard boxes, plinths
180 × 180 × 180 cm
Kelp, 2013
National Museum of Wales, Cardiff
Courtesy of the artist and T293

p. 127
Installation shot
Kelp, 2013
National Museum of Wales, Cardiff
Courtesy of the artist

p. 127
Overlaid images
Stimulate Surprise
(slide details), 2015
Presentation Deck
7 mins 4 sec
Courtesy of the artist
and Tanya Leighton

pp. 128–129
Installation shot
Kelp, 2013
National Museum of Wales, Cardiff
Courtesy of the artist

p. 129
Overlaid images
Stimulate Surprise
(slide details), 2015
Presentation Deck
7 mins 4 sec
Courtesy of the artist
and Tanya Leighton

pp. 130–131
Installation shot
Stimulate Surprise, 2015
Tanya Leighton, Berlin

Courtesy of the artist
and Tanya Leighton

p. 131
Overlaid images
Stimulate Surprise
(slide details), 2015
Presentation Deck
7 mins 4 sec
Courtesy of the artist
and Tanya Leighton

pp. 132– 133
Installation shot
Stimulate Surprise, 2015
Tanya Leighton, Berlin
Courtesy of the artist
and Tanya Leighton

p. 132
Overlaid images
Snacks; Super Crisp, Pringles, 2015
Perspex, food packaging, stickers
38 × 36 × 14 cm, 34 × 19 × 10 cm
Stimulate Surprise, 2015
Tanya Leighton, Berlin
Courtesy of the artist
and Tanya Leighton

p. 133
Overlaid images
Stimulate Surprise
(slide details), 2015
Presentation Deck
7 mins 4 sec
Courtesy of the artist
and Tanya Leighton

p. 134
Installation shot

Stimulate Surprise, 2015
Tanya Leighton, Berlin
Courtesy of the artist
and Tanya Leighton

p. 135
Installation shot
Stimulate Surprise, 2015
Tanya Leighton, Berlin
Courtesy of the artist
and Tanya Leighton

pp. 134–135
Overlaid image
Trivision Billboard, 2013
Aluminium trivision billboard
300 × 451 × 14 cm
Kelp, 2013
National Museum of Wales, Cardiff
Courtesy of the artist
and Tanya Leighton

pp. 140–141
A Misunderstood Weed (detail), 2016
IBC tank, salt water, seaweed,
plastic, LED lights, pump, filter
100 × 120 × 117 cm
Road Back To Relevance, 2016
Nomas Foundation, Rome
Courtesy of the artist

pp. 142–143
A Misunderstood Weed, 2016
IBC tank, salt water, seaweed,
plastic, LED lights, pump, filter
100 × 120 × 117 cm
Road Back To Relevance, 2016
Nomas Foundation, Rome
Courtesy of the artist

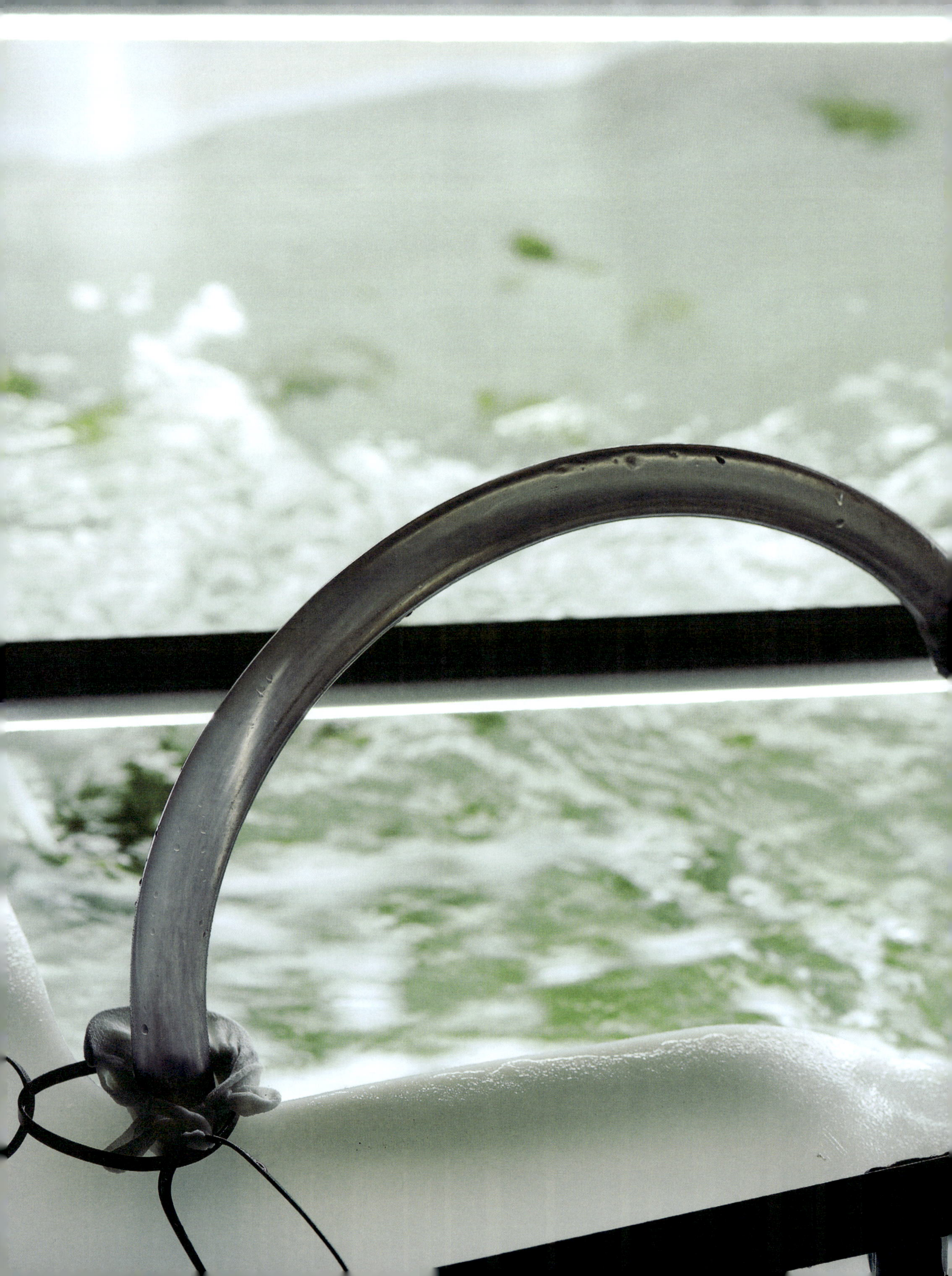

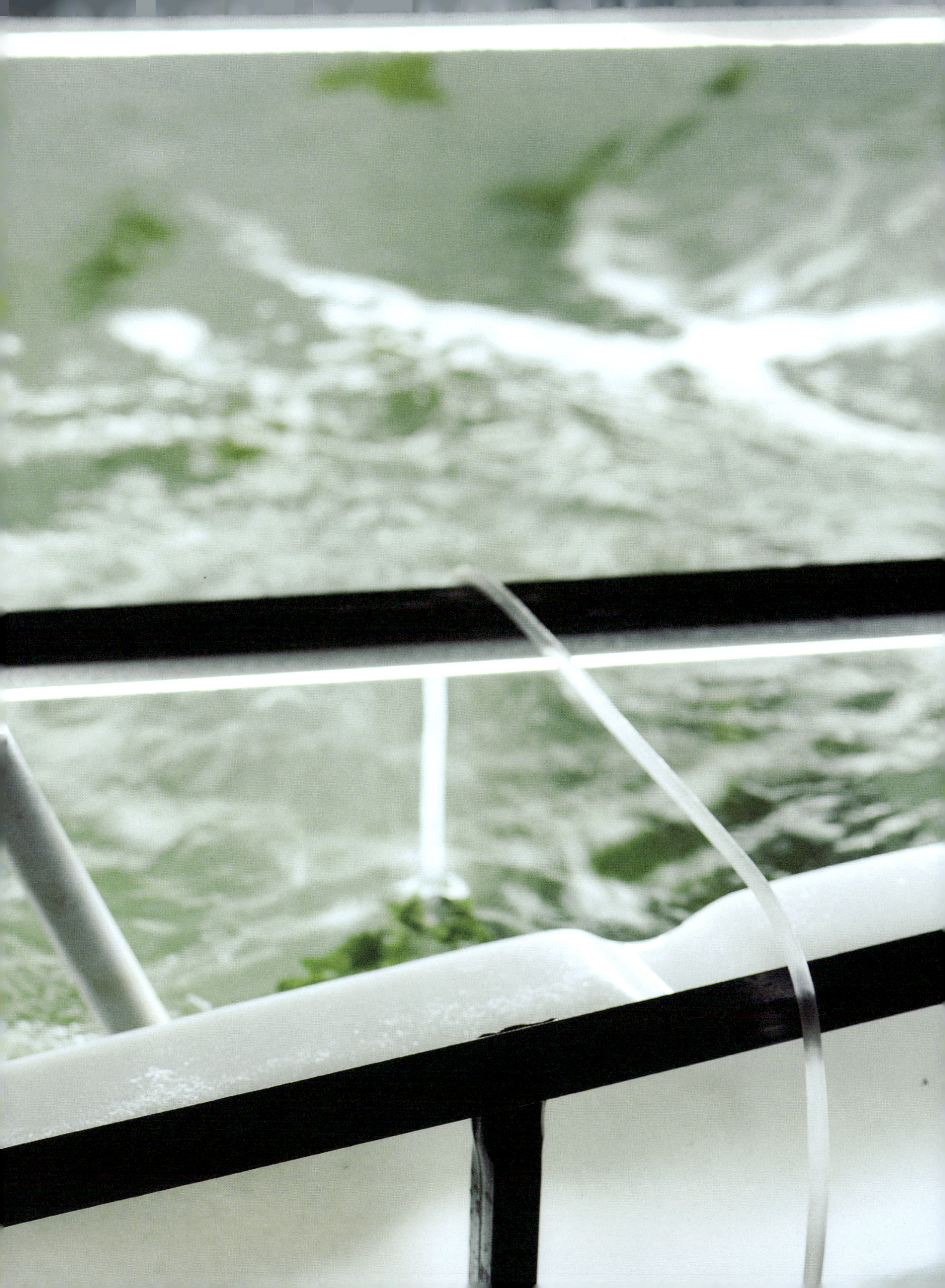

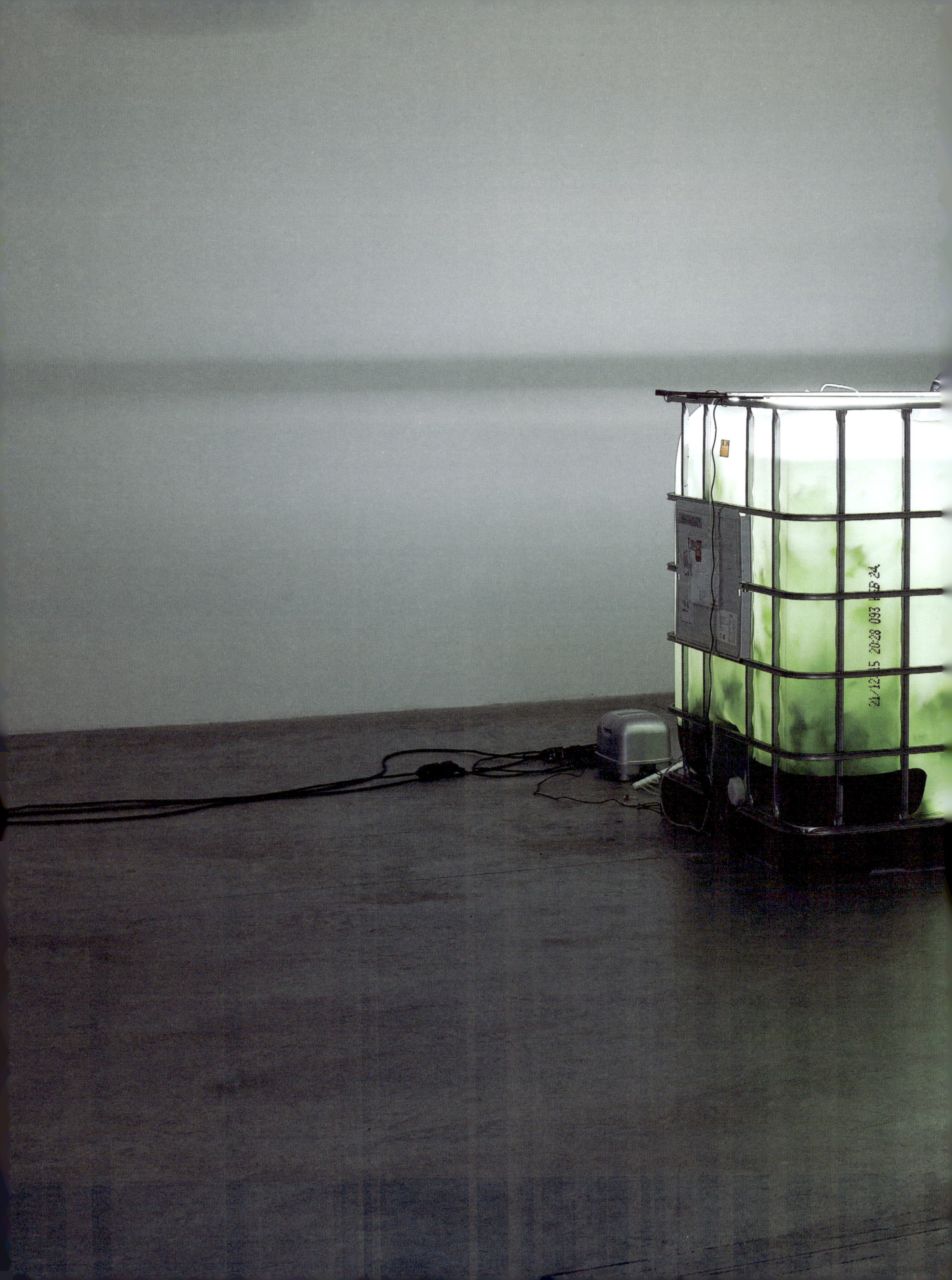

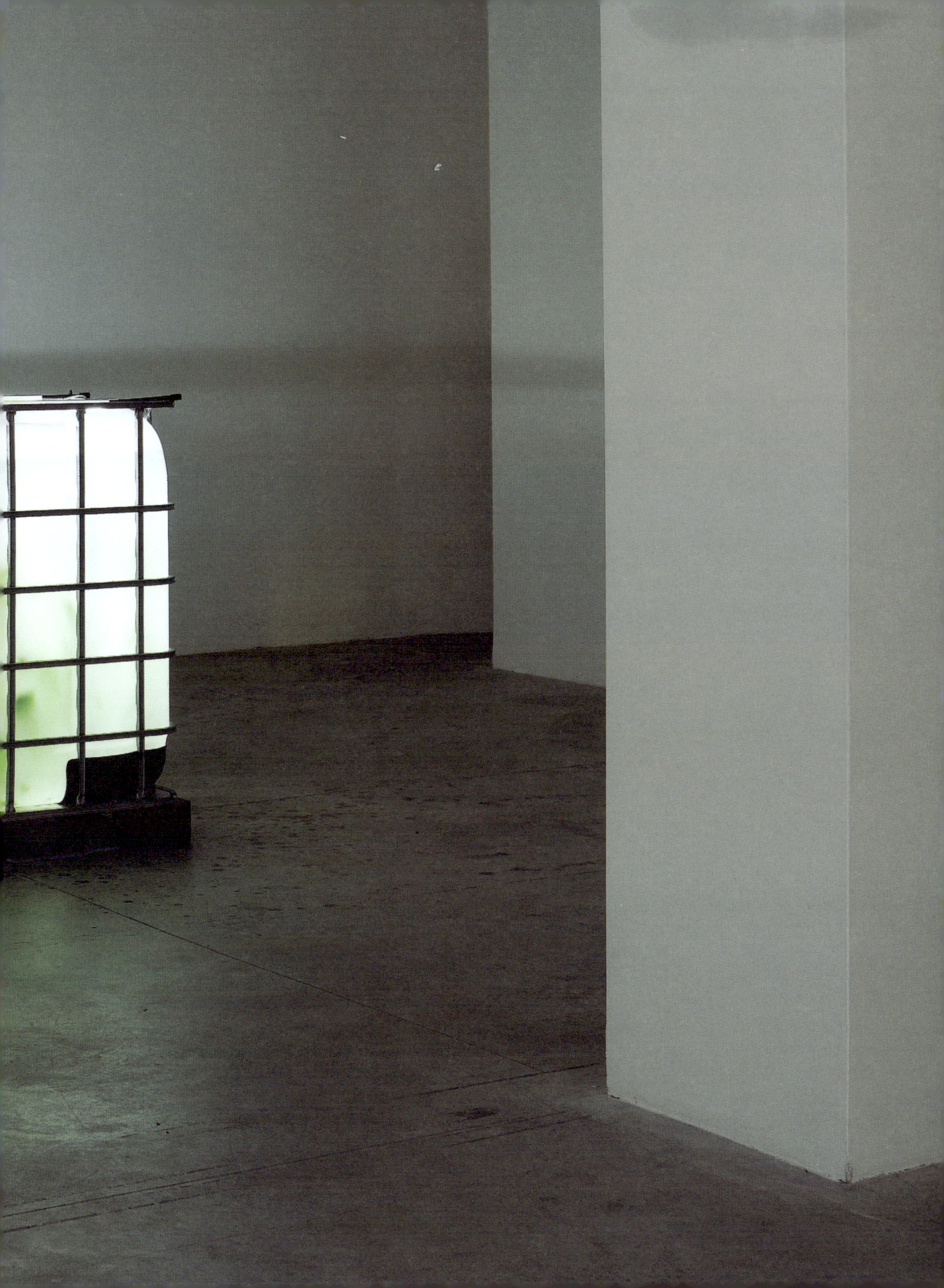

Colophon

This book has been published
on occasion of the exhibition:

Road Back To Relevance

Nomas Foundation, Rome
March–July, 2016

Publisher
Mousse Publishing, Milano

Publishing Editor
Ilaria Bombelli

Copy editing
Lindsey Westbrook, Chiara Moioli

Italian translation
Aurelia Di Meo

Graphic Design
Per Törnberg

Colour Correction
Nicola Leck

Printing
Artigianelli, Brescia, Italy

Photo Credits
Roberto Apa (4–7, 22–23, 46–49, 58 overlaid
image, 76–99, 136–39); Isabelle Arthuis
(104–07); Manish Singh Baghel (32); Jordan
Barse (16–17); John Betancourt (20–21);
Pasquale Di Stasio (38–41); Philippe De
Gobert (108–09); Danilo Donzelli (50–53);
James Ewing (112–15); Hans Georg (47
overlaid image, 116–17 overlaid images);
Wolfgang Günzel (110–11); Michael Hemy
(109); James Horan (18–19, 26–28); Gunter
Lepowski (58–63, 67, 71, 122–23, 130–35);
Richard Trevor Lloyd (24–25); Robin Maggs
(124–29, 134–35 overlaid image); Ben Ness
(42–45, 54–57, 72–75, 100–03, 118–21); Dan
Rees (48–49 overlaid image, 51 overlaid
images, 52–53 overlaid images, 71 overlaid
image; Roberto Ruiz (40 overlaid images);
Kevin Todora (116–17)

Front cover image
Ben Ness

Back cover image
James Horan

A special thanks to
Collezione Agovino, Fondazione Nomas,
Land SRL, MOT International, Múrias
Centeno, T293, Tanya Leighton Gallery

Acknowledgements
Marty Adelstein, Alessandra Arancio,
Vela Arbutina, Lisa & David Barse,
Sol Calero, Dan Chandler, Maria Elena Croci,
Saim Demirican, Claudia Fiasca, Leslie Fram,
Elisa Genovesi, Ilaria Gianni, Danny Goldberg,
Ben Gregory, Massimo Lauro, Aude Levere,
Richard Trevor Lloyd, Simona Merra,
Arun Nayar, Ben Ness, Chris Phillips,
Marion Rees, Dieter Roelstraete, Craig Rose,
Mark Sandleson, Raffaella & Stefano Sciarretta,
Ashwin Thadani, Nicholas Thornton,
Sung Tieu, Rosalia & Humberto Ugobono,
Sarah Williams

Printed May 2016

ISBN 9788867492176
€ 28